Studies in Economic Transition

General Editors: Jens Hölscher, Reader in Economics, University of Brighton; and **Horst Tomann**, Professor of Economics, Free University Berlin

This series has been established in response to a growing demand for a greater understanding of the transformation of economic systems. It brings together theoretical and empirical studies on economic transition and economic development. The post-communist transition from planned to market economies is one of the main areas of applied theory because in this field the most dramatic examples of change and economic dynamics can be found. The series aims to contribute to the understanding of specific major economic changes as well as to advance the theory of economic development. The implications of economic policy will be a major point of focus.

Titles include:

William Bartlett, Sanja Malekovic, Vassilis Monastiriotis (*editors*)
DECENTRALISATION AND LOCAL DEVELOPMENT IN SOUTH-EAST EUROPE

Tilman Bruk and Hartmut Lehmann (*editors*)
IN THE GRIP OF TRANSITION
Economic and Social Consequences of Restructuring in Russia and Ukraine

Lucian Cernat
EUROPEANIZATION, VARIETIES OF CAPITALISM AND ECONOMIC PERFORMANCE IN CENTRAL AND EASTERN EUROPE

Bruno Dallago and Ichiro Iwasaki (*editors*)
CORPORATE RESTRUCTURING AND GOVERNANCE IN TRANSITION ECONOMIES

Bruno Dallago (*editor*)
TRANSFORMATION AND EUROPEAN INTEGRATION
The Local Dimension

Hella Engerer
PRIVATIZATION AND ITS LIMITS IN CENTRAL AND EASTERN EUROPE
Property Rights in Transition

Saul Estrin, Grzegorz W. Kolodko and Milica Uvalic (*editors*)
TRANSITION AND BEYOND

Daniela Gabor
CENTRAL BANKING AND FINANCIALIZATION
A Romanian Account of how Eastern Europe became Subprime

Oleh Havrylyshyn
DIVERGENT PATHS IN POST-COMMUNIST TRANSFORMATION
Capitalism for All or Capitalism for the Few?

Iraj Hoshi, Paul J.J. Welfens and Anna Wziatek-Kubiak (*editors*)
INDUSTRIAL COMPETITIVENESS AND RESTRUCTURING IN ENLARGED EUROPE
How Accession Countries Catch Up and Integrate in the European Union

Björn Jindra
INTERNATIONALISATION THEORY AND TECHNOLOGICAL ACCUMULATION
An Investigation of the Multinational Affiliates in East Germany

Mihaela Keleman and Monika Kostera (*editors*)
CRITICAL MANAGEMENT RESEARCH IN EASTERN EUROPE
Managing the Transition

David Lane (*editor*)
THE TRANSFORMATION OF STATE SOCIALISM
System Change, Capitalism, or Something Else?

David Lane and Martin Myant (*editors*)
VARIETIES OF CAPITALISM IN POST-COMMUNIST COUNTRIES

Jens Lowitzsch
FINANCIAL PARTICIPATION OF EMPLOYEES IN THE EU-27

Enrico Marelli and Marcello Signorelli (*editors*)
ECONOMIC GROWTH AND STRUCTURAL FEATURES OF TRANSITION

Sönke Maatsch
CENTRAL AND EAST EUROPEAN MIGRANTS' CONTRIBUTIONS TO SOCIAL PROTECTION

Tomasz Mickiewicz
ECONOMIC TRANSITION IN CENTRAL EUROPE AND THE COMMONWEALTH OF INDEPENDENT STATES

Tomasz Mickiewicz
ECONOMICS OF INSTITUTIONAL CHANGE SECOND EDITION
Central and Eastern Europe Revisited

Milan Nikolić
MONETARY POLICY IN TRANSITION
Inflation Nexus Money Supply in Postcommunist Russia

Julie Pellegrin
THE POLITICAL ECONOMY OF COMPETITIVENESS IN AN ENLARGED EUROPE

Stanislav Poloucek (*editor*)
REFORMING THE FINANCIAL SECTOR IN CENTRAL EUROPEAN COUNTRIES

Johannes Stephan (*editor*)
TECHNOLOGY TRANSFER VIA FOREIGN DIRECT INVESTMENT IN CENTRAL AND EASTERN EUROPE

Horst Tomann
MONETARY INTEGRATION IN EUROPE

Pasquale Tridico
INSTITUTIONS, HUMAN DEVELOPMENT AND ECONOMIC GROWTH IN TRANSITION ECONOMIES

Milica Uvalic
SERBIA'S TRANSITION
Towards a Better Future

Hans van Zon
RUSSIA'S DEVELOPMENT PROBLEM
The Cult of Power

The full list of titles available is on the website:
www.palgrave.com/economics/set.asp

Studies in Economic Transition
Series Standing Order ISBN 978–0–333–73353–0
(*outside North America only*)

You can receive future titles in this series as they are published by placing a standing order. Please contact your bookseller or, in case of difficulty, write to us at the address below with your name and address, the title of the series and the ISBN quoted above.

Customer Services Department, Macmillan Distribution Ltd, Houndmills, Basingstoke, Hampshire RG21 6XS, England

---

Decentralization and Local Development in South East Europe

Edited by

Will Bartlett
Senior Research Fellow in the Political Economy of South East Europe, London School of Economics and Political Science, UK

Sanja Maleković
Senior Research Associate, Institute for International Relations, Zagreb, Croatia

and

Vassilis Monastiriotis
Senior Lecturer in the Political Economy of South East Europe, London School of Economics and Political Science, UK

palgrave
macmillan

Softcover reprint of the hardcover 1st edition 2013 978-0-230-35563-7

First published 2013 by
PALGRAVE MACMILLAN

Palgrave Macmillan in the UK is an imprint of Macmillan Publishers Limited, registered in England, company number 785998, of Houndmills, Basingstoke, Hampshire RG21 6XS.

Palgrave Macmillan in the US is a division of St Martin's Press LLC, 175 Fifth Avenue, New York, NY 10010.

Palgrave Macmillan is the global academic imprint of the above companies and has companies and representatives throughout the world.

Palgrave® and Macmillan® are registered trademarks in the United States, the United Kingdom, Europe and other countries.

ISBN 978-1-349-34717-9 ISBN 978-1-137-29565-1 (eBook)
DOI 10.1057/9781137295651

This book is printed on paper suitable for recycling and made from fully managed and sustained forest sources. Logging, pulping and manufacturing processes are expected to conform to the environmental regulations of the country of origin.

A catalogue record for this book is available from the British Library.

A catalog record for this book is available from the Library of Congress.

Transferred to Digital Printing in 2013

Contents

List of Figures and Tables

Figures

Tables

Notes on Contributors

Editors

Will Bartlett is Senior Research Fellow in the Political Economy of South East Europe at the London School of Economics and Political Science and Honorary Professor at both the London School of Hygiene and Tropical Medicine and the School for Policy Studies, University of Bristol. He has an MA in Economics from the University of Cambridge, an M.Sc. from the University of London and a Ph.D. from the University of Liverpool. He has lectured in Development Economics and Comparative Economic Systems at the Universities of Southampton, Bath and Bristol, and from 1983 to 1986 was Research Fellow at the European University Institute in Fiesole, Italy. His current research covers economic and social development in South East Europe. His book *Europe's Troubled Region: Economic Development, Institutional Reform, and Social Welfare in the Western Balkans* was published by Routledge in 2008. His research has been funded by the UK's Economic and Social Research Council, the Leverhulme Trust and the British Academy and he has published widely in refereed academic journals. He has also applied his research knowledge in practice as a consultant and senior advisor to the European Commission, European Parliament, European Training Foundation, World Bank, OECD and other international organizations.

Sanja Maleković is Senior Research Fellow in the Institute for International Relations, Zagreb. She holds a Ph.D. from the Faculty of Economics, Zagreb, on *The New Approach to Regional Development in Croatia* (1997). She has been visiting lecturer at the Postgraduate Course on European Studies at the University of Padua (EU Cohesion Policy) and is currently lecturer at the Postgraduate Course on EU Economics at the Faculty of Economics in Zagreb. She has been engaged as team leader and expert on a number of projects supported by the EC, UNDP, World Bank, ILO, and Croatian central and regional government institutions related to regional development policy, the development of entrepreneurship, as well as evaluation of development programmes. Her most recent research contributions relate to local and regional development, regional policy and decentralization, regional competitiveness and evaluation of development programmes.

Vassilis Monastiriotis is Senior Lecturer in the Political Economy of South East Europe at the European Institute, London School of Economics and Political Science. He is also affiliated to LSE's Hellenic Observatory, the LSE research unit on South Eastern Europe and the ESRC Spatial Economics Research Centre. His research focuses on economic policy and performance at the regional, national and supranational levels, with emphasis on labour markets, economic growth and the macro-economy. He has published numerous articles in economics and regional science journals and received various distinctions, including the Moss Maden Medal in Regional Science (2008) and a European Investment Bank Award (2001). He has a Ph.D. in Economic Geography (LSE), an M.Sc. in Economics (University of Macedonia) and a B.Sc. in Economics (Aristotle University of Thessaloniki). He is the Co-editor of Spatial Economic Analysis (Taylor & Francis), Editor of GreeSE Papers (Hellenic Observatory), Committee Member of the British and Irish Section of the Regional Science Association International and member of various professional associations and editorial boards.

Authors

Ivo Bićanić is Professor at the Faculty of Economics, University of Zagreb, Croatia and is also teaching the Executive MBA programme at the University of Zurich. His research focuses mainly on economic growth, economic convergence and entrepreneurship in former transformation economies. He completed a B.Phil. in Economics at Oxford University. In 1994 he was a Senior Visiting Fellow of St Antony's College, Oxford and was a Scholar at the Woodrow Wilson centre in Washington, DC and in 1995 had an Eiuniadi Fellowship at Cornell University. From 1996 to 2007 he was Recurrent Visiting Professor at the Central European University in Budapest. He has contributed to edited volumes and written articles on topics of economic history; the transformation, comparative growth and economic inequality – in some he concentrated more on the Croatian experience and in others on a comparative approach. He is currently involved in completing an extensive study of growth diagnostics for the Croatian Employers' Association and is a member of the University Committee on Research and Technological Development.

Vesna Bojičić-Dželilović is Senior Research Fellow in the Department of International Development at the London School of Economics and Political Science. Her main areas of research include political economy of post-communist transition, conflict and post-conflict reconstruction, human security and civil society. She teaches and writes on these issues in the context of South East Europe. She has published articles, book chapters and policy papers and co-edited four books. She holds a Ph.D. in Economics and Master's in Development Economics.

Lars Burema is a project manager with the European Centre for Minority Issues (ECMI), Kosovo. He is currently managing a two-year project on the legal empowerment of marginalized communities in Kosovo, with a specific focus on addressing discrimination issues. Mr Burema has also managed ECMI Kosovo's project on supporting minority communities in Kosovo's local government reform process. He has a long-standing interest in post-conflict development, which he has explored through work and study. Previously, he has co-authored the study 'Eyes Wide Shut? The Impact of Embedded Journalism on Dutch Newspaper Coverage of Afghanistan'. He has a Master's degree in 'Conflict, Security and Development' from King's College London and a BA in Social Science from University College Utrecht.

Bruno Dallago, Ph.D. in Economics, is Professor of Economics at the University of Trento, Dean of the Faculty of Sociology and Academic Director of the Graduate School on Local Development. He was President of the European Association for Comparative Economic Studies; Visiting Professor at various universities, including the University of California at Berkeley, USA; the University of North Carolina at Chapel Hill; Hitotsubashi University, Tokyo; and has acted as a consultant to various international organizations. He is the author and editor of several scholarly books and journal articles. He researches comparative and institutional economics, the transforming economies of Central and East Europe, SMEs and entrepreneurship.

Englantina Gjini has acquired her interdisciplinary Master's degree in Comparative Local Development (Economics, Law, Sociology and Politology) at the University of Trento, Italy and University of Regensburg, Germany in 2008. She has worked as Project Coordinator for international organizations such as UNDP, UNICEF, PHARE Programme and SwissContact. She has a long experience as an Executive Director of ZMIMSC Foundation (The Regional Centre for Development and Monitoring of Infrastructure, Environment and Civil Society) centred in Gjirokastra Region, Albania. In this position she has initiated and directed several projects on local development, public policy and decentralization. Currently, she is studying at the University of

Toronto, School of Graduate Studies, Canada on Public Policy and Governance Master's programme and Advanced Diploma on Social Services Administration programme.

Dubravka Jurlina Alibegović has a doctorate in Economics from the University of Zagreb. She is Senior Research Associate and Head of Department for Regional Economics, Sustainability and Governance at the Institute of Economics, Zagreb. Previously, she worked as Deputy Minister in the Ministry of Science and Technology of the Croatia. She is a member of the Governing Board of the European Urban Research Association (EURA), the Croatian Section of the European Regional Science Association (ERSA), and the Croatian Network of Experts in Local and Regional Development. She was a member of the EU negotiation team for Croatia's accession to the European Union for Chapter 22: Regional policy and coordination of structural instruments. She is a member of the council for financing science and higher education in Croatia, and a member of the national commission for implementation of decentralization and reform of local and regional self-government units in Croatia. She has published a number of professional and scientific papers. She is a lecturer of Postgraduate Courses on Local Public Finance and Budgeting, and Local Development at the University of Zagreb.

Marija Kolin is Senior Research Fellow at the Institute for Social Sciences in Belgrade, Serbia. She holds an MA and a Ph.D. from the University of Belgrade in Social Anthropology and Sociology. During 2002–3 she was awarded a Fulbright Visiting Scholar Fellowship at the Georgetown University, Washington, DC. Ms Kolin works in numerous national and international research projects focused on social policy, social economy, civil society and gender issues. She has published several books and articles in Serbia and abroad. Her recent research spans women's participation in the labour market, social inclusion and European integration. She is a lecturer in the Centre of Gender Studies at the Faculty of Political Sciences, Belgrade. Ms Kolin has worked as a consultant on various EU projects in Serbia and the Western Balkans, and has acted as project evaluation assessor for the Delegation of the European Commission in Belgrade. She has evaluated research proposals for the European Commission Directorate General for Research & Innovation.

Cristina Matiuta is Associate Professor at the University of Oradea, Romania and head of the Department of Political Science and Communication. She graduated Political Science at Babes-Bolyai

University, Cluj-Napoca, Romania in 1996 and obtained her doctorate degree at the same university in 2004, with a thesis about the Relationship between Liberalism and Nationalism and Romania's Problems of Modernity. She teaches courses on Political Parties, Civil Society and Theory and Practice of Democracy. She has been a visiting researcher at the Université Libre de Bruxelles, Belgium, Faculty of Political Science (November 2002–February 2003), Institute of Federalism, University of Fribourg, Switzerland (March–July 2007) and a visiting lecturer at the University of Alicante, Spain (April 2008) and the University Federico II, Napoli, Italy (April–May 2010). She is Editor-in-Chief of the *Journal of Identity and Migration Studies* and author of three books and various articles in refereed journals. She has been involved as researcher in several national and international research projects in the field of active citizenship, governance, identity and migration.

Dragiša Mijačić is a Ph.D. candidate at the Maastricht Graduate School of Governance, Maastricht University and UNU-MERIT, the Netherlands, with a research focus on governance, decentralization and local/regional development. His research interests cover the impact of different types of institutional arrangement at the regional level on economic development. Mr Mijačić holds a joint Master's degree in development studies from the University of Trento and Free University of Bozen/Bolzano, Italy. He has worked as a policy researcher and development consultant, for the European Commission, and various international organizations across South East Europe. Mr Mijačić serves as Executive Director of the Institute for Territorial Economic Development (InTER), an independent think tank established with the mission of promoting and advancing sustainable socio-economic territorial development in the Western Balkans. He has published in the fields of socio-economic territorial development, decentralization, clusters, strategic planning, project-cycle management and donor-assistance monitoring and evaluation.

Vedrana Pribičević is currently employed as lecturer at the Zagreb School of Economics and Management, Croatia, where she teaches Microeconomics, Macroeconomics and Mathematical Methods in Economics. She received her MA in Economics from the Faculty of Economics and Business, University of Zagreb in 2007. Currently, she is a Ph.D. candidate at the same institution. Her academic interests encompass economic growth and economic inequalities.

Marija Risteska holds a Ph.D. in political science. She is the founder and works as Senior Analyst at the Centre for Research and Policy Making.

Her research work is in the area of public administration reform, public management, good governance, policy transfer and European integration. She teaches public policy, comparative public administration and public management at NY College in Skopje. Besides numerous policy studies on European integration of Macedonia, and good governance in health, education, gender and migration, Marija has edited the book *Mapping the Leaders in Macedonia and Albania: Can Elites Promote Positive Social Change?* and co-edited the books *European Law for SMEs* and *The Macedonian Question: 20 Years of Political Struggle into European Integration Structures*. She has contributed to public sector reforms in Macedonia on public policy development, strategic planning and better regulation. Ms Risteska has ten years of consulting experience with the EU and UN agencies.

Božidar Šišević holds a BA in Economics from the Faculty of Economics in Podgorica, and an MSc in Development Economics from Strathclyde University. He was Fulbright scholar from 1979–80, at the University of Texas, Austin, Indiana University, Bloomington and the University of California, Berkley. Mr Šišević spent most of his professional career at the Institute for Socio-Economic Research in Podgorica, doing research on human resource development, employment and unemployment, development of small and medium enterprises and entrepreneurship, regional economics, agricultural and rural development. At the Faculty of Economics in Podgorica he also lectured on Entrepreneurship and Small and Medium Enterprises Development. In 1979 he was appointed Executive Director of the Montenegro Development Agency. He has served as advisor to different government officials on human resource development, employment and unemployment, development of SMEs and entrepreneurship. The last ten years he has been working as a team leader at the National Observatory of Montenegro and Centre for Human Resource Development at the Employment Agency of Montenegro, mostly performing research on the labour market employment and training need analyses, vocational and adult education and training, social economy and social entrepreneurship, and the informal economy.

Lana Srzić is an independent consultant with expertise in post-conflict reconciliation and economic development, with a regional focus on South East Europe. She has worked for, among others, the United Nations Economic Commission for Europe (UNECE), the ILO and the Swiss Federal Department of Foreign Affairs. Ms Srzić holds a First Class Honours Bachelor's Degree from the University of Oxford in Modern History and Politics and a Ph.D. in International Relations from the Graduate Institute of International and Development Studies, Geneva.

Preface

The decentralization of administrative power and responsibility has been carried out in several post-communist countries in South East Europe (SEE) in recent years, aiming to consolidate democratic systems, strengthen local governance, promote local economic development, provide public services more responsive to local needs and contribute to the resolution of the ethnic conflicts which have afflicted the region since the collapse of the former Yugoslavia. However, decentralization may fail to achieve the desired effects if the administrative and financial capacity to implement the delegated or devolved responsibilities is inadequate. If not managed carefully, it may simply strengthen local elites and increase ethnic tensions rather than distribute power and influence widely among the local population.

In order to investigate these issues and in view of the potential importance of decentralization for promoting inclusive growth in the new economic environment that has followed the onset of the global economic crisis and its severe impact on the region, the research unit on South East Europe – LSEE – initiated a research project on 'Decentralisation and Regionalisation in South East Europe: Political, Economic, Social, and International Relations Aspects' funded with the generous support of the Latsis Public Benefit Foundation. The project, which was carried out in 2009–11, aimed to compare policies towards decentralization and regionalization in SEE based on original field research and data analysis. The results of the research project have been published as a set of LSEE Papers on Decentralisation in South East Europe, and revised versions of three of these papers dealing with issues related to decentralization appear as chapters in this book.

As part of the research project, LSEE co-organized a conference in Zagreb, Croatia, on 10–11 May 2010 in collaboration with the Institute for International Relations (IMO) under the direction of the editors of this volume. The conference on 'Regional Policy and Decentralisation in South East Europe' aimed to bring together the latest and best research on the issue of decentralization and regional development policy by leading scholars from around the whole region. The conference received generous support from the Friedrich Ebert Stiftung and the National Bank of Greece. We are especially grateful to Mirko Hempel of the Friedrich Ebert Stiftung Zagreb, George Andreou of the National

Bank of Greece, and Sanja Tisma, Director of IMO, for their personal contributions to the success of the conference as well as to all the participants, including paper presenters and discussants. Three papers from the conference were published in 2011 in Volume 35 Number 2 of the journal *Southeastern Europe*, while a selection of other papers presented at the conference that deal with the issue of decentralization have been subsequently revised and edited for publication in this volume. The editors are grateful to all the participants at the Zagreb conference for their valuable contribution to the discussion of the papers presented there. Finally, we are grateful for the administrative support provided by Ivan Kovanovic at LSEE and the encouragement and support of Ellie Shillitoe and Geetha Williams at Palgrave Macmillan throughout the writing and preparation of the book for publication.

Part I
Introduction

1
Decentralization Paradigms in South East Europe: An Introduction

Will Bartlett, Sanja Maleković and Vassilis Monastiriotis

Introduction

The countries of South East Europe entered the period of transition in the 1990s with very different legacies of government. Albania, Bulgaria and Romania had experienced highly centralized systems of government, while in Yugoslavia a more devolved form of government had been adopted through the system of socialist self-management (Dubey, 1975). This involved the decentralization of most government functions apart from defence and monetary policy to the federal republics. Within republics, many government responsibilities were decentralized to the level of municipalities with their own tax-raising powers, although genuine autonomy was constrained by the institutions of the one-party state.

Following the fall of the communist systems in these countries, and the onset of the process of political and economic transition, the evolution of systems of government differed. In the formerly centralized countries decentralization legislation was introduced in the early 1990s in Albania (Sewell and Wallich, 1995), Bulgaria (Martinez-Vazquez, 1995), and Romania (Jakob, 1995). The opposite trend took effect in the former Yugoslavia where, following its break-up in 1991, the successor states centralized many functions of government to the level of the new states, the erstwhile republics. After the end of the wars and conflicts in former Yugoslavia, interest in decentralization was not regained until the successor states felt sufficiently well established to relinquish some powers to the local level. This happened after the democratic changes that took place in Croatia and Serbia in 2000 with the fall of the Tudjman and Milošević regimes and the coming to power of political parties with a greater commitment to the consolidation of democracy than had previously been the case. Policy interest in decentralization has been reinforced in several other successor states of former Yugoslavia at the same time, largely as a way of defusing ethnic conflicts as in Macedonia and Kosovo, or as part of the state-building process as in Bosnia and Herzegovina.

The influence of EU enlargement and accession processes has also led to a parallel policy interest in regionalization and the establishment of EU-style regional divisions, mainly for statistical purposes. In the EU member states in the region (Bulgaria and Romania) this regionalization process has naturally aligned with the activities of EU regional policies. The countries of the Western Balkans have developed regional profiles in accordance with EU principles (the so-called NUTS regions[1]) in anticipation of future engagement with the EU regional development funds. However, while regionalization is largely an artefact of an administrative top-down approach to regional and local development practiced by the EU through the distribution of structural funds to member states, the decentralization process has been envisaged more often as a bottom-up process aiming to assist democratization and popular engagement in the political process at the local level. This approach holds the promise of releasing local energies for productive entrepreneurship and generating economic growth and 'home-grown' development potential, while at the same time addressing local specificities and permitting the peaceful expression of ethnic and cultural differences. Even so, decentralization has several potential drawbacks, including the possibility that a lack of administrative capacity may prevent the process from fulfilling its hoped-for potential and that it may even widen spatial disparities and worsen inequalities within countries. This book addresses these issues in a region in which the need for new dynamic sources of economic growth and the sustainable continuation of peaceful conflict resolution is of paramount importance for stability of the European continent as a whole.

Decentralization of government to regional and local levels, in both its administrative and fiscal forms, has taken place to different extents in the countries of South East Europe (Kandeva, 2001; Šević, 2008). It is a standard observation that decentralization has three main forms. In the least extensive form, central government powers may be simply 'deconcentrated' to local level with local offices of the central government providing centrally financed services at this level. A more extensive form of decentralization involves the 'delegation' of government functions from the centre to lower levels of government: while the broad aims of policy continue to be set by the central government which often supervises the delivery of services and provides most of the finance, the local level has autonomy in how services are to be provided and may also have some independent tax-raising powers. Both deconcentration and delegation can be observed in the countries in South East Europe. In Croatia, for example, one finds both central government offices and departments of democratically elected county administrations in most large cities, with each being responsible for delivering elements of local public services (Ivanisević et al., 2001). The institution of the Prefect plays a similar role in Albania and Romania. The most extensive from of decentralization is the 'devolution' of responsibility for defining, financing and providing services to lower levels of government. This latter form of decentralization was practised in the former Yugoslavia but has been rarely replicated apart from under the government arrangements in the rather special case of Bosnia and Herzegovina (Jokay, 2001; Fox and Wallich, 2008). The Bosnian case is an example of extensive devolution in which the powers of central government have been restricted to essential elements such as national defence and the regulation of the national currency and monetary policy.

Decentralization has been pursued for various reasons. One essential reason for decentralization has been to support local economic development and contribute to the creation of a competitive market economy. Decentralization of central government powers to local level may strengthen local governance and lead to an improved local business climate which may in turn incentivize increased local investment in physical and human capital giving rise to an 'economic dividend' due to decentralization. Improved local public infrastructure may also raise the attractiveness of a local economy to outside investors. The role of decentralization in promoting local economic development in South East Europe is addressed in Part I of this book.

Decentralization is also often applauded for its ability to bring government closer to the people and to match local preferences for an optimal mix of local taxation and expenditure or a mix of public services suited to the needs of the local population. It is thought that preferences can be better satisfied by local governments due to their greater awareness of local conditions compared to government at the central level (Oates, 1972). This benefit of decentralization is associated with variation in the demand for local services across jurisdictions and in the differing costs of providing such services. The key argument (sometimes referred to as the 'decentralization theorem') is that decentralization promotes allocative efficiency in the consumption of public services. This is held to be especially important in cases where the preferences across local communities are heterogeneous. Examples include cases where ethnic affiliations imply strong cultural differences and where ethnic rivalry has been a prominent feature of the political landscape. The role of decentralization in potentially defusing ethnic tension is further discussed in Part II.

Yet, while decentralization may promote local economic development, enhance allocative efficiency in consumption and diminish ethnic tensions over the distribution of public goods, it also has several potential drawbacks. These include a worsening of the efficiency of public administration due to the weak administrative capacity of local governments combined with a possible loss of effectiveness of public services due to an increase in corruption and a possible worsening of spatial inequality. The case for decentralization assumes that all units of local self-government have similar administrative capacity and similar levels of information and know-how. The issues of weak administrative capacity at local level, corruption and elite capture are dealt with in Part III of this book.

Decentralization is also commonly thought to have negative effects on the spatial distribution of income since wealthy localities generally have a larger tax base and can raise more tax revenue than poorer ones. If these tax revenues are used to invest in local economic development, a widening of income differentials may take place. There is then a role for central government in making compensating transfers, known as equalization grants, to poorer local authorities to redress imbalances due to an initial unequal distribution of resources. Whether these are sufficient to counteract the almost inevitable increase in inequality between different regions of a country is an empirical issue. Part IV of the book provides empirical evidence on the relationship between decentralization and spatial inequalities in three countries in South East Europe: Croatia, Serbia and Bulgaria.

The following sections of this chapter review the contributions of the book's chapters in these interrelated thematic areas, regarding the relationship between decentralization and local development, ethnic conflict resolution, administrative capacity and the issue of spatial inequality.

Local economic development

Traditional approaches to local economic development favoured state intervention to correct market failures. Regional development funds and agencies have often been established to counteract the unfavourable effects of market forces on regional inequalities: the Yugoslav Federal Fund for Less Developed Regions was an example of this approach. In recent years this approach to promoting local economic development from the outside has fallen into disfavour. In contrast, new theories of local economic development emphasize the role of institutions in mobilizing local 'endogenous' resources such as entrepreneurship, skills and innovation to support the growth of local economies (Pike, Rodriguez-Pose and Tomaney, 2006). These theories emphasize the importance of effective local institutions, strong social relations, productive social capital and positive interpersonal trust in creating a supportive environment for local development. Such institutions are more likely to emerge and be effective in an environment of extensive decentralization whether of the delegation or devolution variety (de Mello, 2011). High trust relations help to reduce the transaction costs of doing business and thus promote economic growth; low trust environments increase the need for formal contracts, contract monitoring and recourse to ineffective judicial systems, all of which increase the transaction costs of doing business. In this view, local institutions which complement each other are needed to support business networks and clusters, local innovation systems, and education and training systems to support the skills of the local labour force. However, institutions that support endogenous development are unlikely to emerge at the local level in an environment characterized by high levels of ethnic tension or widespread social exclusion. In Bosnia and Herzegovina, for example, the breakdown of social capital and trust relations have had negative effects on the development of the SME sector (Rus and Iglić, 2005).

In Chapter 2, Bruno Dallago analyses the role of decentralization in supporting economic growth and promoting political freedom in the transition (or transformation) countries of South East Europe. He argues that when an economy undergoes relentless change it suffers pervasive uncertainty, which poses dangers for the sustainability of transformation. Decentralization and local development can be a guarantee against such risks. However, in the Balkans it has led in some cases to a segmentation of the territory, the society and the economy, and has generated serious inequalities. Comparison with the model of transformation adopted in Poland and Slovenia suggests that while policy should focus on the creation of local opportunities by mobilizing local endogenous resources it should also be supplemented by attracting external resources to finance infrastructure development and investment in human capital. Since ethnic tensions are a danger for stability and development in the region, local development policies that include support for transborder actions and regional cooperation may also play an important role. He concludes that cooperation among central and local governments is needed to achieve favourable outcomes that should also be complemented by cooperation among local governments to enhance accountability.

Much attention has been given to the relationship between decentralization and economic growth. By improving local responsibility and accountability, it is thought the decentralization can support local economic development, which in turn should raise overall growth in the economy (Oates, 1993). Empirical evidence on this point is ambiguous. Some studies have found a positive relationship between decentralization and economic growth in advanced economies (Iimi, 2005), while others have found a negative relationship (Rodriguez-Pose and Ezcurra, 2011). Still others have found no evidence of any relationship between the two variables (Rodriguez-Pose and Bwire, 2004; Bodman, 2011). For transition economies, Rodriguez-Pose and Kroijer (2009) found a negative association between fiscal decentralization and economic growth in a sample of 16 countries in Central and Eastern Europe, although the degree of local tax-raising powers appeared to have a positive effect on economic growth.

In Chapter 3, Dubravka Jurlina Alibegović quantifies the impact of decentralization on economic growth in the transition economy of Croatia, which launched a partial decentralization of public functions in 2001. The major change was in the distribution of income tax revenues, with a larger part of those revenues being attributed to local governments to cover expenditures on decentralized functions in primary and secondary education, health care, social welfare and fire protection. Equalization grants were established for the decentralized functions of local government units with insufficient resources. The empirical analysis identifies a positive relationship between the extent of fiscal decentralization and the rate of economic growth, suggesting that more decentralization would be beneficial for the Croatian economy.

Institutional theories emphasize the system of local governance as a key factor influencing local economic development. Local governance systems comprise not just the formal institutions of local self-government and the political parties which control them but also other actors such as small businesses, entrepreneurs, NGOs and external actors such as the central government, foreign investors, foreign donors who also influence local decision-making. Where local institutions are relatively weak, it may be difficult to build political coalitions to support the process of endogenous local development. In such a situation external actors – including central government bodies, foreign investors and international donors – often exert undue influence and may undermine the development of local institutions supportive of local economic development.

In Chapter 4, Will Bartlett and Božidar Šišević analyse the effects of decentralization policies in Montenegro on the development of the less developed municipalities in the North East region. This region underwent a severe process of deindustrialization during the economic transition period in the 1990s and the early 2000s. Many of the local wood processing factories closed down, leading to the paradox of widespread unemployment and closed factories amid an area of abundant forest resources. International aid programmes funded by the EU and bilateral donors sought to revive the prospects of the region, but with little success. The region had previously been supported by development funding from what had been the central government in Belgrade. Although the Ministry of Economy has recognized the regional development problems and has designed regional development programmes aimed at reducing regional inequalities by redistributing resources across the regions more evenly, the authors argue that Montenegro is still a relatively centralized state and that decentralization reforms have had little impact on regional development. A further problem in fostering local development lies in the way that privatization took place in Montenegro, which failed to attract foreign direct investment to the region. On the basis of their observations and analysis drawn from in-depth interviews with key actors in the North East region, the authors propose the creation of a local development partnership council that would coordinate the development projects of the less developed municipalities.

Decentralization and conflict resolution in ethnically divided societies

As pointed out before, decentralization has been widely promoted as a means to ensure that local public services meet local needs and are adjusted to local preferences, rather than being imposed from the centre in the form of a diktat. Ethnic differentiation is a prime source of preference heterogeneity and has therefore often led to calls for greater local autonomy in ethnically divided societies. Where these calls have been resisted, ethnic conflict has often been the result and in the extreme case has led to secessionist movements becoming active as in the former Yugoslavia, with Kosovo being only the most recent example.

Decentralization has therefore often been used as a tool of peace building in ethnically diverse communities across the world (Brancati, 2009) and has been a prime measure for conflict reduction in several countries of South East Europe.

In Bosnia and Herzegovina, the Dayton Peace Agreement of 1995 brought an end to a vicious ethnic war and created a complex system of entities and cantons that institutionalized ethnically based local governments across the country. In Macedonia, decentralization was a basic component of the Ohrid Framework Agreement that ended the civil conflict between ethnic Albanian and ethnic Macedonian factions in 2001 (Mojsovska, 2011). It involved a change of municipal boundaries, improved minority language rights in municipalities with significant Albanian communities and a staged extension of devolved powers of government to more capable municipalities. In Kosovo, decentralization on ethnic lines was an integral feature of the Ahtisaari Plan that was accepted by the parliament of Kosovo when announcing its unilateral declaration of independence in February 2008.[2] This created several new municipalities for geographically isolated Serb minority communities, and provided extensive decentralized functions for secondary health services to Serb majority municipalities. The cases of Bosnia and Herzegovina and Kosovo are analysed in detail in Chapters 5 and 6 respectively, and a comparative analysis is provided in Chapter 7.

In Chapter 5, Vesna Bojičić-Dželilović presents an overview of the decentralization process in Bosnia and Herzegovina. She argues that strong political interests have cemented new territorial divisions created through war. Based on fieldwork and available studies, she discusses the factors that constrain the work of local administrations and the consequences for effective public service delivery. Efforts to shift the decentralization discourse to issues of economic development and improved mobilization of developmental resources by focusing on regional governance have been unsuccessful. She emphasizes that while uneven access to public services has been a general outcome of decentralization, its specific feature is that communities and individuals that were the worst affected by the war are also at the greatest disadvantage in the current institutional set-up. This is significant in that it reveals some of the limitations of the 'devolution' form of decentralization as a route to conflict resolution. She further argues that the greatest challenge to implementing decentralization in the context of the country's ethnically distorted politics and unfinished state-building continues to be the appropriate balancing of the local and higher scales of government through locally driven democratic debate. With such an approach, decentralization could be made to work towards the internal reintegration of the state while contributing also to the well-being of the nation.

The case of Kosovo is taken up by Lars Burema in Chapter 6 who analyses the potential for decentralization as a mechanism for defusing inter-ethnic tension, focusing on the case of southern Kosovo.[3] He contrasts the 'consociational' approach to managing diversity based on power-sharing and group autonomy with the 'integrationist' approach focused on the creation of a multi-ethnic identity through shared political, social and civil institutions. The main focus is placed on the Kosovo Serb community, which is the largest and politically most important minority, and the one most affected by the decentralization process. The analysis assesses the potential dangers of decentralization against its positive effects on levels of participation and integration of the Serb community. He argues that decentralization in the southern part of Kosovo has increased the involvement of both Kosovo Serb community members and political parties in the political process. While decentralization may in some circumstances strengthen secessionist tendencies, no move towards secessionism has been reported so far (although it should be pointed out that the situation is rather different in the north of Kosovo). The second danger of decentralization is that it might promote discrimination against minorities, increasing inter-ethnic tensions. However, considering the complex problems faced in Kosovo in implementing legislation, he concludes that fears of an emergence of discriminatory practises towards local minorities in the southern part of Kosovo have not materialized. The third potential danger is that decentralization might reinforce ethnic identities and create further tensions between the Albanian and the Serbian-led institutions. He argues that decentralization, while recognizing ethnic differences, has proven itself to be quite successful in improving the integration of the Serb community. In conclusion, the author highlights three key factors that are likely to determine the success of decentralization as a mechanism for improving inter-ethnic relations: employment opportunities need to be increased, infrastructure needs to be developed and all this needs to be done in close consultation with the local community.

Regional inequalities are often seen as a factor leading to secessionist impulses in the context of ethnically divided societies. Fiscal decentralization coupled with large fiscal transfers to regions inhabited by ethnic minorities is one approach to dealing with such problems, as in the Trentino-Alto Adige region in Italy, for example. Yet the effectiveness of fiscal decentralization in reducing ethnic tension seems to be greatest in richer countries with low levels of inequality (Tranchant, 2009; Murshed and Tadjoeddin, 2008) while it seems to encourage ethnic conflict where inequalities are high (Bakke and Wibbels, 2006). Consequently, if decentralization has the effect of leading to greater spatial inequalities, its potentially ameliorating impact on ethnic tensions may be offset. It is this interaction between the extent of inequalities and the nature of decentralization that seems to determine the incidence of ethnic conflict (Brown, n.d.). This insight calls for comparative analysis of cases of decentralization in ethnically divided societies to investigate the effect of decentralization on conflict resolution in countries with different levels of development and different level of spatial inequality. Since the level of development is lower in Kosovo than in Bosnia and Herzegovina, while the level of inequality is similar[4] one might expect more difficulties in Kosovo in using decentralization as a tool of ethnic conflict resolution.

The two cases are compared in Chapter 7 by Lana Srzić based on the 'consociational' and 'integrative' approaches to the analysis of decentralization in ethnically divided societies. She argues that in the Bosnian case decentralization resulted from a process of internal agreement following the war brokered by the international community but supported by a legacy of coexistence and cooperation based on a common culture and language. In Kosovo, however, a different legacy of conflict and cultural separation has underpinned the more difficult search for a workable structure of governance. In contrast to the views of Burema in the previous chapter, Srzić argues that in Kosovo the centrality of ethnicity in decentralization has been detrimental to establishing a functional state. Decentralization is seen through an ethnic prism, either as an instrument to improve the relative position of one's ethnic group, or as an internationally imposed structure potentially harmful to ethnic group interests. Echoing the arguments put forward by Bojičić-Dželilović in Chapter 5, she argues that the complex decentralized structure in place in Bosnia and Herzegovina with its lack of a clear hierarchy among governmental units has been a serious obstacle to economic development. Srzić concludes that the current structures in both Kosovo *and* Bosnia and Herzegovina have caused a deadlock, a lack of accountability and a constant power struggle on the basis of ethnicity. She proposes that a new model of governance is needed that would link decentralization to crucial issues such as job creation and poverty reduction and would demonstrate the potential benefits of decentralization for economic development, ethnic conflict resolution and improved governmental accountability.

Decentralization and implementation deficits

Much of the literature on decentralization has been devoted to the issue of implementation deficits. It is widely recognized that one of the disadvantages of decentralization is that local governments may not have the capacity to implement local programmes as effectively as central governments as they have fewer managerial resources both in terms of manpower and facilities (Prud'homme, 1995). Economies of scale in administration and in the production of services also mean that average costs of administration may be higher in smaller municipalities than in larger ones, and higher for all local government units than for the central government. Capital cities usually have far greater capacity to offer reliable services to the public than do municipalities in peripheral areas. On the other hand central government may have less information about local needs and resources. As Bardhan points out: 'information asymmetry thus works both ways: the central government may not know *what* to do; the local government may not know *how* to do it' (Bardhan, 2002: 189).

A main aim of decentralization has been to reduce the power of the central state, which had been discredited in the countries that had laboured under highly centralized systems of government under communism. As explained previously, this applied mainly to Albania, Bulgaria and Romania in the 1990s and to the Yugoslav successor states in the period after 2000. Decentralization of government can therefore be seen as a political parallel to economic decentralization from state-owned planned economies to market-based private ownership economies. However, decentralization may merely strengthen local elites rather than distributing power and influence widely among the population. Local governments are often captured by local business interests and by the top echelons of the political parties in power locally. In such a case, it may be that the provision of local public services is oriented to satisfying elite interests rather than meeting the preferences of the local population more broadly (Bardhan and Mookherjee, 2006). Examples include cases in which local roads are developed in proximity to the residence of important local politicians and neglected elsewhere. Furthermore, local government officials may be more corrupt than officials at the central level, and so the overall incidence of corruption may increase with decentralization further diminishing the effectiveness of local administration (Prud'homme, 1995). However, the empirical evidence is ambiguous with some studies showing that fiscal decentralization is actually associated with lower levels of corruption (Ivanyna and Shah, 2011; Fiorino,

Galli and Padovano, 2012). This section of the book presents a number of case studies that address the issue of local administrative capacity and the difficulties facing local governments in responding to local needs and facilitating local development in the way intended by the architects of decentralization reforms. A number of innovative solutions are presented by the authors of the various chapters ranging from a greater emphasis on social enterprise to the promotion of policy entrepreneurship at the local level.

In Chapter 8, Cristina Matiuta compares the legal framework for decentralization policies in Romania and Bulgaria and examines the extent to which legal provisions are implemented. She underlines three main factors which have slowed the implementation of decentralization: (i) the problem of human resources, (ii) corruption and (iii) political interference in the local public administration. The main challenge for both countries is the capacity to ensure the effective implementation of relevant regulations and strategies. She considers that a solution could be found through more effective management, coordination and cooperation between institutions in charge of the reforms and the development of partnerships between relevant stakeholders. She demonstrates that some positive changes have been introduced in recent years in response to pressure from the EU to implement the *acquis communautaire*. Although both countries have significantly improved civil servants' qualifications, further changes in the administrative culture and the modernization of the administrative apparatus are required. Firstly, information and media campaigns are needed to foster public cooperation in the process of decentralization. Secondly, improved monitoring of decentralized public services is necessary. Thirdly, a closer link is needed between the process of decentralization and local economic development policy, including measures to increase the absorption of EU funds at the local level. All of this should be accompanied by efforts to enhance the transparency and accountability of public institutions to tackle the widespread problem of corruption that threatens to undermine the potential benefits of decentralization.

In Chapter 9, Englantina Gjini explores the policy towards decentralization in Albania and the main difficulties that have been encountered in turning the policy into a practical reality. She argues that in order to succeed, decentralization in Albania required a new institutional design, effective coordination and devolved fiscal responsibilities. In 1999, the Strategy for Decentralization and Local Autonomy set out a long-term vision for the development of local government. Yet local governments still do not have the capacity to carry out their new functions effectively because the necessary financial resources have not been fully transferred along with their administrative responsibilities. Furthermore, the implementation of the Law on the transfer of property to local authorities was haphazard and despite the regulations little has happened. She concludes that the integration of administrative and fiscal decentralization in Albania requires a far greater political commitment than has been the case up to now, as well as the committed participation from both the central and local governments.

In the face of deficits in local administrative capacity, governments are increasingly turning to the 'third sector' of social enterprises and non-profit enterprises with a social purpose to fill some of the gaps. In Chapter 10, Marija Kolin argues that a major problem in Serbia's underdeveloped regions is a lack of financial resources and administrative and professional capacities that would ensure that local programmes reach a wide range of beneficiaries. She suggests that, given the weak capacity of local public administration, the capacity of local 'third-sector' service providers should be expanded. Kolin identifies a variety of third-sector service providers in Serbia and provides a detailed insight into their structure and the scope of targeted beneficiaries. She points out that while the state provision of welfare remains the dominant model, non-governmental organizations are increasingly becoming supplemental actors in the provision of local services. She argues that greater attention should be given to strengthening the local welfare system and to promoting alternative community services using instruments such as community foundations, partnerships and third-sector funds, and to the development of innovative local financial institutions that could support the development of third-sector organizations at the local level.

In the face of low administrative capacity it is often argued that local administration may be improved through institutions of public–private partnership, involving the private sector more in the design of local economic development strategies. In Chapter 11, Dragiša Mijačić examines whether improved dialogue between the public and private sectors at the local level in Serbia could support more effective strategic planning. Mijačić presents the results of field research conducted between 2009 and 2010 in the Autonomous Province of Vojvodina with local self-government institutions that were or had been involved in the strategic planning process and with representatives of private sector enterprises in two cities and three municipalities. His research demonstrates that private sector representatives were generally more aware of the existence of a strategic plan and its objectives in municipalities in which a participatory approach had been implemented. Participatory planning appears to contribute to the transparency of local administration and increases trust in local authorities. However, the research also revealed a rather negligible participation of the private sector in the actual process of strategic planning, which may partly be attributed to inability of local businesses to create jobs, generate wealth or contribute to local economic development. Furthermore, there was no evidence of improved public–private dialogue on any important issues, whether related to the implementation of the strategy or to any other question. The reasons may be found in the traditional lack of trust between the actors on both sides as well as in procedural issues. Mijačić concludes that in order to increase the trust between the actors and their sense of ownership it is necessary to establish a permanent forum for public–private dialogue at the local level.

Could administrative capacity be improved by encouraging 'policy entrepreneurship' within local self-government institutions? This would seem to be the way forward to ensure that local administrations respond sensitively and effectively to local needs, given an appropriate delegation of decision-making authority to local government officials. In Chapter 12, Marija Risteska assesses how the decentralization process affects policy entrepreneurship in Macedonian municipalities since the decentralization reform of 2005. She considers the hypothesis that in a decentralized environment local policymakers, including public service managers, become 'policy entrepreneurs' who strive to match the design of the public services offered by municipalities with the preferences and needs of their constituents. She assesses local policymakers' potential to engage in policy entrepreneurship in the social sector, focusing on childcare services. She argues that while the management of these services was fully transferred to municipalities in the second phase of decentralization, policymaking remained under the competence of the central government. Moreover, financial resources allocated for the enlarged set of competences were allocated according to the pre-existing distribution of assets rather than needs.

Risteska concludes that this policy may further widen the disparities between rural and urban areas. Could officials in municipalities without childcare institutions act as policy entrepreneurs and establish new childcare institutions in response to local needs? Risteska points out the obstacles to this solution among which are the lack of financial resources and a lack of guidance and support for policy entrepreneurship from the central government. She concludes that in order to enable municipalities to make more effective use of their transferred competences and to encourage them to establish new local public services it is necessary to

(i) redistribute finances to ensure more balanced development, (ii) set up an appropriate institutional framework and provide the necessary guidance from the central government and (iii) strengthen cooperation between local and central government.

Spatial inequalities

Decentralization is often held to have strong negative implications for spatial inequalities. As argued earlier, such inequalities may interact adversely with ethnic differences in an environment of decentralized governance, such that if inequality increases ethnic tensions there may be adverse effects on local economic development. Spatial inequalities seem to have widened in many post-communist economies during the transition period in the 1990s as market opening encouraged agglomeration in capital cities and a relative decline of less developed areas (Blokker and Dallago, 2009; Petrakos, 2001). For example, regional differences in unemployment rates in transition countries have generally been far greater than in the West (Boeri and Scarpetta, 1996); this has been explained by low labour mobility (Bornhorst and Commander, 2006) and by spatial differences in education and skills (Jurajda and Terrell, 2009). The phenomenon of widening spatial disparities has also been observed in transition economies of South East Europe (Leitner and Stehrer, 2009). Whether decentralization has contributed to an increase in spatial inequalities in transition economies and elsewhere is less clear. Canaleta, Arzoz and Garate (2004) find a strong negative correlation between decentralization and regional inequality in a sample of OECD countries, while in a study of several countries in the European Union, Ezcurra and Pascual (2008) find that fiscal decentralization is similarly associated with a reduction of regional inequality within countries. Costa-Font (2010) also finds a reduction in regional inequalities in welfare provision in Spain following devolution of power to the provinces. However, Rodriguez-Pose and Ezcurra (2010) demonstrate that while fiscal decentralization is associated with a reduction in regional inequalities in advanced countries, it is associated with increased regional inequalities in low- and middle-income countries, and it is the latter group to which the countries of South East Europe belong.

In Chapter 13, Vassilis Monastiriotis investigates the extent and scale of spatial disparities in Serbia and Bulgaria. Combining district- and municipal-level data covering the period 1995–2008, he examines three dimensions of inequality. Firstly, he investigates the degree of disparity at different scales (regional and local) and the relative importance of each scale for overall inequality (both within and between regions). Secondly, he investigates the extent and scale of spatial clustering in the form of geographical concentration of front-runner and lagging areas. Thirdly, he identifies trends of divergence, the persistence of disparities and their geographical manifestation. Based on the evidence obtained from these analyses, Monastiriotis identifies significant differences in the patterns of spatial inequality in Bulgaria and Serbia. In Bulgaria, inequalities appear to be located mainly within regions rather than between them. Several parts of the country have dynamic centres of economic growth, but there are relatively weak linkages within regions that would spread this growth more widely. In Serbia the picture is quite different, with a substantial north–south polarization that seems to be deepening over time. While not addressing the issue of whether decentralization is implicated in these differences directly, Monastiriotis provides implicit evidence on the relationship between decentralization and inequality. One implication seems to be that decentralization in Serbia has not been associated with in an increase in spatial inequalities, although it has also failed to unleash local endogenous growth potential in the poor southern part of the country; a more radical policy seems to be needed to address this issue. In Bulgaria, even though decentralization has not been a priority of government policy (Meurs, 2008),[5] spatial disparities have increased. In this case, centrally managed policy to promote economic growth appears to have created several distinct growth poles but without having much effect on local pockets of poverty and underdevelopment throughout the country.

Looking at the long view, spatial inequalities in South East Europe appear to be surprisingly resilient. In Chapter 14, Ivo Bićanić and Vedrana Pribičević investigate the persistence of regional inequalities and identify the difficulties in reducing such deep-seated patterns. They focus on the example of Croatia both within the former Yugoslavia and as an independent country. During the pre-transition period, regional discrepancies were influenced by development inertia, social engineering and exogenous shocks. Socialism failed to narrow the gap between the more and the less developed regions. With the disintegration of Yugoslavia, Croatia faced new borders as points of spatial discontinuity. Bićanić and Pribičević use two different indicators to identify long-run tendencies of spatial inequalities: the Gini index, an intuitive measure of inequality and the Theil index, which provides measures of inter- and intra-regional inequalities. The data reveal a gradual decrease of intraregional inequality over time, with increasing heterogeneity at the same time in the Northwest region, including Zagreb, Croatia's capital.

Conversely, the Adriatic region becomes less diverse over time, while the Eastern region lags behind substantially. The results suggest that spatial inequalities are deeply entrenched between Croatia's regions. The chapter draws conclusions relating to the ability of policies of decentralization and regional development to mitigate such inequalities.

Conclusions

The decentralization of government has often been promoted as a way to remove the power of the central state from interference in the functioning of the nascent market economy that has been created in the transition economies of Central and South East Europe through privatization and the deregulation of the entry of new small firms (Bird, Ebel and Wallich, 1995; Kandeva, 2001). The enthusiasm for decentralization has been focused on its potential role in promoting local economic development, delivering local services more attuned to local needs and in doing so resolving ethnic rivalries and conflicts. However, as shown in the chapters of this book, this is often a less successful process than has been expected by its proponents.

Recent theories of economic growth have pointed to the important role played by 'endogenous' development, based on the mobilization of local resources and energies. This certainly seems relevant in the current context of post-crisis recovery as the region cannot expect to rely on such large inflows of capital and financial resources from the outside as it did in the pre-crisis period (Bartlett and Monastiriotis, 2010). Decentralization is often seen as making an important contribution to the mobilization of local resources for economic development. However, as the contributions to this book show, while it may be a necessary ingredient it may not be a sufficient policy instrument on its own to support local economic development in South East Europe. While there is some evidence that decentralization supports economic growth more developed countries such as Croatia, elsewhere the linkage is less apparent. Decentralization has often failed to remove the element of political interference and political connectedness of the state and the new business elites, which control the often highly monopolized private market economy. State capture, either at central or local level, has been a persistent feature of economic institutions that have emerged in the region and has undermined the competitiveness of the emerging economies. Possible solutions to these defects lie in a greater empowerment of the local level of government through enabling and supporting inter-municipal cooperation and the development of cooperation between the public and private sectors at the local level especially small business associations and local social enterprises to counteract the influence of dominant large enterprises and local elites. The introduction of freedoms and incentives for local officials to engage in 'policy entrepreneurship' could further support the development of a policy environment more responsive to local needs and the emergence of local 'productive entrepreneurship' in the private sector.[6]

Opinions differ as to whether decentralization can provide an effective route to ethnic conflict resolution and its sustainability. As the chapters in this book demonstrate there is ample scope for disagreement over the causes of continuing ethnic rivalries and the factors that might prevent them from becoming once again inflamed. It is indeed plausible that the design of the structure of local governance is an important factor in resolving such ethnic tensions. From the analyses presented in the book, it would seem that the interaction of political and economic factors is critical. In southern Kosovo, for example, where political participation has been achieved even in a context of widespread poverty, ethnic tensions appear to be dissipating. In the northern part of Kosovo, however, local economic interests appear to support the maintenance of an ethnic enclave outside the rule of law of the central (Kosovo) government. There, despite an extensive system of enhanced autonomy, ethnic conflicts have recently been roused again over a dispute over control of border posts. In Bosnia and Herzegovina, arguably with the most decentralized government structure in the region, and with a legacy of ethnic coexistence more embedded than in Kosovo, ethnic rivalries appear to be held in check rather than diminished through the institutional arrangements for decentralization. In Bosnia, ethnically based political interests appear to be reinforced by devolution rather than being resolved, entrenching uneven access to public services and reinforcing inherited inequalities. It therefore seems that there is no easily discernible relationship between decentralization and ethnic conflict resolution, with much depending on the specificities of the case and the political motivations of the actors involved. Contributory factors to embedding successful decentralization practices seem to be success with job creation, development of local infrastructure, and the encouragement and facilitation of a wide participation of all interest groups in the institutions of local governance.

A fundamental difficulty with the process of decentralization in South East Europe has been the ubiquitous problems of implementation and an absence of administrative capacity at the local level. One solution that suggests itself is the contracting out of local service provision to social enterprises, but this in turn requires investment to enable and incentivize the entry of new providers. No doubt this could be facilitated in cases where local officials have the freedoms and abilities to engage in imaginative and innovative processes of policy entrepreneurship, but these actors are frequently constrained by the very lack of implementation and limitations of capacity which successful policy entrepreneurship would go some way to redress. Equally, a greater coordination and cooperation between the public and private sectors would no doubt overcome some of the information problems which prevent local officials from responding effectively to the needs of local economic actors. Participatory planning is a sound idea, but it is doubtful whether it can be implemented effectively in an environment in which there is a lack of trust between different local actors and in which political interests seek to capture positions in local government so that 'participation' may easily turn into partisan 'control' or 'capture'. There is moreover a fine line between participation and corruption, and between policy entrepreneurship and local elite capture. The sensitivity of central government to these issues goes a long way to explain their reluctance to back up the formal legal frameworks of administrative decentralization with effective fiscal decentralization that would fully enable local officials to implement their newfound powers without a controlling oversight from the centre. The case studies presented in this book suggest that there may be some significant differences in these issues between countries that are EU member states and those that are not. In Bulgaria and Romania the influence of the EU structural funds, and of EU practices that are transferred through their implementation may serve to strengthen the applicability of the principles of decentralization. In the EU 'candidate' and 'potential candidate' states, there are simply insufficient resources to enable experiments with democratic local participation and control to stray much from central government priorities. Even so, this distinction should not be taken too far. Entrenched problems of corruption and state capture at local level seem to persist in both cases.

Spatial inequalities have increased throughout the transition countries in Central and Eastern Europe, and much evidence suggests that decentralization is associated with increased spatial disparities in both advanced and transition countries. However, the evidence provided in this book appears to indicate that the situation may be rather different in the Yugoslav successor states. In both Croatia and Serbia it seems that spatial inequalities have not increased during the transition period or with the introduction of decentralization, but rather have been sustained and persistent over time under a variety of political regimes. The difference may be associated with the fact that a decentralized system of governance was practiced in the former Yugoslavia, albeit within a one-party state, and so there is consequently less contrast with an earlier high degree of centralization as practiced in Bulgaria and other transition countries in Central and Eastern Europe under Soviet-style communism. Such persistent inequalities are, however, associated with specific historical and political conditions, which are not impervious to change. To the extent that inequalities interact with ethnic rivalries and tensions to create political instability and undermine the development of local social capital and trust relations, they potentially have an adverse impact on future economic development. The persistence of such inequalities should therefore inspire much greater attention from policymakers and calls for greater priority to policy action on this important issue.

Whether decentralization or the associated policies of regionalization have much of a role to play in overcoming such deep-seated structural conditions remains an open question. It is hoped that this book will provide a stepping stone and perhaps an inspiration towards further research on the impact of decentralization in South East Europe and to the design of appropriate policies that could contribute to future economic growth and the improvement of social welfare in the region.

Notes

1. NUTS – the Nomenclature of Territorial Units for Statistics – is the standard classification used by the EU and its statistical office, Eurostat, for the definition of territorial units within countries. The 'NUTS2' level of territorial classification referred to in several chapters in this book is the regional level used of the application of EU regional policies.
2. The 'Ahtisaari Plan' was submitted under the title 'Comprehensive Proposal for the Kosovo Status Settlement' in March 2007. The Plan envisaged that Serb municipalities would enjoy 'enhanced responsibilities', including authority over health care and higher education, the right to appoint police commanders and responsibility for their own cultural and religious affairs.
3. The northern municipalities, being almost entirely populated by ethnic Serbs, do not recognize the state institutions set up by the Kosovo government and seek greater integration with Serbia.
4. The Gini coefficient, a measure of income inequality, was 33.3 in Bosnia and Herzegovina in 2009 and 30.0 in Kosovo in 2007 (World Bank, 2007, 2009).
5. 'In 2002 Bulgarian local governments still had limited revenue autonomy and faced numerous limitations on their ability to independently adjust spending. In many ways, local governments served as agents of the central state rather than agents of the local population' (Meurs, 2008: 29).

6. The term 'productive entrepreneurship is used here the sense of Baumol (1990) to indicate the absence of rent-seeking, corruption and brigandage.

References

Bakke, K. M. and Wibbels, E. (2006) 'Diversity, disparity and civil conflict in federal states', *World Politics*, 59(1): 1–50.
Bardhan, P. (2002) 'Decentralisation of governance and development', *The Journal of Economic Perspectives*, 16(4): 185–205.
Bardhan, P. and Mookherjee, D. (eds) (2006) *Decentralisation and Local Governance in Developing Countries: A Comparative Perspective*, Cambridge, MA: The MIT Press.
Bartlett, W. and Monastiriotis, V. (eds) (2010) *South East Europe after the Crisis: A New Dawn or Back to Business as Usual?* London: London School of Economics.
Baumol, W. J. (1990) 'Entrepreneurship: Productive, unproductive, and destructive', *Journal of Political Economy*, 98(5): 893–921.
Bird, R. M., Ebel, R. D. and Wallich, C. I. (1995) *Decentralisation of the Socialist State: Intergovernmental Finance in Transition Economies*, Washington, DC: The World Bank.
Blokker, P. and Dallago, B. (eds) (2009) *Regional Diversity and Local Development in the New Member States*, Basingstoke: Palgrave Macmillan.
Bodman, P. (2011) 'Fiscal decentralization and economic growth in the OECD', *Applied Economics*, 43(23): 3021–35.
Boeri, T. and Scarpetta, S. (1996) 'Regional mismatch and the transition to a market economy', *Labour Economics*, 3(3): 233–54.
Bornhorst, F. and Commander, S. (2006) 'Regional unemployment and its persistence in transition countries', *Economics of Transition*, 14(2): 269–88.
Brancati, D. (2009) *Peace by Design: Managing Interstate Conflict through Decentralisation*, Oxford: Oxford University Press.
Brown, G. (n.d.) 'Federalism, decentralisation and horizontal inequalities', *CRISE Policy Briefing No. 3*, Centre for Research on Inequality, University of Oxford
Canaleta, C. G., Arzoz, P. P. and Garate, M. R. (2004) 'Regional economic disparities and decentralisation', *Urban Studies*, 41(1): 71–94.
Costa-Font, J. (2010) 'Does devolution lead to regional inequalities in welfare activity?' *Environment and Planning C: Government and Policy*, 28(3): 435–49.
De Mello, L. (2011) 'Does fiscal decentralisation strengthen social capital? Cross-country evidence and the experiences of Brazil', *Environment and Planning C: Government and Policy*, 29(2): 281–96.
Dubey, V. (1975) *Yugoslavia: Development with Decentralisation*, Baltimore: The John Hopkins University Press.
Ezcurra, R. and Pascual, P. (2008) 'Fiscal decentralisation and regional disparities: evidence from several European Union countries', *Environment and Planning A*, 40(5): 1185–201.
Fiorino, N., Galli, E. and Padovano, F. (2012) 'Does fiscal decentralisation and government fragmentation affect corruption in different ways? Evidence from a panel data analysis' *International Center for Public Policy Working Paper 12–17*, Atlanta: International Center for Public Policy, Andrew Young School of Policy Studies, Georgia State University.

Fox, W. and Wallich, C. (1998) 'Bosnia-Herzegovina: Fiscal federalism after Dayton', in R. M. Bird and F. Villaincourt (eds) *Fiscal Decentralisation in Developing Countries*, Cambridge: Cambridge University Press, pp. 271–300.

Iimi, A. (2005) 'Decentralisation and economic growth revisited: An empirical note', *Journal of Urban Economics*, 57(3): 449–61.

Ivanisević, S., Koprić, I., Omejec, J. and Simović, J. (2001) 'Local government in Croatia', in E. Kandeva (ed.) *Stabilization of Local Governments*, Budapest: Open Society Institute, pp. 179–240.

Ivanyna, M. and Shah, A. (2011) 'Decentralisation and corruption: New cross-country evidence', *Environment and Planning C: Government and Policy*, 29(2): 344–62.

Jakob, F. A. (1995) 'Decentralisation and local government finance in Romania', in R. M. Bird, R. D. Ebel and C. I. Wallich (eds) *Decentralisation of the Socialist State: Intergovernmental Finance in Transition Economies*, Washington, DC: World Bank, pp. 223–50.

Jokay, C. (2001) 'Local government in Bosnia and Herzegovina', in E. Kandeva (ed.) *Stabilization of Local Governments*, Budapest: Open Society Institute, pp. 89–140.

Jurajda, S. and Terrell, K. (2009) 'Regional unemployment and human capital in transition economies', *Economics of Transition*, 17(2): 241–74.

Kandeva, E. (ed.) (2001) *Stabilization of Local Governments*, Budapest: Open Society Institute.

Leitner, S. and Stehrer, R. (2009) 'Inequality in selected SEE countries: A decomposition analysis of trends and determinants', Paper prepared as part of the Global Development Network (GDN) project *Inequality and Fiscal Policy in Transition Countries*.

Martinez-Vazquez, J. (1995) 'Intergovernmental fiscal relations in Bulgaria', in R. M. Bird, R. D. Ebel and C. I. Wallich (eds) *Decentralisation of the Socialist State: Intergovernmental Finance in Transition Economies*, Washington, DC: World Bank, pp. 183–222.

Meurs, M. (2008) 'Decentralisation and development in post-socialism: Local characteristics and outcomes in post-socialist Bulgaria', *Post-Communist Economies*, 20(1): 11–32.

Mojsovska, S. (2011) 'Decentralisation and regional policy in the Republic of Macedonia: Developments and perspectives', *LSEE Paper on Decentralisation and Regional Policy No. 4*, London: London School of Economics and Political Science.

Murshed, S. M. and Tadjoeddin, M. Z. (2008) 'Is fiscal decentralisation conflict abating? Routine violence and district level government in Java, Indonesia', *MICROCON Research Working Paper No. 7*, Brighton: MICROCON.

Oates, W. (1972) *Fiscal Federalism*, New York: Harcourt Brace Jovanovic.

Oates, W. (1993) 'Fiscal decentralisation and economic development', *National Tax Journal*, 46(2): 237–43.

Petrakos, G. (2001) 'Patterns of regional inequality in transition economies', *European Planning Studies*, 9(3): 359–83.

Pike, A., Rodriguez-Pose, A. and Tomaney, J. (2006) *Local and Regional Development*, London: Routledge.

Prud'homme, R. (1995) 'The dangers of decentralisation', *World Bank Research Observer*, 10(2): 201–20.

Rodriguez-Pose, A. and Bwire, A. (2004) 'The economic (in)efficiency of devolution', *Environment and Planning A*, 36(11): 1907–28.
Rodriguez-Pose, A. and Ezcurra, R. (2010) 'Does decentralisation matter for regional disparities? A cross-country analysis', *Journal of Economic Geography*, 10(5): 619–44.
Rodriguez-Pose, A. and Ezcurra, R. (2011) 'Is fiscal decentralisation harmful for economic growth? Evidence from the OECD countries', *Journal of Economic Geography*, 11(4): 619–43.
Rodríguez-Pose, A. and Kroijer, A. (2009) 'Fiscal decentralization and economic growth in Central and Eastern Europe', *Growth and Change*, 40(3): 387–417.
Rus, A. and Iglić, H. (2005) 'Trust, governance and performance: The role of institutional and interpersonal trust in SME development', *International Sociology*, 20(3): 371–91.
Sewell, D. and Wallich, C. I. (1995) 'Fiscal decentralisation and intergovernmental relations in Albania', in R. M. Bird, R. D. Ebel and C. I. Wallich (eds) *Decentralisation of the Socialist State: Intergovernmental Finance in Transition Economies*, Washington, DC: World Bank, pp. 251–80.
Šević, Ž. (ed.) (2008) *Local Public Finance in Central and Eastern Europe*, Cheltenham: Edward Elgar.
Tranchant, J.-P. (2009) 'Fiscal decentralisation, institutional quality, and ethnic conflict: A panel data analysis, 1985–2001', *Conflict, Security and Development*, 8(4): 491–514.
World Bank (2007) *Kosovo Poverty Assessment*, Washington, DC: The World Bank.
World Bank (2009) *Protecting the Poor During the Global Crisis: 2009 Bosnia and Herzegovina Poverty Update*, Washington, DC: The World Bank.

Part II

Decentralization and Local Development

2

Puzzles in Local Development and Transformation in South East Europe

Bruno Dallago[1]

Introduction

The overall economic aim of transformation in South East Europe (SEE) over the last 20 years has been to support sustained economic growth. This required states to ensure conditions for the pursuit of freedom and the creation of innovating institutions, organizations and structures. Local development should have played a central role in this, on its own merit and in consideration of the centralized nature of the pre-transformation economic system.

Local development includes all the conditions fostering performance and transformation in a given subnational territory: enterprise foundation, growth and restructuring; the production, use and management of human, social and physical resources (the territory); structural change; and the activity of governments (both local and national). Local development is critically important for the success of transformation for different reasons: it mobilizes dispersed resources, fosters entrepreneurship and the economic utilization of social capital, allows policies to better respond and adapt to asymmetric shocks coming from the integration in the world economy, decreases transaction costs through the strengthening of trust, and adapts infrastructure to local circumstances. Perhaps most important, local development is the cradle and necessary condition for streamlining formal and informal institutions and coordinates them to support productive entrepreneurship and activity.

One important question for the success of transformation, then, is to define what is needed for fostering local development. Within the general framework of economic freedom, the starting point is to combine a respect for general economic principles of good economic management with an adaptation of policies to local circumstances. Such a conjugation requires both an understanding of the nature and features of the new situation through interpretation and a definition of problems and their solutions through relevant analysis. Both of these are fundamental bases for effective innovation.

This chapter considers what went wrong with transformation through the lens of local development. The chapter starts by considering Dani Rodrik's (2007) stimulating observation that reform policy should both follow general principles of adopting good economic management and adapting to local circumstances (Section 1). It considers the proposition that a socially advantageous outcome also requires a deep and broad-based interpretive process that involves both technical expertise and genuine social and political participation (Section 2). It goes on to argue that when an economy undergoes relentless change, and suffers pervasive ambiguity and uncertainty, animal spirits are often activated in the form of entrepreneurship (Section 3). Such animal spirits have much to do with the freedoms and unfreedoms that may easily follow from the ensuing changes and may jeopardize the sustainability of transformation. Local development is one important guarantee against such risks (Section 4). Taken together, the four dimensions of economic management, interpretation, entrepreneurship and local development strongly influence economic performance (Section 5). Section 6 concludes.

Transformation and local development

A standard approach to the analysis of economic development is that growth takes place when institutions are closely aligned so as to reduce uncertainty, facilitate social interaction, provide strong incentives for economic activity and keep enforcement effective and its costs low (Sautet, 2005). Existing entrepreneurial abilities are thus allocated to productive uses fostering growth.

Growth-reviving reform policy should be based on general principles of good economic management (Rodrik, 2007). These include protection of property rights, contract enforcement, market-based competition, appropriate incentives, sound money, and debt sustainability among others. Reform policy should also give importance to local circumstances (involving careful choice of the location of investment, encouragement of good labour relations in line with local traditions and support for cooperation between firms and local governments) because opportunities and constraints differ according to the specific environment in which policies are implemented. Institutions are based on 'considerable local knowledge' (Rodrik, 2007: 42), and proceed through 'a process of discovery about local needs and capabilities' (Rodrik, 2007: 166). Institutions map into different policy packages, having different costs and benefits depending on prevailing political constraints, levels of administrative competence, and local market failures.

The skill of reformers is to find the package of institutions that minimizes the costs and difficulties and maximizes the benefits for a particular economy under the constraint of path dependence. A deep and broad-based interpretive process is required involving both technical expertise and genuine social and political participation. However, during transformation the coordinates necessary for identifying and streamlining general principles and local features are ambiguous and uncertain due to institutional transformation, incompleteness and weak enforcement (Dallago, 1996).

Consequently, effective policies require both analytic problem solving (e.g. how to decrease costs, which investment should be implemented, where to obtain financial resources, where to build roads and infrastructure and how to design performance-friendly taxation) and interpretation (e.g. which kind of development strategies are most appropriate to a given territory, which form of enterprise is the most effective, and when and how to innovate).

Although important, too much detailed attention to interpretation may foster foot dragging, which local development may be able to attenuate, based as it is on local social capital and local control. Such features are important particularly for the transformation of sticky and incrementally changing informal institutions. Local development is important also for promoting small- and medium-sized enterprises (SMEs) and supporting local governments, both of which are particularly well placed to foster interpretation and adaptation to local circumstances, being closer to local processes and embedded in local features.

During transformation, territorial differences and economic and social inequality tend to increase substantially (Eurostat, 2010a) due to the 'spontaneous' processes that are unleashed. These included the agglomeration of economic activities and domestic and foreign capital, and the weakening capacity of governments to finance welfare expenditure. Growing inequalities associated with transformation create clashing perceptions, interests and strategies, leading to congestion of opportunities (e.g. in the privatization process or in personal connections) on one side and a lack of opportunities on the other (Sen, 1999).

Typical territorial patterns of transformation have encompassed five main factors (Blokker and Dallago, 2009). These can be summarized as (a) polarization through a faster development of regions with large urban centres and the decline of peripheral regions, (b) metropolization which has replaced traditional urban–rural divides, (c) the East–West divide arising from new opportunities of transborder cooperation, (d) decentralization and local democracy which is still developing in some countries and (e) new regional trajectories which are developing through the restructuring of different sectors at varying speeds.

Development programmes that have sought to attract foreign investments have been mostly analytic in nature. In spite of EU and government efforts, they have lacked coordination involving neighbouring localities and central governments and have sometimes disregarded sound general principles such as accounting for the opportunity cost of granting subsidies to foreign investors.

Insufficient attention to the principles of interpretation and experimentation at the local level have often made it difficult to devise sustainable national strategies, which led to uncoordinated actions and in the long run causing a waste of opportunities. Consequently, SMEs are generally ailing in many localities while industrial parks, financial support and business incubators have remained rather ineffective in most transformation countries in the region.

Despite differences in name (regions, provinces, counties, municipalities, communes and villages), two- or three-tier government systems have been established in most transformation countries in order to take into account different local circumstances and their institutionalization. In SEE, local self-government units have similar design, powers and functions, although other features may differ such as the number of inhabitants) (see Table 2.1). Special status is usually given to the capital city and in some cases to large secondary cities (Woelk, 2005).

Laws on local self-government are the result of relatively recent constitutional and administrative reforms and usually reflect the principles of the European Charter of Local Self-Government (ECLSG). However, in reality top-down relations often prevail whereby rights and authority are vested in the state, which delegates them when appropriate. Usually intermediate local government levels function as territorial branches of the central administration. In some cases (e.g. Serbia) this level has neither autonomy nor elected bodies. In general there also is a central ministry for local development or government.

Most local authorities suffer from a lack of financial and technical capacity for the implementation of their functions. This depends primarily on the low level of own source revenue in the form of local tax revenues and income from fees and charges (see Table 2.2)[2] and the dominance of financial transfers from the central government and

Table 2.1 Territorial organization in SEE

Country	Territorial authorities (counties or regions)	Local authorities			Number of settlements	Number of settlements	Population
		City status	District	Total		Per municipality	
Albania	12	65	308	373	3052	8.2	9811
BiH							
	10	–	79	79	3343	42.3	36,110
Republika Srpska	7	2*	61*	63	2721	43.2	23,220
Bulgaria^	264						28,670
Croatia	21	127	429	556	6752	12.1	8070
Kosovo	–	–	33	33	1466	44.4	55,001
Macedonia	–	–	84	84	1767	21.0	24,668
Montenegro	–	–	21	21	1256	59.8	31,749
Romania^	41			3180			6750
Serbia	1	23	122	145	4720	32.6	50,654
Slovenia	–	11	199	210	6028	28.7	9539

Notes: * In Republika Srpska, the city of Banja Luka is a district-type municipality with city status and appears under both headings. ^ Existence of structured sub-municipal level (communities, localities).
Source: Pálné Kovács and Grünhut (2011: 348); from CIA Factbook (2010); CEMR-Dexia (2011).

Table 2.2 Size of local governments in SEE, 2003 (2009 data in parenthesis)

	Government expenditures as a share of GDP (%)	**Local expenditures as a share of GDP (%)**	**Local expenditures as a share of general government expenditures (%)**
Albania	27	6.7	23
Bulgaria	38 (40.6)	6.5 (8.2)	16 (20.3)
Croatia	49	7.5	15
FYROM	27	1.8	7
Romania	32 (41.0)	8.5 (10.1)	25 (24.5)
Serbia	25	5.6	25
EU27	(50.8)	15.5 (17.2)	33.9 (33.8)

Source: OECD (2007); Local Innovations for Growth in Central and Eastern Europe (2007). For 2009 data: CEMR-Dexia (2011).

shared taxes. Moreover, most local authorities have weak technical capacities for fund raising, economic development and strategic planning. They also lack investment capital: although usually permitted since the mid or last years of the past decade (according to the network of associations of local authorities of SEE), local authorities lack credibility and expertise in financial markets.

Local governance includes the exercise of political authority and the use of institutional resources to coordinate and manage the process of making decisions, allocating funds and delivering services at the local level. Local governance includes the activity of local governments, but it extends also to the local effect of other kinds of government (e.g. the national government) and other actors (including the citizens, their social and political organizations, businesses, and the like). The actual features of local governance have important consequences for the ability of local governments to pursue the interests of local constituencies and foster local development. Overall, local governance is weak both administratively and financially and the relation with central governments uneasy. Such a situation weakens the chances for growth-reviving reform policy, thus preventing the effective implementation of Rodrik's principle.

Analysis, interpretation and innovation

Innovation requires both analysis and interpretation (Lester and Piore, 2004). Analysis is a rational approach organized around projects which works best when alternative outcomes are well understood, clearly defined and distinguished from one another, and when communication among the parties consists of the precise exchange of pieces of information. Interpretation is a process ongoing in time and without clear end points, making use of fluid, context-dependent, undetermined communication. Interpretation uses ambiguity as a resource and sets directions of innovation in order to make people with different interests and perspectives come to share a common vision and understanding.

Analysis and interpretation involve different kinds of skills and ways of working together with other economic and social actors, yet they must be managed simultaneously to sustain innovativeness and competitiveness. When the interpretive process is missing, the range among which choices are made is too narrow and analytical processes may lead to choosing the best alternative within a bad lot. However, interpretation is inherently fragile since it requires trust, cooperation, transparency and disclosure, which may be at odds with a competitive and transforming environment. This problem can be solved by building public spaces for interpretation, including firms, universities, political organizations, media, civic organizations and international agencies.

Transformation can be usefully represented as a radical process of institutional innovation. During transformation uncertainty is pervasive, as reference models and relevant knowledge are missing, coordination through the economic system is fuzzy, feasible and sustainable goals are unclear and the path to be followed is blurred. Along with precise analysis and problem-solving, such a daunting aim also requires interpretation which involves broad and socially converging perspectives of the problems at stake, far-reaching and imaginative discussion of feasible and sustainable alternatives, debate and interaction among involved parties to collect ideas and streamline goals and action, anticipation of the interrelation among individual changes that are introduced, and the coordination of expectations. Unfortunately, during transformation public spaces were jeopardized leaving little room for interpretation. The resulting institutional ambiguity allowed much value to be captured by uncooperative and secretive actors. Consequently, interpretation can easily end up in a strategic game to defend privileges and capture value.

Local development can provide a solution through its diffused character supporting a common understanding. Interpretation requires that different stakeholders share a common view of processes and have common basic interests. When the society and the economy are territorially polarized, economic and social stratification are also divided. Polarization prevents actors from finding a common language, and hence prevents interpretation and innovation. Much of the effort of elites in booming territories is directed at defending their privileges, while the attention of losers is addressed to survival and perhaps to changing inequalities to their advantage.

In SEE, particularly in former Yugoslavia, other factors contributed to hampering and derailing analysis and interpretation – including war, political and social tensions, and distributive issues. These slowed down reform and focused analysis and interpretation on international, interregional, and interpersonal distributive issues (Dallago and Uvalic, 1998; Kostova, 2007; Lazic, 2007). Political and social tensions, wars and widespread corruption have diverted analysis and interpretation towards distributive issues and establishing systems of governance designed to guarantee gains.

As a consequence, territorial disparities have widened dramatically, while the change of elites has been minimal in some cases, and broad but fragmented in others. In Serbia, for example, the majority of elite entrepreneurs originated in the former socialist nomenklatura and even succeeded in securing elite positions for their children (Lazic, 2007). Less linear and more heterogeneous has been the emergence of elites in Bulgaria (Kostova, 2007), which went through a nearly complete renewal in the 1990s; the outcome is a fragmented and weak economic elite. In Croatia, the new elite showed initial continuity in that it originated primarily from the former socialist managers and later on through links with the dominant political party (Barrett, 2007).

Entrepreneurship

Akerloff and Shiller (2009) highlight a third issue having to do with motivations and the relationship with ambiguity and uncertainty – that is, with the role of animal spirits. This situation is particularly important for business people when society goes through a process of relentless change, particularly in periods of crisis and even more so during transformation. Animal spirits explain such events as the changing thought patterns and modes of doing business, entrepreneurial attitudes, the loss of trust and confidence, the sense of fairness that inhibits the wage and price flexibility that could possibly stabilize an economy and the role of corruption.

Animal spirits have much to do with entrepreneurship. The allocation of entrepreneurial capabilities needs an institutional framework that promotes socially productive entrepreneurship (Baumol, 1993). This requires also that formal and informal institutions are aligned.

In transformation countries, in spite of some success with innovation (Aidis and Welter, 2008; Fabrizio, Leigh and Mody, 2009), the dominant pattern involved the weakening of the structures of production and foreign trade. This aspect is perhaps most evident in SEE.

Other important features are the low number of SMEs[3] (Table 2.3) (OECD-EBRD, 2003; Blokker and Dallago, 2009) together with their mostly backward nature and the existence of a widespread underground economy (Schneider and Buehn, 2009). One important reason for this is the unfavourable regulatory environment (Table 2.4).

Fries, Lysenko and Polanec (2003) find a strong association of business obstacles and added costs and constraints on business such as corruption, with private security protection and reliance on internal sources of finance. Corruption and state capture are widespread in SEE, although there are important differences between countries. Based on the BEEPS surveys from 1999 and 2002, Steves and Rousso (2003) analyse the anti-corruption activities of 24 transformation countries in the period 1999–2002, including SEE. The overall intensity of the anti-corruption index divides SEE into four groups of countries. High intensity reformers include Albania, Croatia, Bulgaria and Romania. Medium-high intensity anti-corruption countries include Moldova, and Serbia and Montenegro, although Serbia and Montenegro score high on new legislative reforms. The medium-low reform group includes Bosnia and Herzegovina, and FYR Macedonia. No SEE country is included in the low reform group of countries.

Although countries in SEE present distinct situations, entrepreneurship is not a strong feature. This is reflected in both the low numbers of enterprises compared to other former transformation countries and in the traditional or survival features of many among them. In spite of important improvement in various countries, the ingenuity of people and organizations alike is still reflected in good part in illegal or illicit practices. Although these support the survival of businesses, they end up for distorting competition and the development of enterprises and localities alike.

Institutions and equity

Freedoms are one of the basic aims of transformation, but unfreedoms may easily follow from actual changes. According to Sen (1999: 3), '[d]evelopment can be seen ... as a process of expanding the real freedoms that people enjoy'. Freedoms depend upon many factors, including gross domestic product (GDP), social and economic arrangements, political and civil rights, and the removal of major sources of unfreedom, such as

Table 2.3 Number of SMEs in the Western Balkans (2009–12)

	Albania	**Bosnia**	**Macedonia**	**Montenegro**	**Serbia**
Active enterprises	73,702	33,136	61,925	21,127	83,631
Total number of SMEs	73,644	32,835	61,794	21,085	83,122
SME/population	26.0	8.8	30.0	34.1	11.4
Share of employment in SMEs	83%	62%	44%	72%	60%

Source: SBA Factsheets 2012, European Commission (data for Albania refer to 2009; for Macedonia and Serbia to 2010). Data for Montenegro are from MONSTAT for 2011 and for Bosnia and Herzegovina from the Statistical Agency of BiH, First Release: Statistical Business Register June 2012. Population data are taken from Eurostat and for Bosnia and Herzegovina from the World Bank.

Table 2.4 Ranking on ease of doing business (2011)

1	Singapore	63	Czech Republic
5	USA	70	Poland
17	Estonia	66	Montenegro
22	Germany	80	Italy
26	France	82	Albania
38	Macedonia	84	Croatia
41	Slovakia	89	Serbia
42	Slovenia	90	Moldova
46	Hungary	110	BiH
51	Bulgaria	119	Kosovo
56	Romania	123	Russia

Source: World Bank (2011).

poverty, tyranny, restricted economic opportunities and systematic social deprivation.

Although transformation has created freedoms, transformation processes have also caused the appearance of previously unknown or unimportant unfreedoms such as unemployment, poverty and minority discrimination. Moreover, undeveloped institutional frameworks prevented the unfolding of developmental effects. Freedom of enterprise resulted in booming numbers of new enterprises, spin-offs, and entry of foreign companies (OECD-EU, 2007; McIntyre and Dallago, 2003). However, many of these enterprises only existed on paper (see Table 2.3) and many of those really existing were established out of necessity and striving for survival. Relatively few enterprises were established to capture opportunities and were often uncompetitive.

Freedoms in SEE have gone through a bumpy road and this is perhaps the most daunting of the four issues discussed here. Along with increased political freedoms, there have been seriously increasing territorial disparities, booming income and wealth inequalities, rapidly growing unemployment, decreased opportunities for much of the population, while welfare support is weaker than in other transformation countries. These outcomes show important differences throughout the region and have been linked only in part to a transitional depression that was particularly severe and prolonged in SEE. As in other transformation countries they have given rise to growing dissatisfaction and unhappiness.

Territorial disparities have increased remarkably (see Table 2.5) as a consequence of dismantling socialist investments, market agglomeration processes, including the uneven inflow of foreign direct investment, the

Table 2.5 Dispersion of regional GDP at NUTS2 level, per inhabitant

	2000	2007
EU27	32.7	28.3
Bulgaria	17.6	35.4
Croatia	17.8*	18.6
Romania	25.3	28.5

Notes: * 2001. For a given country the dispersion of regional GDP is defined as the sum of the absolute difference between regional and national GDP per inhabitant, weighted by the regional share of population and expressed as a percentage of national GDP per inhabitant.
Source: Eurostat (2010a).

different bargaining power of local governments, the weakness of the new states and local administrations, the lack of public resources, and the dismantling of welfare systems (Blokker and Dallago, 2009).

The data in Table 2.5 show interregional disparities that are lower than absolute disparities, since they include the effect of depopulation of backward regions. If we disregard demography, territorial disparities appear larger. For instance, territorial disparities in Serbia are among the largest in Europe (Isakovic and Stefanovic, 2011), particularly between the northern and southern parts of the country and between rural and urban areas, and have been increasing over the last few years. The ratio of the most developed and the least developed municipalities is 1:15. The poverty index in 2007 ranged from 3% in the urban area of Belgrade up to 18.7% in the rural areas of South East Serbia. In 2006, registered unemployment rate in South-Serbia was 45% in the Jablanica District and 43.6% in the Pčinja District, compared to 31.1% on average for Serbia. For both districts the employment rate was approximately 10% lower than national average (ILO Country Report). Within the EU, the dispersion of regional GDP per inhabitant (in PPS, NUTS level 2 in 2008) in Bulgaria was second only to Hungary and was immediately followed by Slovakia and Romania (Eurostat, 2011).

The estimate of regional GDP in Croatia also exhibits great disparities in GDP per capita. More than half (53.1%) of the national GDP was produced in only four territorial units – the City of Zagreb (30.1%), the County of Primorje-Gorski Kotar (8.1%), the County of Split-Dalmatia (7.9%) and the County of Istria (6.3%). The government has identified 'Areas of Special State Concern', mostly the war-affected areas in the East and the South of the country and some other economically depressed regions. Donor programmes, which until now have focused their activities on the capital, are increasingly targeting these regions (Bićanić and Pribičević, 2009).[4]

Political and economic freedoms have led to changes in the social stratification and the composition of elites as stressed previously (Lane, Lengyel and Tholen, 2007). The rapid increase of various unfreedoms, including unemployment and poverty has led to dramatic increases in personal income disparities, such as the consequence of privatization, differences in returns to human capital and the bargaining power of various social and professional groups, and an increase in international openness (Table 2.6). Per capita income inequality was fairly low when transformation started with the partial exception of former Yugoslavia. After 1989, pre-tax disparities increased rapidly in most transformation countries, particularly in the Southern part of former Yugoslavia, the Baltic countries, Hungary and Poland, although not in Slovenia and the Czech Republic (EBRD-World Bank, 2006).

Pre-tax distribution may be substantially modified through the fiscal and welfare systems. Different countries have followed divergent routes: Croatia and to a lesser extent Montenegro, Bosnia and Herzegovina, and Serbia have built more generous welfare systems. Macedonia retains a social insurance system from former Yugoslavia; and as of the beginning of 2012 Kosovo has created a new social assistance and compulsory pension system, Albania has created a new social insurance system combined with a decentralized system of social assistance (see Table 2.7).

Growing distributive disparities have also been the consequence of decreased employment opportunities, which pushed many employees (particularly the unskilled and women) to leave the labour market, and of the different chances in the labour market following structural change. Lost employment, disrupted welfare, increased distributive disparities, inflation along with political turmoil and wars in some countries pushed a sizeable part of the population into poverty. In some countries (e.g. Albania and Romania) one-fourth of the population is below poverty line, although in other countries (e.g. Serbia and Montenegro) and generally in Central Europe the situation looks better (Eurostat, 2010b).

These events generated dissatisfaction and doubtful or negative economic and political effects (e.g. voting for undemocratic parties and undertaking risky borrowing also in foreign currencies to support lifestyles). Unhappiness is associated with lack of growth and the perception of losses of income and wealth, but also depreciation of human capital stock accumulated under central planning, deteriorating public goods, and rising income inequality (Guriev and Zhuravskaya, 2009: 166). Improved economic performance since the late 1990s has been

Table 2.6 Some indicators of malaise in South East Europe

	Unemployment rate (2007)	**Gini index (2007)**	**Poverty (%) (2007)**	**HDI 1990**	**HDI 2010**	**Underground economy, % of GDP, 2006**
Albania	12.5	26.7 (2005)	25	0.647	0.719	35.1
BiH	29	56.2	20	0.698[a]	0.710	35.3*
Bulgaria	6.3	30.7	14.1	0.678	0.743	36.4
Croatia	14.8	29 (2008)	11 (2003)	0.690[b]	0.767	34.2
Kosovo	40	30 (2006)	37	–	–	–
Macedonia	35 (2008)	39 (2003)	22	0.634[b]	0.701	36.9*
Montenegro	14.7	30	7	0.755[a]	0.769	–
Romania	3.6 (2008)	32	25 (2005)	0.688	0.767	37.5
Serbia	18.8	30	6.5	0.719[a]	0.735	37.3*[c]

Notes: (a) 2005. (b) 1995. (c) with Montenegro. * 2004/2005.
Source: World Bank; CIA (The World Factbook); EBRD; UNDP (Human Development Report 2010); Schneider and Buehn (2007).

Table 2.7 Social security and social protection (2003)

Country	Total social protection	Education*	Total social expenditure (expenditure on social protection) as % of GDP
Albania	8.8	2.9	11.7
BiH	21.4	–	–
Bulgaria	17.6	3.9	21.5
Croatia	26.5	4.2	30.7
Kosovo	10.3	–	–
Macedonia	12.0	–	–
Montenegro	23.0	5.9	28.9
Romania	16.1	4.0	20.1
Serbia	20.9	3.5	24.4
EU25	28.0	–	–

Note: * Includes all educational expenditures.
Source: Bartlett and Xhumari (2007); ILO (2005).

insufficient to convince many voters in those countries that it was worth doing, and SEE fares worse than both Central and East Europe (EBRD-World Bank, 2006; EBRD, 2010, 2011). The global economic crisis has further worsened the situation.

Clearly growing disparities, poverty, unemployment, dissatisfaction and split societies tend to depress the room for and role of animal spirits, make shared interpretation and analysis more difficult and give political strength to populist policies to the detriment of general principles of good governance and economic management.

Local features and macroeconomic performance

Various components of macroeconomic performance have been shown to increase regional disparities in transition countries. In particular, the process of opening up and integrating competitive markets and structural change have been considered as favouring metropolitan areas and regions with strong industrial basis and closer to the main markets (Petrakos, 2001). Relevant macroeconomic factors for local development and regional disparities include the spatial consequences of foreign capital and trade, macro-geographical adjustment, aggregate economic performance, and structural change.

The overall effect of regional disparities is under the influence of weak macroeconomic performance, which went to the disadvantage primarily of peripheral regions. Not only SEE includes some of the poorest countries in Europe. It also includes some of the countries that have had a particularly bumpy road to transformation and economic performance. Indeed, by 2007, the last normal year before the world crisis, none of the Balkan countries reached the level of production that one could have expected deriving from a normal post-transformation recovery, Croatia being a partial exception. The worst performance is that of Bulgaria whose GDP is still below the level attained in 1989.

The international crisis hit a serious blow in all the countries, although it has been more serious in some than in others. Performance in some countries and entities continued to improve after the serious transitional depression and is still doing so (Albania and Kosovo), while in other countries it reached its peak in 2008 (Croatia and Romania). Finally, in the remaining countries GDP peaked in 2008, decreased in the following year and then either increased in 2010 (Bosnia and Herzegovina, Macedonia, Montenegro, and Serbia) or stagnated (Bulgaria). These GDP dynamics – depression–growth–depression – hit certain areas of the countries less (typically the capital cities) and others more (typically the agrarian periphery) and contributed to an increase in territorial disparities in all transformation countries, although with substantial inter-country differences, as seen previously.

Studies on the local consequences of macroeconomic performance have been pursued particularly for Central and East European countries as members of the European Union. These also include Romania and Bulgaria. However, there is also evidence for the entire Balkan area that indicates that following transition the concentration of economic activities in a limited number of core regions or development axes is a general feature and that interregional disparities have increased (Petrakos, 2001, Heidenreich, 2003).

Although the pattern is rather similar to all transformation countries, this concerns primarily the outstanding role of the capital cities. Indeed, the development of border regions adjacent to the main European markets, albeit present, is less important in the Balkan countries than in Central and East European new member countries. A further typical feature is that disparities tend to be particularly concentrated at the level of very small areas. This latter feature is particularly damaging for local development since it weakens the generation of agglomeration and specialization economies and spillovers (Monastiriotis and Petrakos, 2009). It is this pattern of local development, together with weak local policies and the effect of political tensions and military events that explain the spatial concentration of poverty and deprivation, generally higher in rural areas than in urban areas (Rovolis, 2011).

For instance and although the dominant position of the capital city is a common feature to all transformation countries, in Romania and Bulgaria it is the peripheral regions that usually have inferior performance, while in Central European transformation countries it is the Western regions having superior performance. However, in both Romania and Bulgaria there are variants to this pattern, in particular to the advantage of the Black Sea region. In Romania and Bulgaria the evolution of regional disparities within each country have clearly increased over time. This pattern is general also in the Western Balkans, where capital cities become more dynamic while rural areas become impoverished (Petrakos, 2001; ETF, 2007; Bartlett, 2009).

Conclusions

The process of transformation in SEE shows various similarities with Central and Eastern Europe. However, it also features important differences, due to the bumpier political, social and economic road and, in various cases, the lower level of development. Interestingly, in the most decentralized pre-transformation country of the region, former Yugoslavia, the successor post-transformation countries and entities have featured a high level of centralization.

Along with a degree of differentiation among South East European countries and in spite of important Western support for some countries, although not for others, two different sets of puzzles should be noticed. These are only in part typical of transformation countries.

The first puzzle, indeed a true failure of transformation policies, is the general failure of catching up with growth. Considering the entire transformation period, Bulgaria represents the most impressive failure, since by 2010 the country was unable to reach the 1989 economic level of production. Other countries suffered serious drawbacks, including Romania and Macedonia. Albania's economy recovered fairly, while Croatia and Montenegro offer a mixed picture, as much as Serbia. Finally, the performance of Bosnia and Herzegovina and Kosovo has been rather impressive in the last decade. However, if one considers the massive inflow of foreign support and the economically positive effect of post-war reconstruction, their performance appears much less impressive. Under these conditions, it is hard to consider economic transformation as satisfactory.

However, the awkward outcome appears fully when one looks inside the economy, in particular at the local level. Local development in the Balkans appears unfavourable and distorted for both the overall development perspectives and the well-being and chances of the population. It led to a segmentation of the territory, the society and the economy with serious inequalities likely to be permanent.

This outcome is only in part an inevitable consequence of transformation. In spite of their geographical extension and unfavourable initial conditions (e.g. regional concentration of heavy industry with high territorial disparities, particularly in Poland) Slovenia and Poland have decreased territorial differences (dispersion of regional GDP per inhabitant in PPS, NUTS level 2) during the last decade, fairing even better than most Western European countries, where disparities actually increased (Eurostat, 2010a; OECD, 2010). The same can be said to a certain extent of concentration of production in capital cities. In the Balkans the picture is much gloomier. Among the EU member countries, in Bulgaria territorial disparities simply exploded compared to the rest of the EU. They also increase substantially in Romania. The availability and comparability of data in the Western Balkans is rather problematic. Yet the available information suggests that the situation is similar, if not worse in various cases, to that of those two countries.

There are different reasons behind this deep segmentation of the territory, among which liberalist policies, the agglomeration of FDI and domestic investment, the lack of policies devoted to foster local development, and the uneasy relation between the central and local levels in most of SEE stand out. Local development in these circumstances has often abdicated its democratic, economically stabilizing and development supporting role to become an instrument fostering growing territorial and social disparities and diminished opportunities for many.

Some Central European transformation countries, particularly Poland and Slovenia, and more recently also Slovakia provide some hints for policy that could be useful for SEE. These relate to the four missing dimensions considered in this chapter and include basic undertakings (e.g. streamlining formal and informal institutions, reforming the state), and actions and policies for fostering local development (e.g. policies for fostering productive entrepreneurship, improving infrastructure, investing in education and vocational training, checking unfreedoms such as unemployment and poverty).

Based on some relatively successful transformation cases and taking advantage of mistakes, some lessons can be drawn and suggestions advanced for future reforms and policies complying with the missing dimensions.

One important reason for the difficulties with effective transformation has been that formal institutions have been too often implemented in an abrupt top-down fashion. This has created a rupture between formal and informal institutions, leading to costly but ineffective enforcement of formal institutions. While formal institutions became less effective, informal ones nurtured growing underground and even criminal economies. Ineffective public administration and ailing productive entrepreneurship followed. The best way to streamline formal and informal institutions is to follow Rodrik's (2007) advice with a plus. Formal institutions require that reforms should be based on general principles of good economic management, and implemented giving attention to local circumstances and the opportunities and constraints that these create. Effective interpretation, careful analysis and cooperation between different levels of government are consequently required. The plus has to do with the human factor. While it is true that human ingenuity is nowhere in short supply, a lack of expertise and capabilities may make the policy ineffective in practice. Policy support for entrepreneurs and for administrators and not only for enterprises may be required, as well as strong support for broad-based education and vocational training.

Cooperation among local governments and their social and economic responsibility and accountability should complement cooperation among central and local governments. This would serve to save resources and provide a favourable background for the development of infrastructure. Local voters should also learn that well-being must be created locally, although support and solidarity based on shared and consistently enforced rules should have a role.

Local development is diffused and democratic by its very nature. Unfreedoms in the form of poverty, destitution, unemployment and disparities hamper local development. Reforms and policies should create a context conducive to diffused development, streamlined through proper incentives and shared goals of formal and informal institutions and through their effective enforcement. Such an approach would require the compensation of losers, providing them with new opportunities. It would also require incentives for socially productive enterprise and for increased investment in human capital. Direct intervention should be limited to exceptional and transitory cases, even when a region is particularly depressed and the population poor. Incentives and opportunities always create better and more resilient outcomes. Policies should also pay attention to the mobility of resources.

The goal should be first to create local opportunities and then attract resources from outside the territory. Diffused infrastructure development is usually the best solution, along with investment in human capital. In

SEE a solution to the problem of ethnic tensions is a precondition for stability and development. Local development actions, including supporting transborder and regional cooperation, may therefore also play an important role to this end.

Notes

1. This research was funded by the Autonomous Province of Trento, as the sponsor of the OPENLOC research project under the call for proposals 'Major Projects 2006'. The author thanks Ms Chiriac for precious research support and Will Bartlett for careful revision of the original manuscript and precious suggestions.
2. See also www.nalas.eu/borrowing/annex2.html for the general financial framework of local development.
3. The number of SMEs per 1000 inhabitants in South East Europe is much lower than in Central Europe and in EU19 (EBRD (2004)).
4. OECD: http://www.oecd.org/dataoecd/25/42/43469966.pdf

References

Aidis, R. and Welter, F. (eds) (2008) *Innovation and Entrepreneurship: Successful Start-ups and Businesses in Emerging Economies*, Cheltenham: Edward Elgar.

Akerloff, G. A. and Shiller, R. J. (2009) *Animal Spirits: How Human Psychology Drives the Economy, and Why it Matters for Global Capitalism*, Princeton and Oxford: Princeton University Press.

Barrett, E. (2007) 'The role of informal networks in the privatisation process in Croatia', in D. Lane, G. Lengyel and J. Tholen (eds) *Restructuring of the Economic Elites after State Socialism: Recruitment, Institutions and Attitudes*, Stuttgart: *ibidem*-Verlag, pp. 211–39.

Bartlett, W. (2009) 'Economic development in the European super-periphery: Evidence from the Western Balkans', *Economic Annals*, LIV(181): 21–44.

Bartlett, W. and Xhumari, M. (2007) 'Social security policy and pension reforms in the Western Balkans', *European Journal of Social Security*, 9(4): 297–322.

Baumol, W. J. (1993) *Entrepreneurship, Management, and the Structure of Payoffs*, Cambridge, MA: The MIT Press.

Bićanić, I. and Pribičević, V. (2009) 'Multiple shocks and changes in the development gradient of Croatia's regions', in P. Blokker and B. Dallago (eds) *Regional Diversity and Local Development in the New Member States*, Basingstoke: Palgrave Macmillan, pp. 272–93.

Blokker, P. and Dallago, B. (eds) (2009) *Regional Diversity and Local Development in the New Member States*, Basingstoke: Palgrave Macmillan.

CEMR-Dexia (2011) *EU Subnational Governments: 2009 Key Figures*, 2010/2011 edition, Council of European Municipalities and Regions.

CIA (2010) *The World Factbook 2010*, Washington D.C.: Central Intelligence Agency.

Dallago, B. (1996) 'Investment, systemic efficiency and distribution', *Kyklos*, 49(4): 615–41.

Dallago, B. and Uvalic, M. (1998) 'The distributive consequences of nationalism: The case of former Yugoslavia', *Europe-Asia Studies*, 50(1): 71–90.
EBRD (2004) *Spotlight on South-Eastern Europe*, London: EBRD.
EBRD (2010) *Life in Transition: A Survey of People's Experiences and Attitudes*, London: European Bank for Reconstruction and Development.
EBRD (2011) *Life in Transition: After the Crisis*, London: European Bank for Reconstruction and Development.
EBRD-World Bank (2006) *Life in Transition Survey*, London: European Bank for Reconstruction and Development.
ETF (2007) *Labour Markets in the Western Balkans: Challenges for the Future*, Turin: European Training Foundation.
Eurostat (2010a) *Eurostat Regional Yearbook 2010*, Luxembourg: Eurostat.
Eurostat (2010b) *Regions and Cities Database*, Luxembourg: Eurostat, http://epp.eurostate.ec.europa.eu/portal/page/portal/region_cities/regional_statistics/data/database
Eurostat (2011) *Eurostat Regional Yearbook 2011*, Luxembourg: Eurostat.
Fabrizio, S., Leigh, D. and Mody, A. (2009) 'The second transition: Eastern Europe in perspective', *IMF Working Paper WP/09/43*, March.
Fries, S., Lysenko, T. and Polanec, S. (2003) 'The 2002 business environment and enterprise performance survey: Results from a survey of 6,100 firms', *Working Paper No. 84*, European Bank for Reconstruction and Development.
Guriev, S. and Zhuravskaya, E. (2009) '(Un)happiness in transition', *Journal of Economic Perspectives*, 23(2): 143–68.
Heidenreich, M. (2003) 'Regional inequalities in the enlarged Europe', *Journal of European Social Policy*, 13(4): 313–33.
ILO (2005) *Social Security Spending in South Eastern Europe: A Comparative Review*, Budapest: International Labour Office.
Isakovic, M. and Stefanovic, D. (2011) 'Regional inequalities in Serbia', *Development and Transition*, UNDP, 22 September.
Kostova, D. (2007) 'Dynamics of the 1990s: Change and continuity of the Bulgarian economic elite', in D. Lane, G. Lengyel and J. Tholen (eds) *Restructuring of the Economic Elites after State Socialism: Recruitment, Institutions and Attitudes*, Stuttgart: *ibidem*-Verlag, pp. 153–68.
Lane, D., Lengyel, G. and Tholen, J. (eds) (2007) *Restructuring of the Economic Elites after State Socialism: Recruitment, Institutions and Attitudes*, Stuttgart: *ibidem*-Verlag.
Lazic, M. (2007) 'Post-socialist transformation in Serbia: Changing recruitment patterns of economic elite', in D. Lane, G. Lengyel and J. Tholen (eds) *Restructuring of the Economic Elites after State Socialism: Recruitment, Institutions and Attitudes*, Stuttgart: *ibidem*-Verlag, pp. 115–26.
Lester, R. K. and Piore, M. J. (2004) *Innovation: The Missing Dimension*, Cambridge, MA: Harvard University Press.
McIntyre, R. J. and Dallago, B. (eds) (2003) *Small and Medium Enterprises in Transitional Economies*, Basingstoke: Palgrave Macmillan.
Monastiriotis, V. and Petrakos, G. (2009) 'Local sustainable development and spatial cohesion in the post-transition Balkans: In search for a developmental model', *GreeSE Paper No. 29*, Hellenic Observatory Papers on Greece and Southeast Europe, LSE, November.
OECD (2007) *Local Innovations for Growth in Central and Eastern Europe*, Paris: OECD, edited by Sylvain Giguère, November.

OECD (2010) *Regional Statistics and Indicators*. http://www.oecd.org/gov/regionaldevelopment/regionalstatisticsandindicators.htm.

OECD-EBRD (2003) *South East Europe Region: Enterprise Policy Performance, a Regional Assessment*, Paris and London: OECD.

OECD-EU (2007) *Enterprise Policy Development in the Western Balkans: Report on the Implementation of the European Charter for Small Enterprises in the Western Balkans*, Paris: OECD.

Pálné Kovács, I. and Grünhut, Z. (2011) 'Specifics of the governmental system', in G. Horváth and Z. Hajdú (eds) *Regional Transformation Processes in the Western Balkan Countries*, Pécs: Centre for Regional Studies of the Hungarian Academy of Sciences, pp. 307–49.

Petrakos, G. (2001) 'Patterns of regional inequality in transition economies', *European Planning Studies*, 9(3): 359–83.

Rodrik, D. (2007) *One Economics, Many Recipes*, Princeton and Oxford: Princeton University Press.

Rovolis, A. (2011) 'Poverty and security in the Balkans: National, regional and social dimensions', *Southeast European and Black Sea Studies*, 11(4): 403–19.

Sautet, F. E. (2005) 'The role of institutions in entrepreneurship: Implications for development policy', *Mercatus Policy Primer No. 1*, Washington, DC: Mercatus Center.

Schneider, F. and Buehn, A. (2007) 'Shadow economies and corruption all over the world: New estimates for 145 countries', *Economics*, 24 July.

Schneider, F. and Buehn, A. (2009) 'Shadow economies and corruption all over the world: Revised estimates for 120 countries', *Economics*, 27 October.

Sen, A. (1999) *Development as Freedom*, New York: Anchor Books.

Steves, F. and Rousso, A. (2003) 'Anti-corruption programmes in post-communist transition countries and changes in the business environment, 1999–2002', *Working Paper No. 85*, October, London: European Bank for Reconstruction and Development.

Woelk, J. (2005) 'Transformation bottom-up? Local government reforms in the Western Balkans compared', University of Trento, *CAST Working Papers No. 4*, November.

World Bank (2011) *Doing Business 2010: Reforming through Difficult Times*, Washington, DC: World Bank and IFC and Palgrave Macmillan.

3

Less is More: Decentralization in Croatia and Its Impact on Regional Development

Dubravka Jurlina Alibegović

Introduction

Fiscal decentralization tendencies and local government reform can be seen in countries throughout the world, including industrialized countries, developing and transition countries (Smoke, 2001; Shah, 2004). An important goal of these reforms is to redefine the role of the public sector and to improve its performance. The reason is that a higher level of decentralization of administrative power and responsibility[1] is expected to result in an increase in public sector efficiency,[2] in the improvement of local and regional governance,[3] as well as in the promotion of local and regional economic development.[4]

The main goal of decentralization is to improve the lives of local citizens. Its success depends on the institutional, economic, fiscal and political context in which local governments operate. Decentralization provides local and regional self-government units with greater autonomy in providing public services to their citizens, yet there are no general and identical solutions for all countries (Smoke, 2001). This chapter provides an analysis of decentralization reforms and their effects on the regional and local development process in Croatia. It investigates the relationship between the level of decentralization and the level of regional development. The second section describes the decentralization of public functions and the current level of regional development. The third section analyses the relationship between decentralization measured as the sub-national share of total government revenues and the level of regional development measured as the regional gross domestic product (GDP) per capita. Conclusions are presented in the last section.

Where are we now?

In the theoretical literature, decentralization is generally described as a process in which selected public functions are assigned to sub-national units and fiscal decentralization is defined as the assignment of revenue sources and expenditure functions to sub-national levels of government.[5]

In July 2001 Croatia initiated a partial decentralization of its public functions.[6] The reforms have been directed in two areas of decentralization. The first area was the delegation of administrative and professional tasks from the central government (ministries) to the local and regional self-government units. The second area was fiscal decentralization in the framework of which part of public expenditures (for primary and secondary education, health care and social welfare) were transferred from the central government budget to large cities and counties and the financing of fire protection was transferred to cities and municipalities. Additional share of income tax for financing decentralized public functions were reassigned to counties and cities.

In the first phase of fiscal decentralization, 32 financially stronger cities,[7] the City of Zagreb and all of the 20 counties[8] were assigned additional responsibilities to provide some public functions locally. This means that expenditures for primary and secondary education, for health care and for social welfare, as well as capital investments, were transferred to these units of local and regional self-government.

The model of decentralization included several changes in revenue sources so as to increase local budget revenues corresponding to the greater responsibilities assigned to the sub-national level of government. The first of these changes was to permit new municipal and city taxes, as well as different levels of surtax on income tax depending on the size of the municipality. The distribution of revenues shared between the state and the sub-national government has also been changed. The major change was in the distribution of income tax revenues, with a larger part being allocated to the local (34%) and to the regional governments (10%).[9] An additional part of the income tax revenue (10.4%[10]) was reserved to cover expenditures for decentralized functions in primary (2.9%) and secondary education (2.0%), health care (2.5%), social welfare (2.0%) and fire protection (1.0%).[11] Equalization grants for decentralized functions have been established (21% of the income tax[12]) for local government units with insufficient resources to carry out their decentralized function in order to meet the required minimum service standards determined by the central government. Most of the decentralized functions (particularly wage costs and contributions for employees in primary and secondary education as well as in the health care sector) remain the financial responsibility of the central government.

In spite of all decentralization efforts, Croatia is still a highly centralized country as measured by standard indicators of the level of decentralization such as the share of the sub-national government in the consolidated general government and the share of the sub-national government in GDP.[13] The share of revenues and expenditures of sub-national government in the total government budget, as well as the share of revenues in GDP – before and after 2001 – could indicate the extent of fiscal decentralization that has taken place. Data presented in Table 3.1 show that the share of revenues and expenditures of local budgets in the consolidated budget of the general government and in GDP is relatively small. In 2000, the year before the launch of the decentralization process in Croatia, the share of the local budget revenues in the consolidated revenues of the general government budget amounted to 10.9% while their share in GDP amounted to 4.6%. In 2001 the process of decentralization started.[14] Data for 2002, the first year after the launch of decentralization, indicates that the share of local budget revenues in consolidated revenues of the general government budget actually decreased to 10.0%, while their share in GDP decreased to 4.0%. Both 2003 and 2004 data also indicate a falling level of fiscal decentralization.

Table 3.1 Revenues and expenditures of the sub-national government in revenues and expenditures of the consolidated general government and in GDP

Year	Revenues			Expenditures		
	Outturn in 000 HRK	Structure in %	% of GDP	Outturn in 000 HRK	Structure in %	% of GDP
2000	8,155,966	10.93	4.62	8,263,723	10.04	4.68
2001	6,953,953	8.82	3.64	7,321,974	8.71	3.84
2002	8,332,799	10.06	4.00	8,335,141	9.52	4.00
2003	8,456,146	9.40	3.72	9,239,693	9.66	4.07
2004	9,407,683	9.75	3.83	8,599,052	9.12	3.50
2005	10,458,468	10.14	3.96	9,713,927	9.66	3.67
2006	11,901,172	10.60	4.16	10,469,579	9.72	3.66
2007	13,379,019	10.56	4.26	11,819,047	9.95	3.76
2008	14,747,477	10.95	4.31	13,650,745	10.48	3.99
2009	14,031,661	10.86	4.21	13,927,532	10.12	4.18

Source: The Ministry of Finance and the author's calculation.

However, in the following years the shares of sub-national budgets gradually increased, and by 2009 the respective shares amounted to just 10.9 and 4.2%, barely equal to the position in 2000.

These data indicate that the decentralization process has not resulted in any greater participation of sub-national government in the total government revenues and expenditures or in a greater share of these revenues and expenditures in GDP. We can conclude that the responsibilities for financing the delivery of public services are firmly in the hands of the central government, which receives the largest part of public revenues and spends the largest part of public expenditures. In other words, sub-national governments still do not have enough autonomy in the delivery of public services and participate in a minor share of public revenues and expenditures. Of course, the data do not indicate how successfully either the central government or the sub-national governments perform their duties in the delivery of public services and their delegated administrative and professional tasks. In other words, the data cannot demonstrate which level of government is a better provider of public functions. This also means that we cannot make a simple conclusion about whether the goals of the decentralization process in Croatia – efficient public services delivery, strengthening of local and regional governance, as well as an increase in local and regional economic development – have been achieved.

Croatia is also a centralized country from the point of view of other measures of the level of decentralization.[15] These measures are expenditure responsibilities, revenue-rising authority and fiscal autonomy of sub-national governments. Expenditure responsibilities of governments imply the division of responsibilities among state, regional and local governments that follow by adequate revenue sources. In Croatia, most of the existing public functions[16] remain under the jurisdiction of the central state. This is also the case even with those public functions that are partially decentralized (education, health, social protection and fire protection) since responsibility and financing are divided between the central, regional and local levels of government. According to the functional classification of the budget, it can be observed that local government is mostly concerned about (and finances) housing and community amenities, preschool and primary school education, general public services and road traffic.

Local governments remain largely dependent on external sources of financing such as grants and borrowing and the rates of shared taxes and of county taxes are completely prescribed by the central government. While the municipal or city authorities on the whole determine the rates of municipal, town and city taxes, they do so within the framework of the limits set by the central government. Local governments are able to influence a few sources of finance. For example, they determine the tax rate on the use of land independently and autonomously determine the rates of surtax on income tax within the limits set by the central government. Local government units access additional revenues on the basis of special acts and decisions of government, such as charges and fees, which are autonomous revenue of sub-national government. Sub-national government units independently set the rates of such non-tax revenue and collect this revenue independently. The main non-tax revenue consists of municipal utility charges and contributions for the construction and maintenance of the utility infrastructure.

Comparison with other developed and transition countries provide an indication of the level of a particular country in regards to the decentralization process. We can therefore compare fiscal decentralization indicators in Croatia with selected countries. This comparison highlights the relatively low level of fiscal decentralization in Croatia. While sub-national government in Croatia received around 10% of the revenues of the consolidated general government, the share of such revenues in other countries is far higher: 28.9% in the Czech Republic, 29.5% in Hungary, 38.5% in Poland, 36.6% in the Netherlands and 57.2% in Denmark (Figure 3.1). These data

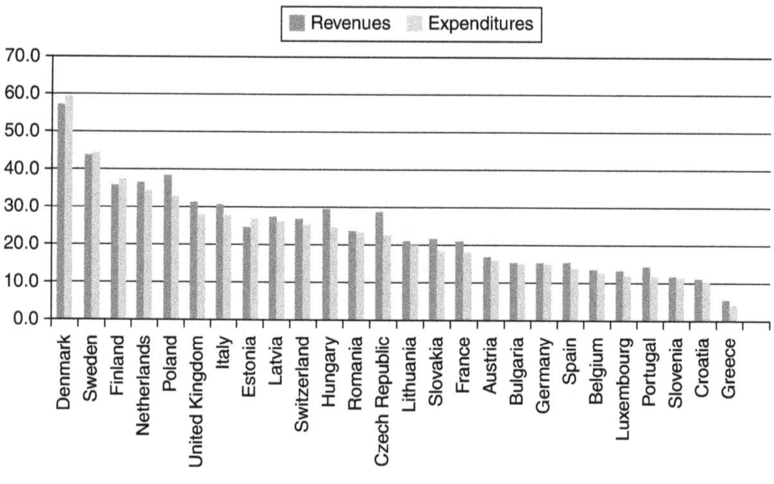

Figure 3.1 Revenues and expenditures of the sub-national governments in revenues and expenditures of the consolidated general government in 2006 (% of total)

Source: IMF (2010), Ministry of Finance and author's calculation.

show that Croatia remains a highly centralized country compared with the European Union's new member states, as well as compared with the old member states of the EU. Decentralization reforms in a particular country are the consequence of the different institutional, economic, fiscal and political context in which local governments operate. In some of the selected countries (e.g. Denmark) the decentralization reform initiatives have been continuously implemented over a number of years and comprehensive reforms in the public sector have been undertaken several times and interpretation of the comparative data should bear this in mind. As previously explained, there is no general solution concerning the extent of decentralization, applicable for all countries and it should not be thought that Croatia should necessarily strive to increase the level of fiscal decentralization to conform to the pattern observed in EU countries. The future of intergovernmental fiscal relations and the decentralization process in Croatia will depend on the decision of future decisions of governments at both central and local level in Croatia depending on the circumstances of the time and the aims and objectives of the government.

Relationship between decentralization and regional development

Previous research has focused mainly on expenditure-based measures of decentralization. On the other hand, in most countries, local and regional economic development is not an obligatory function of local and regional governments. However, many sub-national governments feel responsible not only for providing the public services prescribed by law, but also for the overall well-being of their local communities. This also includes an attempt to stimulate local and regional economic development. Since the major aim of this chapter is to give an answer to the key research question concerning the relationship between the current level of decentralization and the existing level of regional development, this part of the chapter will quantify this impact of decentralization by relating a certain measure of decentralization to the economic outcomes on the regional level in Croatia.

The level of regional development in Croatia is presented in Figure 3.2. The data show that there are marked regional inequalities in Croatia measured by GDP per capita. The City of Zagreb is the most developed part of the country and GDP per capita in the City of Zagreb is 3.5 times higher than in the County of Slavonski Brod-Posavina,

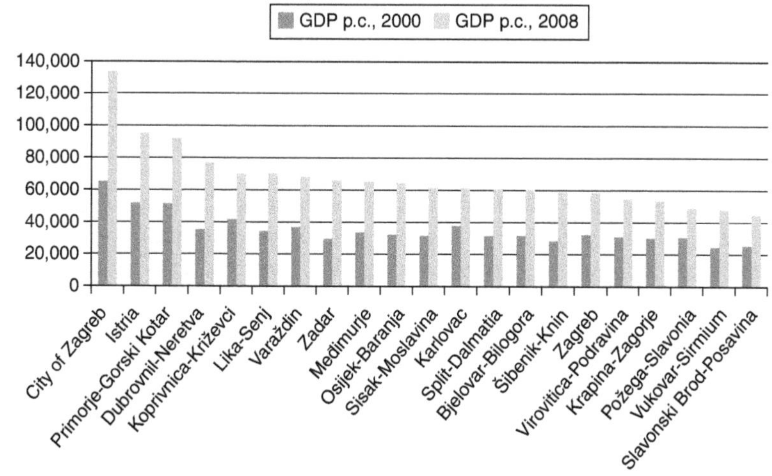

Figure 3.2 Gross domestic product per capita in the Croatian counties (in HRK, current prices)
Source: Central Bureau of Statistics.

which is the county with the lowest level of GDP per capita in 2008 (see Figure 3.2).

Sub-national governments are closest to the citizens. They are well informed about local needs and preferences and they are usually in a position to adjust their budgets and costs of public services to these preferences and needs. Sub-national governments should therefore be given the authority to introduce their own sources of revenues (tax and non-tax). This is a fundamental feature of the theory of fiscal decentralization (Oates, 1972).

Researchers have tried to quantify the impact of decentralization by relating some measure of decentralization to the economic outcomes of economic growth (Davoodi, Xie and Zou, 1995; Davoodi and Zou, 1998; De Mello, 2000; Ebel and Yilmaz, 2002). In this chapter I apply the methodology of Ebel and Yilmaz (2002) in order to identify the relationship between decentralization measured as the sub-national share of total government revenues and the achieved level of regional development, measured as regional GDP per capita.

Empirical analysis

Sub-national governments are as a rule faced with the problem of inadequate financing. Most are unprepared or unable to raise funds necessary for local economic development. In addition, the central state often sets limits on the borrowing capacity of local governments. Thus, it is important that local and regional governments have the capacity to introduce their own tax and non-tax revenues to provide enough resources for financing both current public needs as well as for financing local investment projects.

The existing structure of sub-national revenues in Croatia is explained in the following paragraphs. Three sources of sub-national revenues are identified: tax revenues, intergovernmental transfers (grants) and non-tax revenues.

Tax revenues are divided into two groups – own taxes and shared taxed (see Table 3.2). Own taxes are those for which the sub-national governments can control the tax rate or tax base. In this analysis revenues from municipal, city and county taxes are considered as own taxes and consist of the following: tax on goods and services, tax on vacation homes, tax on a business, tax on the use of land, tax on inheritance and gifts, tax on motor vehicles, tax on boats and vessels, and tax on games of chance. Shared taxes are those in which the sub-national governments have limited or no control over the rate and tax base and the state government determines how to share the revenues. Here I include the revenues from income tax and the surtax on income tax in the revenues from shared taxes.[17]

Intergovernmental transfers are provided as block grants and it is not possible to distinguish the proportion of intergovernmental transfers that is conditional from that which is general-purpose. In addition, it is not possible to make a distinction between transfers that are distributed according to objective criteria in comparison to ones that are based on discretionary measures.[18] Intergovernmental transfers are provided to finance local and regional needs and are usually designed to favour local and regional self-government units with poor fiscal capacity.

Non-tax revenues include revenues from business operations, property and administrative fees. Local and regional self-government units are officially authorized to introduce numerous other revenues on the basis of special acts and decisions of government, such as charges and fees, which are included in the non-tax revenues of their budget.

Table 3.2 provides a comparison of fiscal statistics reported in the data base of the Ministry of Finance for all of 20 Croatian counties and the City of Zagreb for the fiscal year 2000 (year before the beginning of the process of decentralization), for the year 2002 (the first year after the start of the process of decentralization) and 2010 (the last available data on the outturn of the sub-national government budgets) showing the detailed structure of sub-national government revenues.

Table 3.2 Structure of sub-national revenues (%)

	2000				2002				2010			
	Own taxes	Shared taxes	Grants	Non-tax	Own taxes	Shared taxes	Grants	Non-tax	Own taxes	Shared taxes	Grants	Non-tax
City of Zagreb	2.31	59.41	0.00	23.89	4.91	47.93	0.84	24.80	4.91	65.02	0.62	27.35
Zagreb	4.73	42.23	4.00	34.79	7.03	42.66	13.45	24.60	5.34	61.44	8.02	21.18
Krapina-Zagorje	5.49	45.04	15.90	24.74	6.45	52.94	15.68	18.83	4.60	65.70	12.58	14.37
Varaždin	4.88	46.43	4.21	31.04	6.53	40.62	19.94	17.52	4.68	61.32	9.50	20.39
Koprivnica-Križevci	3.26	32.90	4.82	53.47	4.70	26.00	24.70	20.39	2.90	47.23	14.07	32.93
Međimurje	5.06	37.31	10.48	26.68	6.63	30.20	28.14	21.94	4.78	56.82	9.74	23.31
Bjelovar-Bilogora	4.16	39.91	10.87	35.06	6.49	50.68	12.95	23.77	4.13	59.46	13.45	19.18
Virovitica-Podravina	3.55	37.20	14.60	33.59	4.82	28.97	32.40	26.46	2.26	40.02	34.33	19.42
Požega-Slavonija	4.87	40.23	21.69	21.01	4.78	48.37	20.82	15.83	3.05	56.31	22.23	16.40
Slavonski Brod-Posavina	4.82	38.60	9.86	29.45	6.34	31.50	33.80	21.67	3.65	56.68	16.94	18.20
Osijek-Baranja	3.24	43.96	8.12	30.29	5.67	35.80	25.19	22.99	4.04	51.44	17.35	23.21
Vukovar-Sirmium	2.61	36.69	26.04	26.85	3.76	27.66	37.57	22.03	2.71	50.41	19.50	21.06
Sisak-Moslavina	2.65	33.74	14.08	41.40	3.46	32.22	28.05	30.87	2.58	54.65	10.36	28.35
Karlovac	4.33	39.01	20.98	24.29	5.37	36.09	26.18	15.74	3.82	60.84	13.24	17.79
Primorje-Gorski Kotar	4.71	31.16	4.21	46.02	9.18	33.34	5.00	41.84	7.46	45.11	4.86	37.44
Lika-Senj	5.89	32.42	22.16	27.53	7.99	25.37	31.90	23.55	5.91	47.41	13.66	27.46
Zadar	6.31	33.10	14.54	33.15	9.56	33.85	13.43	28.46	7.83	41.96	12.45	29.56
Šibenik-Knin	6.84	39.69	20.31	24.64	9.94	26.84	29.47	21.25	8.73	47.02	15.95	25.39
Split-Dalmatia	4.68	34.14	6.32	35.40	7.58	37.44	6.16	34.64	7.92	48.76	9.25	30.67
Istria	6.16	28.98	2.54	34.29	10.18	29.33	10.53	31.97	10.32	38.76	7.01	33.68
Dubrovnik-Neretva	5.43	32.94	15.13	32.63	9.51	43.88	11.40	22.63	7.23	49.18	14.43	26.36

Source: Ministry of Finance.

The structure of revenues indicates that most of the counties' budget revenues derive from shared taxes over which they have little control. However, the more developed counties with cities or towns that are a centre of business activities and in which many business firms are registered generally have a higher portion of shared taxes in their budget. The County of Krapina-Zagorje has the highest proportion of shared taxes (65.7%) along with the City of Zagreb (65%). The revenue structures of the less developed counties are characterized by high proportions of revenue derived from grants, which increased sharply in 2002. For example, the share of grants in the County of Vukovar-Sirmium has increased from 26% in 2000 to 38% in 2002.

Own-tax revenues have consistently formed a relatively low proportion of total revenues of local and regional governments in Croatia. In the county of Istria own-tax revenues amounted to 10.3% of total tax revenues in 2010. The budgets of the other counties have an even lower share of own-tax revenues indicating that local and regional governments have very little revenue autonomy or policy control. Overall, non-tax revenues amount to 37.4% of the total revenues in county budgets, while some counties have a very low share of non-tax revenues in their total revenues (Krapina-Zagorje, Požega-Slavonija, Brod-Posavina, Bjelovar-Bilogora and Virovitica-Podravina).

All the previously mentioned types of sub-national government revenues are variables in a model that was developed to analyse the impact of fiscal decentralization on regional development. In this research several different models were created. In all of these models fiscal decentralization was defined as the revenue autonomy of the sub-national government.[19] In the rest of this chapter I present the results of this model in order to analyse the impact of fiscal decentralization on regional development. After selecting the variables, an estimation equation is presented, which has been estimated by applying a panel data estimator known as the Panel Generalized Least Squares (GLS) method of estimation using a fixed effect model. The estimated model takes the following form:

$$GDP = \alpha + \beta_1 own\_tax + \beta_2 tax\_sharing + \beta_3 grants + \beta_4 non\_tax + \beta_5 pop\_growth + \beta_6 emp + \varepsilon$$

where *GDP* is gross domestic product per capita in local currency by counties for the period 2000–8, *own_tax* is the share of own-tax revenue in total sub-national government revenues; *tax_sharing* is the share of income tax and surtax on income tax in total sub-national government revenues; *grants* is the share of grants and transfers received from the state government and other public authorities in total sub-national government revenues; *non_tax* is the share of non-tax revenues (revenues from business operations, property and administrative fees and charges) in the total sub-national government revenues; pop_growth is estimated annual population growth rate by counties; *emp* is number of employed persons by counties.

Regional GDP per capita is the dependent variable in the model while different measures of fiscal decentralization, measured as the share of own-tax revenue, non-tax revenue, tax sharing and grants in total sub-national revenues are the independent variables. Several other variables are included as independent variables.

Estimated results

Table 3.3 presents the estimated results from the analysis. A strong relationship between the level of decentralization and the level of regional development can be observed in the model. This is the most important conclusion and provides an appropriate answer to the key research question. In the model, the strongest impact is evident for sub-national government share of own-tax revenues in total sub-national government revenues. This result confirms that a higher level of regional development is linked to higher shares of the own-tax revenues of the sub-national government. This fiscal decentralization variable is statistically significant at the 1% level, suggesting that greater revenue

Table 3.3 Decentralization and regional development

Dependent variable	**GDP**	
Regressors	**Estimated coefficients**	
Constant	5643.93	(0.544)
Share of own-tax revenue	591.73***	(3.51)
Share of tax sharing (income tax)	–141.66	(–1.22)
Share of grants	–199.90*	(–1.76)
Share of non-tax revenue	–47.08	(–0.45)
Population growth	993.81	(0.48)
Employed persons	0.23**	(2.22)
Number of observations	126	
R-squared	0.97	

Notes: Coefficients marked *** are significant at a level of 1%, ** at a level of 5%, * at a level of 10%, while *t*-values are presented in brackets.
Source: Author's calculation.

autonomy of sub-national governments is statistically associated with higher levels of regional and local development. Moreover, the level of grants in local revenues is negatively associated with the level of regional development. Of course, to some extent this reflects the equalization purpose of such grants, which are directed towards the poorer regions. However, the finding that higher levels of own-tax revenues are so strongly correlated with the development level does provide some evidence to suggest that the fiscal autonomy of sub-national government has a positive influence on regional development.

Among several other variables in the model, employment and population growth are included as control variables to provide an additional explanation of the relationship between the level of decentralization and regional development. While population growth is not statistically significant, the level of employment also appears to have a strong influence on the level of regional development as could be expected. The overall fit of the model as represented by the 'R^2' statistic is also very high suggesting that a large part of the variation in the level of regional development can be explained by the level of decentralization and by the level of employment.

Conclusions

The decentralization process is often considered to be crucial in enabling local and regional government units to manage their development. This research presented in this chapter has shown that higher levels of decentralization of administrative power and responsibilities as well as fiscal autonomy are expected to exert a positive influence on local and regional economic development. This suggests that to the extent that government is interested in promoting local and regional development it should seek to promote the process of decentralization in Croatia in a way which implies more independence of local self-government units, both in performing their tasks as well as in the collection of revenues.

Despite the potential for generating local economic development, the sub-national level of government in Croatia has relatively little fiscal autonomy. This suggests that the decentralization process in Croatia has not yet achieved its full potential in promoting efficient public service delivery, strengthening local and regional governance, or generating local and regional economic development. In order to do so, a greater participation of sub-national governments in the total government revenues (and expenditures) would be needed.

The results further suggest that the relatively low level of decentralization in Croatia does not imply the need for any less responsibility

Appendix: Data sources

Variable	County	Source
Share of own tax revenue	21 counties	Ministry of Finance
Share of tax sharing (income tax)	21 counties	Ministry of Finance
Share of grants	21 counties	Ministry of Finance
Share of non-tax revenue	21 counties	Ministry of Finance
Total expenditures	21 counties	Ministry of Finance
Population growth	21 counties	Central Bureau of Statistics
Employed persons	21 counties	Central Bureau of Statistics
GDP	21 counties	Central Bureau of Statistics

for sub-national government to provide public services at the local and regional level. On the contrary, it means that local and regional self-government units should take on more duties and responsibilities in providing local public services. This should be backed up by a far higher level of revenue autonomy of sub-national governments as the statistical results suggest that this would assure higher levels of regional and local development.

We can conclude that *less* participation of state government in the total government revenues (expenditures) and in GDP and an *increase* in the level of decentralization is highly likely to provide a much-needed stimulus for local and regional economic development. An expected result of the process of decentralization would be a more positive economic outcome on the local and regional level in Croatia.

Notes

This chapter is a result of the research projects '002-0022469-2468 Sustainable Development, Innovation, and Regional Policy of the Republic of Croatia (Održivi razvoj, inovacije i regionalna politika Republike Hrvatske)' financed by the Ministry of Science, Education and Sports of the Republic of Croatia.

1. Economists argue whether a decentralized fiscal system poses a danger to macroeconomic stability. Shah (2005) concludes that decentralization based on transparent fiscal rules is associated with improved fiscal performance.
2. In a recent study of 21 OECD countries, Adam, Delis and Kammas (2008) concludes that public sector efficiency increases with fiscal decentralization.
3. Based on cross-country data on 78 countries, De Mello and Barenstein (2001) show that the relationship between decentralization and governance depends on how sub-national expenditures are financed.
4. The literature on the relationship between decentralization and growth is inconclusive. For example, Bahl and Linn (1992) find a positive correlation between decentralization and the level of development while Davoodi and Zou (1998) find a negative effect of fiscal decentralization on growth.

5. The definition is based on the following papers: Buier and Kletzer (1992), Casella and Frey (1992), Grossman and West (1994), Ehdaie (1994), Inman and Rubinfeld (1992), Musgrave and Musgrave (1993), Oates (1972, 1977, 1993, 1999), Tanzi (1995), De Mello (2000), Ebel and Yilmaz (2002), Bird and Wallich (1992, 1993, 1994).
6. The Decentralization Programme for the period 2004–7 adopted by the Government of the Republic of Croatia (2004) describes this process as the first phase of fiscal decentralization in Croatia.
7. The criteria for the selection of cities, which, together with the counties and the city of Zagreb, took over the financing of the decentralized expenditures for primary education, were that these cities have more than 10,000 inhabitants, or are county capitals, and that the income tax per capita in 1999 was higher than 400 HRK.
8. The total number of the 53 selected local and regional government units that have been assigned decentralized functions represents only 9% of the total number of local and regional self-government units in Croatia. On the other hand, the local budgets of the 53 selected cities and counties represent the majority (around 70%) of all the local budgets in Croatia.
9. The share of income tax revenues allocated to the local and regional governments was gradually increased. The last change in the distribution of the income tax was on 1 July 2008. Since then cities participated with 55% and counties with 15.5% in income tax revenues. The City of Zagreb has the status of a city as well as a county and participated with 70.5% in the distribution of income tax revenues.
10. An additional share of income tax revenue for financing decentralized functions allocated to the local and regional governments was gradually increased. Since 1 July 2008 cities and counties participated with 12% in the additional part of the income tax revenues.
11. Since 1 July 2008 cities and counties participated with 3.1% in the additional share of the income tax revenues for financing primary education. Participation of counties in additional share of income tax revenues was 2.2% for secondary education, 3.2% for health care and 2.2% for social welfare financing. Cities participated with 1.3% in additional part of income tax revenues in the financing of fire protection.
12. Since 1 July 2008 equalization grants for decentralized functions were 17.5% of the income tax revenues.
13. Although it is widely accepted in literature that the sub-national share of total government revenue/spending is an imperfect measure of fiscal decentralization, due to pragmatic reasons as well as the availability of comparable data, many researchers use these measures to represent the degree of fiscal decentralization.
14. Unfortunately, the Ministry of Finance only consolidates data and presents for 53 local government units (20 counties, the City of Zagreb and 32 big cities) out of 576 (approximately 70% of local budgets). This is the number of local government units that, by law and government decree, hold decentralized functions in primary and secondary education, social welfare and health care.
15. Based on Jurlina Alibegović and Slijepčević (2010).
16. The classification of government functions was developed by the Organization for Economic Co-operation and Development and published by the United

Nations Statistical Division. Public functions are classified in the following categories: general public services, defence, public order and safety, economic affairs, environmental protection, housing and community amenities, health, recreation, culture and religion, education and social protection.

17. Revenues from profit tax were also shared revenues until the end of 2006. In this analysis the revenue from profit tax is excluded since this exclusion enables the comparison of sub-national governments' revenue structure during the whole period of analysis (2000–8).
18. Data on the sub-national government budgets collected by the Ministry of Finance does not make any distinction among intergovernmental transfers. See the website of the Ministry of Finance: http://www.mfin.hr
19. Based on the methodology defined in Ebel and Yilmaz (2002).

References

Adam, A., Delis, M. D. and Kammas, P. (2008) 'Fiscal decentralisation and public sector efficiency: Evidence from OECD countries', *CESifo Working Paper Series No. 2364.*

Bahl, R. W. and Linn, J. F. (1992) *Urban Public Finance in Developing Countries*, New York: Oxford University Press.

Bird, R. M. and Wallich, C. I. (1992) *Fiscal Decentralisation and Intergovernmental Relations in Transition Economies*, Washington, DC: The World Bank.

Bird, R. M. and Wallich, C. I. (1993) 'Fiscal decentralisation and intergovernmental relations in transition economies', *Policy Research Working Papers Public Economics, WPS 1122*, Policy Research Department, Washington, DC: The World Bank.

Bird, R. M. and Wallich, C. I. (1994) 'Local government finance in transition economies: Policy and institutional issues', in S. Schiavo-Campo (ed.), *Institutional Change and the Public Sector in Transitional Economies*, Washington, DC: The World Bank, pp. 97–128.

Buier, W. H. and Kletzer, K. M. (1992) 'Fiscal policy coordination as fiscal federalism: Economic integration, public goods and efficiency in growing economies', *Center Paper No. 464*, New Haven: Yale University, Economic Growth Center.

Casella, A. and Frey, B. (1992) 'Fiscal federalism and the theory of clubs, federalism and clubs: Towards an economic theory of overlapping political jurisdictions', *European Economic Review*, 36(2): 639–46.

Davoodi, H., Xie, D. and Zou, H. (1995) *Fiscal Decentralisation and Economic Growth in the United States*, Policy Research Department, Washington, DC: The World Bank.

Davoodi, H. and Zou, H. (1998) 'Fiscal decentralisation and economic growth: A cross- country study', *Journal of Urban Economics*, 43(2): 244–57.

De Mello, L. R. (2000) 'Fiscal decentralisation and intergovernmental fiscal relations: A cross-country analysis', *World Development*, 28(2): 365–80.

De Mello. L. R. and Barenstein, M. (2001) 'Fiscal decentralisation and governance: A cross-country analysis', *IMF Working Paper*, Washington, DC: The International Monetary Fund.

Ebel, R. D. and Yilmaz, S. (2002) 'On the measurement and impact of fiscal decentralisation', *Policy Research Working Paper 2809*, Washington, DC: The World Bank.

Ehdaie, J. (1994) 'Fiscal decentralisation and the size of government: An extension with evidence from cross country data', *Policy Research Working Paper No. 138*, Washington, DC: The World Bank.
Government of the Republic of Croatia (2004) *Decentralisation Programme for Period* 2004–2007 (in Croatian), Zagreb: Government of the Republic of Croatia.
Grossman, P. J. and West, E. G. (1994) 'Federalism and the growth of government revisited', *Public Choice*, 79(1–2): 19–32.
Inman, R. P. and Rubinfeld, D. L. (1992) 'Fiscal federalism in Europe: Lessons from the United States experience', *European Economic Review*, 36(2–3): 654–60.
International Monetary Fund (2010) *Government Finance Statistics Yearbook 2010*, Washington, DC: International Monetary Fund.
Jurlina Alibegović, D. and Slijepčević, S. (2010) 'Decentralisation in Croatia: Problems and possible solutions', Paper prepared for presentation at research seminar *On the Way to EU Membership: Present and Future Challenges for Candidate and Potential Candidate Countries*, organized by the University Institute of European Studies (IUEE) and the Spanish Agency of International Cooperation for Development (AECID), Barcelona, Spain, 16–17 December.
Musgrave, R. and Musgrave, P. (1993) *Javne financije u teoriji i praksi*, Zagreb: Institut za javne financije.
Oates, W. E. (1972) *Fiscal Federalism*, New York: Harcourt Brace Jovanovich, Inc.
Oates, W. E. (ed.) (1977) *The Political Economy of Fiscal Federalism*, Lexington; Toronto: Lexington Books.
Oates, W. E. (1993) 'Fiscal decentralisation and economic development', *National Tax Journal*, 46(2): 237–43.
Oates, W. E. (1999) 'An essay on fiscal federalism', *Journal of Economic Literature*, 37(3): 1120–49.
Shah, A. (2004) 'Fiscal decentralisation in developing and transition economies: Progress, Problems and the Promise', *World Bank Policy Research Working Paper Series No. 3282*, Washington, DC: The World Bank.
Shah, A. (2005) 'Fiscal decentralisation and fiscal performance', *World Bank Policy Research Working Paper No. 3786*, Washington, DC: The World Bank.
Smoke, P. (2001) 'Fiscal decentralisation in developing countries: A review of current concepts and practice', *Programme Paper Number 2*, Geneva: United Nations Research Institute for Social Development (UNRISD) Democracy, Governance and Human Rights.
Tanzi, V. (1995) 'Fiscal federalism and decentralisation: A review of some efficiency and macroeconomic aspects', Annual Bank Conference on Development Economics in Washington, DC, 1–2 May, Washington, DC: The World Bank.

4
Regional Policy and Decentralization in Montenegro

Will Bartlett and Božidar Šišević

Introduction

Although Montenegro enjoyed rapid economic growth in the period preceding the onset of the global economic crisis, the process of economic transformation that took place over the previous decade led to severe deindustrialization of the less developed North East region of the country. In this region, most of the local wood-processing factories closed down in the early 2000s, leading to the paradox of widespread unemployment and abandoned factories amid an area of abundant forest resources. International aid projects funded by the EU and bilateral donors have sought to revive the prospects of the region but with little success. The region benefitted little from the pre-crisis economic boom that took place from 2004 to 2008, which was mainly based on a large inflow of foreign direct investment (FDI) to the Coastal region. The North East region has failed to attract new foreign investment in green field development, and has remained underdeveloped with poor infrastructure and regional disparities within the country having widened.[1]

Having adopted a very open neoliberal economic policy in the 2000s, Montenegro was severely affected by the global economic crisis creating a difficult economic climate for regional development policies. Real GDP fell by an estimated 5.7% in 2009, with a relatively weak recovery in 2010.[2] Exports of goods and services fell by as much as two-fifths in 2009. By March 2010, as many as a quarter of companies had their accounts blocked and were unable to repay their loans[3] leading to a significant increase in non-performing loans within the banking system, most of which is now under foreign ownership. Consequently, banks have become more cautious in lending to the business sector. Credit flows fell by 5% in 2009, and by March 2010 the largest bank had ceased providing new credits altogether. So severe has become the banks' aversion to risk in Montenegro that they turned down an offer of a credit line from the European Investment Bank. According to one microfinance institution that we visited, the default rate on loans to small producers in the North East region increased from 1% in 2008 to 10% in 2009. Furthermore, there is high out-migration as people leave the region for the capital city and the coastal areas. Schools in smaller rural areas are closing, and there is very little public investment in cultural activities and the quality of life is relatively low.

Within the context of economic crisis, this chapter focuses attention on the less developed North East region of the country. It investigates the effectiveness of the policy responses to the negative effects of the transition to a market economy. In particular, we examine the effects of decentralization and regional policies on the less developed municipalities in the North East of Montenegro. The research was carried out in March 2010 on the basis of a round of interviews held with senior policy makers in Podgorica and key informants in the North East region of Montenegro. The chapter analyses the reasons for the failure of regional policy and advances some proposals for policy improvements.

Regional disparities in Montenegro

Montenegro is afflicted by high levels of regional disparities. The main policy response has been one of benign neglect that has failed to meet the needs of the North East region, which has consequently entered a spiral of economic decline. The global economic crisis has also had a noticeable impact on the region with unemployment increasing to over 20% in 2011. External demand for Montenegro's exports has fallen, while the reduction in inward foreign investment, which had fuelled the economic boom of the mid to late 2000s, has been even more dramatic. By 2011, the unemployment rate in the northern 'continental' part of the country stood at 26.4%, compared to 12.7% in the central region and 12.5% on the coast (Fabris and Žugic, 2012). Income per capita in the north was €4,900 compared to €17,000 in the central region. The negative effects of the global economic crisis have also been reflected in the reduced national budget, in reduced salaries of employees financed from the central budget, and in reduced transfers from the central government for local infrastructural projects. The crisis has in effect provided a further excuse for neglecting the formulation of an organized industrial policy on a regional level that would involve local economic regeneration of the former industrial base of the region, especially in industries such as wood processing and paper making, food processing, textiles, and the leather industry. In the absence of a concerted effort towards regeneration, there is little local capacity for endogenous development especially in small municipalities. Institutions of inclusive local governance are weakly developed, with much power concentrated in the position of the local mayor. Decentralization has been attempted, yet in practice weakly applied due to the factors outlined in the introduction to this book: weak administrative and fiscal capacity and local elite capture.

In the former Yugoslav system, the North East region of Montenegro benefited from a focused regional policy which established a local industrial economy based on processing the natural forest and agricultural resources of the region, including wood processing, furniture production, food processing, textiles and wool production. Each of these industries employed several thousand people. However, in the 1990s, due to the effects of international isolation brought about by sanctions and the impact of neoliberal transition policies that encouraged unrestricted cheap imports, most of these industries collapsed. Both domestic policymakers and their international advisors argued that Montenegro should develop banking, education and other service industries, and should not care too much about the industrial sector. They also advocated that Montenegro should open its border to cheap imports of industrial and agricultural products. The intention was to benefit consumers and it was thought that forcing domestic producers to compete with foreign imports would stimulate efficiency. However, the local economy was unable to meet this import competition, which contributed to the collapse of the domestic industries. In the wake of this policy, one of the authors visited the North East part of the country in 2004 and found a picture of almost universal desolation, with most factories in the region shut down, high levels of unemployment and a population struggling with day-to-day needs of mere survival (Bartlett, 2006).

The situation in our field research in the North East in March 2010 showed a picture that had changed little. For example, in 2008, Montenegro imported €100 million of furniture, and exported only €5 million despite the abundant resources of wood and a tradition of wood-processing industries. While the North East abounds with high-quality spring water, the net import of drinking water was €15 million. We were also informed that a meat-processing company we visited in Bijelo Polje imports four-fifths of the meat used in the production of its final products, despite the presence of many local farmers willing to supply the company. The situation is the same in several other meat-processing companies in the region. In the period since 2004 most of the defunct companies in both wood processing and food processing have been privatized and some have begun to operate again. New businesses have been created in construction and food processing, and there has been a limited revival of economic activity. However, many factories remain closed. The Berane paper mill, once the largest in the region but closed since 1998, was reopened after privatization to recycle paper waste. However, the new owner has been unable to raise sufficient working capital to keep the plant operating. Unemployment in the region remains high. For example, in Bijelo Polje in 2009 there were over 4000 unemployed people, representing an unemployment rate of 18%, of which almost half (48%) are women, while most have a lower level or vocational education.

In the rest of this section, we illustrate the problems faced by the North East region, which underline the growing regional disparities in the country, by focusing on three key economic sectors: forestry, tourism and local public services.

Forestry

It is estimated that 8% of GDP is generated in the forestry sector in Montenegro. Most of this is produced in the North East region, and thus provides an important source of income for regional development. Yet, owing to the economic recession, revenues from forestry have tumbled. Concession fees to local municipalities fell by 50%, from €7 million in 2008 to €3.5 million in 2009. Most former state-owned sawmills were privatized in 2005–8. This was followed by a process of allocating concessions to the state-owned forest that was divided in Forest Management Units. The owners of the sawmills were allowed to bid for these concessions in order to provide them with a guaranteed supply of raw material. However, the system has not worked well. About half the concession fees were not paid in 2009, which has had a negative impact on the municipal finances. At the same time the concession companies have been responsible for damaging the local roads by their use of heavy lorries laden with logs. The local municipalities are responsible for the repair of local roads, but due to limited financial capacity are unable to maintain them, with adverse consequences for the road quality in many areas. A further adverse effect of the policy has been the deterioration in the quality of the forests, due to neglect and poor management. Often, the quality has fallen so much that the wood products are unsuitable for high quality processing into furniture, and are only usable as fuel, and as 'biomass' for communal heating systems. A major difficulty in using even this limited potential is that the power companies often do not have the right equipment to burn the biomass, which would be a renewable source of fuel for them. Consequently, a German aid agency is assisting the power companies to replace the communal heating equipment so that it is capable of burning the biomass products.

Thus, while forests remain an important local endogenous resource, the wood-processing companies were closed down in the 1990s and early 2000s and so the resource was unused for many years. While the wood-processing companies were eventually privatized and reopened in the mid-2000s, the concession system has proved to be unsuitable, benefiting only the elite of new owners who profit from short-term exploitation of the forest, damage the local roads and undermine sustainable local economic development.

Tourism

Tourism is mainly developed on the coastal region, where much investment has been directed in recent years leading to a property boom. In the North East, however, what tourism infrastructure there was in former Yugoslavia is in a parlous state of repair. Many hotels were occupied by refugees in the 1990s and early 2000s and were badly damaged and require significant reinvestment to operate effectively as tourism venues. International donors such as GIZ[4] have been actively promoting tourism as a source of economic regeneration and growth. However, according to the Ministry of Tourism, there is a problem of overlap between donor projects.[5] The Ministry has developed a policy of sustainable development that has social, environmental as well as economic goals. Regional tourism plans for the North East around the Prokletije area depend upon inter-municipal cooperation to achieve their aims. The 'Hiking and Biking' tourist project aims to develop 6000 kilometres of trails through the mountains in the North, while other programmes of local tourism development aim to create local jobs and reduce out-migration. The tourism strategy is supported by the donor organization GIZ.

Local municipalities benefit from an 18% tourism tax, and have established Local Tourism Organizations. Yet these are underfunded owing to the restricted tax base as there are so few tourists coming to the region. While local municipalities are responsible for the development of local trails and roads, the central government is responsible for main roads in the region. However, roads are often poorly signposted which is likely to discourage tourism development. The Ministry does not have sufficient funds to erect the necessary signposts and is expecting support for this from USAID. In addition, roads are poorly maintained. In the ski resort of Kolašin, although the town centre has been regenerated with new infrastructure and housing units, the road to the resort is full of potholes and almost impassable.

International donors such as GIZ and USAID view tourism as a future growth engine for local economic development in the region. Nevertheless tourism will only ever benefit a small proportion of the population, while tourist areas are being ruined by unregulated real estate development. Donors have too high expectations for the capacity of tourism to underpin local economic development. Without investment in local infrastructure, without training local people and without favourable financing the tourism sector has little chance of success and will not be able to become the motor for local economic development. According to a recent report of the IMF, Montenegro should not rely on tourism as a major engine of growth, as the sector is highly vulnerable to political risk from events in neighbouring countries in the wider region. The case of tourism illustrates the failure of policy transfer from international donor organizations, based upon a too optimistic view of the potential for tourism as a source of endogenous local development.

Local public services

Local public utility companies owned by each municipality provide local public services, such as water supply and electricity. While the central state pays for infrastructure development, the local public utilities are responsible for maintenance. They derive their income from user charges, but the revenue collection rate is low ranging from 50–90%. Consequently, maintenance is often inadequate. Inefficiencies therefore abound, and in the case of the water companies leakages cause the loss of up to 50% of supply. With very limited local resources for investment, priority in financing local public services was given to those which are financed from the central government budget and donor aid programmes, while those which are less costly and have a bigger public impact are neglected – such as maintenance and smaller reconstructions of the schools and local health centres, local roads and sport centres. The local infrastructure such as water and electricity supply, sewerage system and waste disposal are neglected and work on the edge of minimum standards. Low levels of administrative capacity and lack of sufficient financial decentralization have undermined the ability of the local public utilities to provide efficient services to the local residents. In addition, local elite capture often leads to the distorted allocation of public utilities, as a result of which local elite groups and local politicians are better served than other members of the local population.

Regional policy

Given the extent of regional disparities and the problems faced by the less developed municipalities in the North East, it is hardly surprising that the government's main economic policy documents identify a need to reduce regional disparities. Achieving a more balanced regional development has been emphasized and accepted as a government priority. In achieving this, market forces and the creation of favourable local conditions are expected to be enough to attract potential investors. An important stimulus from the central government has been the supply of low interest loans for investment in the less developed regions. Most regional development programmes of this type have been designed at the national level and implemented in the municipalities. At the time of writing, the Ministry of Economy was in the process of setting up a new Unit for Regional Development, and formulating a Strategy for Regional Development, supported by the Council of Ministers, including the Ministers of Economy and Finance, a Vice-Prime Minister and the Association of Municipalities. A new Law on Regional Development was being drafted, but no political decision had yet been taken to define regions within the country.

A range of policy measures has been adopted to reduce regional disparities. Support is given to entrepreneurship development by the Employment Agency through favourable interest rates to finance investment. Other agencies active in this respect are the Development Fund and the Agency for SMEs. A special programme of the Employment Agency for the North East called 'A Job for You' has provided 5000 individual participants with finance to start a business at reduced interest rates. The programme offers a loan of €5000 for each worker employed, up to a maximum of three workers, at an interest rate of 3% per annum, and with a grace period of one to three years. In addition, employers benefit from wage subsidies for newly employed workers. However, the resources available for the programme are limited, and its impact has been at best marginal. In 2009, 44 new loans were issued under the programme in Bijelo Polje, and 67 people were employed.[6] A further programme called 'Employing School Leavers' is targeted at those who leave secondary school after the minimum period of education, and subsidized their wages for between six months to one year. In 2009 the programme supported the employment of 69 young people.[7] Other programmes support training and retraining of new employees, who are guaranteed employment after three months training, providing the employer with a wage subsidy for up to 30 months. Finally, local public works programmes have been set up by the Employment

Agency in activities such as waste collection, social work, agriculture and cultural production in partnership with local NGOs, the public utility companies and the local municipalities. In Bijelo Polje, in 2009, 16 public works projects employed 150 local people. The job creation programmes 'Looking after Older People' trains unemployed women to provide domestic help to elderly people in their homes. A seasonal employment programme provides employment for unemployed people from the North East on the coastal region in the tourist season. A special programme to support the employment of people who are otherwise 'hard to employ' provides training to build self-esteem, and involved 198 people in 2009 in the municipality. Finally a programme called 'A Chance for Young Managers' has provided support for 14 ambitious young people who want to pursue a career in management, providing them with two months theoretical training and two months practical work experience, leading in most cases to a full-time employment. These programmes are also implemented in other communes according to the size of the communes. The Development Fund, which is more concerned with financing growing companies, invested some resources in these communes under favourable interest rates and grace period.

The EU also has a strong interest in regional policy in Montenegro, as a pre-accession country, on account of the need to harmonize systems to the European regional policy. Montenegro is a single NUTS2 region. The lack of a NUTS3 definition has been problematic for the development of EU-funded Cross-Border Programmes.[8] Montenegro became a candidate for EU membership at the end of 2010. Programming and implementing EU assistance through the IPA programme under 'Component III' for regional development needed to be contracted in a very short time before the funding deadline in 2013, a difficult task due to a lack of administrative capacity. Fortunately, a regional development strategy had already been prepared within the Ministry of Economy with EU assistance. The government based this strategy around several large infrastructure investments. These included hydropower plants in the North East region intended to supply electricity to the whole of South East Europe and Italy, a major highway linking the coast and the North East, as well as other investments in airports and water supply.[9] However, it is thought within the EU Delegation that plans to build a major highway from the capital city to the North East region will not be cost-effective and will fail to create jobs. A project financed through IPA to develop inter-municipal cooperation in the repair and maintenance of local roads was thought to be a far more effective way to absorb some of the EU regional funds in the future.[10]

Decentralization in Montenegro

In addition to the regional policies that aim to redistribute resources more evenly across the different regions of the country, decentralization of power and resources to municipalities is also seen as a way to promote endogenous development on the basis of locally available resources, both human and physical. Yet, Montenegro is a relatively centralized state. Although there are 21 municipalities, most power lies in the hands of the central administration in the capital city, Podgorica, and the municipalities are relatively weak both administratively and financially.

Following advice from USAID, a Law on Local Self-Government was adopted in 2003 to which amendments were passed in subsequent years.[11] The law redefined the competences of municipalities and created a new organizational structure giving them the responsibility for a range of activities relevant to the local population. Public services assigned to municipalities include responsibility for water supply, waste management, sewage, public traffic, social care for old people and disabled persons, childcare, information, culture, and physical recreation and sport. In order to reduce migration of young people from the region there was an attempt to decentralize higher education. The law also provided for the direct election of mayors, giving them considerable autonomy in the local political process, a system under which 'the mayor is king'.[12] Under this system the power of local councils to control the executive was weakened as they lost the capacity to oversee expenditure. With the increasing influence of the EU and the Council of Europe, amendments to the law on local self-government were adopted in 2009 based on the Continental legal approach. Along with a new election law introduced in 2009, the direct election of mayors has been replaced by an indirect election system intended to align the political affiliations of mayors more closely with that of the local council. The Ministry of Justice in collaboration with the Union of Municipalities of Montenegro and the Council of Europe prepared a 'Working Programme on Better Self-Government in Montenegro', and a 'Strategy for the Reform of Local Self-Government 2010–2015' has been adopted. A major goal of the decentralization policy is to encourage inter-municipal cooperation through local Inter-Municipal Councils. A 'Strategy for Sustainable Development' has also been formulated, although this is a very general document that emphasizes the need to use local resources for sustainable development without specifying the specific measures or programmes required.

The financing of municipalities is defined by the Law on Local Self-Government Financing[13] as well as by special laws for taxes, fees and other financial issues related to the municipal budgets. There are four sources of municipal finance (GoM, 2009). Firstly, revenue is raised through local taxes and fees, including a surtax on personal income, a property tax, a consumption tax, a tax on construction land, a registration tax and taxes on lotteries. Local fees include residence fees, administration fees and communal fees. In addition, there are several 'reimbursements' for the use of construction land, for environmental protection and improvement, and for the use of local roads. Secondly, there are 'shared revenues' from personal income tax, property tax and revenues from concessions. Thirdly municipalities receive revenue from an Equalization Fund established in 2007, which is financed on the basis of 11% of personal income tax receipts and 20% of the receipts of the property tax. This fund is distributed to those municipalities with below-average revenues from their own sources and from common sources. Fourthly, municipalities receive conditional grants from the State budget for financing municipal investment projects, according to a multi-annual investment plan.

Even though the process of decentralization has placed local government nominally in charge of service delivery in several important areas, the municipalities in North East Montenegro lack the capacity to deliver the full range and quality of local services due to a lack of financial resources.[14] An analysis carried out by the UNDP in 11 municipalities concluded that municipalities lack administrative and financial capacity and qualified staff and, moreover, are vulnerable to corruption. According to the analysis of the Council of Europe, the central government's Equalization Fund has failed to provide additional resources to the North East region.[15] The Ministry of Finance considers that the problem of lack of administrative capacity of the municipalities is so serious that decentralization is unlikely to be effective and that the main focus of economic development should be the more developed part of the country around Podgorica.[16] In collaboration with the Council of Europe, the government is developing a new strategy for the reform of local self-government. Support from the European Commission through the IPA technical assistance programme may also be influential in this process, as standards will be set in line with the European Charter of Local Self-Government elaborated in 1985 and ratified by Montenegro in 2008.

Conclusion

Regional disparities are severe in Montenegro, which is characterized by a less developed North and a more developed Centre and South. In the North East, deindustrialization has led to the decline of traditional industries such as wood processing, paper production, textiles and food processing. Foreign investment has been concentrated on coastal tourism and property development, causing the neglect of the North East, leading to a polarized pattern of development. Regional policy has been relatively ineffective in tackling the wide regional disparities that exist. In the forestry sector, privatization has benefitted new owners rather than supporting the regeneration of the wood-processing industry and providing employment for the local community. Tourism has been promoted by donor organizations as a sector that could generate local development but has limited potential and might be seen as an example of the failure of policy transfer. Local public services often benefit narrow elite interests to a greater extent than the general population, while expenditure on repair and maintenance of schools and infrastructure such as local roads is often inadequate. Local public utilities such as water supply also often suffer from inefficiencies and a lack of financial capacity.

Despite declared ambitions, strategies and laws, decentralization in Montenegro has been limited and the state remains highly centralized. The decentralization that has taken place has not contributed much to local economic development in the North East. Decentralization policies and practices have been highly politicized, and have led to a distorted allocation of resources from the centre to politically well-connected municipalities. In some cases municipalities have been captured by local elites, and local services are often oriented to satisfying particular interests rather than serving the wider community. Although decentralization has provided municipalities with a range of responsibilities, administrative decentralization has not been accompanied by effective fiscal decentralization, undermining the ability of the local self-government units to deliver effective and responsive public services. Nor do local municipalities have the administrative capacity to carry out effective local economic development programmes. The local officials we met and with whom we discussed this issue had different opinions. Some were in favour of the existing situation with a strong central government with central decision-making as a way of achieving some redistribution of resources from the Budget. Others were in favour of a more radical decentralization that would enable an improved use of local resources.

International donors have assisted in the design of policies to promote local economic development in the North East region. However, the assistance they have provided has been rather ad hoc, with some agencies favouring forestry development, others favouring tourism, and yet others favouring small-scale agriculture (e.g. production of forest fruits).

The government on the other hand has pushed for large-scale infrastructure projects. Donor programmes have been consequently been characterized by a failure of the various attempts at policy transfer that have been carried out from the very different environments of more developed countries.

A further difficulty has been that the privatization process failed to support local economic development as it mainly relied on foreign investment rather than local sources of finance. The process of restructuring of the large industrial enterprises in the less developed regions was poorly organized and these companies failed to attract the foreign investment that was available. The less developed regions do not have the infrastructure or the trained labour force that would attract foreign companies to invest in the local economy. Moreover, since the administrative capacities of the region are limited, officials are often unable to prepare more complex projects that could be financed from EU funds or donor programmes. In our view, given that the government is not keen to establish a local development agency or fund, a way forward might be to establish a dedicated regional development partnership council based on existing legislative provision for inter-municipal cooperation that would bring together all the local actors and their representatives in the North East. Such a council would have the role of preparing and coordinating the implementation of appropriate local economic development projects and development activities of the individually weak local municipalities. Such an approach could be developed as part of the EU IPA programme on regional development that is now open to the country as a candidate state.

Notes

The research was funded by a grant from the Latsis Public Benefit Foundation, for whose support we are extremely grateful. It forms part of a larger project on Decentralization and Regional Development in South East Europe that was carried out at the LSEE research unit at the European Institute of the LSE.

1. Interview, Central Bank of Montenegro, 29 March 2010.
2. Data are taken from the World Bank publication 'South East Europe Regular Economic Report', November 2011.
3. Interview, Central Bank of Montenegro, 29 March 2010.
4. The German Agency for International Cooperation (GIZ – Deutsche Gesellschaft für Internationale Zusammenarbeit).
5. Interview, Ministry of Tourism, March 2010.
6. Interview, Bijelo Polje Employment Agency, 24 March 2010.
7. Ibid.

8. Interview, EU Delegation, Podgorica, March 2010.
9. Interview Deputy PM, Podgorica, 29 March 2010.
10. Interview, EU Delegation, Podgorica, March 2010.
11. Official Gazette no. 42/03, 28/04, 75/05 and 13/06.
12. Comment made during an interview at the EU Delegation, Podgorica, March 2010.
13. Official Gazette no. 44/03.
14. Interview, UNDP Podgorica, March 2010.
15. Interview, Council of Europe, Podgorica, 29 March 2010.
16. Interview, Ministry of Finance, Podgorica, 30 March 2010.

References

Bartlett, W. (2006) 'International aid, policy transfer and local economic development in North Montenegro', in B. Dallago (ed.) *Transformation and European Integration: The Local Dimension*, Basingstoke: Palgrave Macmillan, pp. 142–57.

Fabris, N. and Žugic, R. (2012) 'Regionalisation and regional policy of Montenegro', *Journal of the Geographical Institute 'Jovan Cvijic'*, 62(1): 49–67.

GoM (2009) *Local Self-Government Sector: Integrity and Capacity Assessment*, Podgorica: Government of Montenegro, Directorate for Anti-Corruption Initiative.

Part III

Decentralization in Ethnically Divided Societies

5

Decentralization and Regionalization in Bosnia–Herzegovina: Context, Model and Implementation Challenges

Vesna Bojičić-Dželilović

Introduction

The violent conflict that lasted for three years (1992–5) triggered the territorial and political reconfiguration of the state of Bosnia–Herzegovina. Under the terms of the Dayton Peace Agreement (DPA) Bosnia–Herzegovina was reorganized as an asymmetric federation under the precept that it would provide a framework for inter-ethnic accommodation, create channels for democratic contestation, and ultimately usher in peace and stability. Therefore, the primary motive for decentralization was political – to exploit its alleged potential as an ethnic conflict management tool. This distinguishes the Bosnia–Herzegovina case from those contemporaneous, peacetime situations where the primary concern of decentralization tends to be its functional role in the context of building a multi-level system of governance to improve development outcomes (Schou and Hang, 2005).

The literature on decentralization as a conflict-management tool within the political theory stream has provided ample evidence of its ambiguous role (Roeder and Rothchild, 2005; Brancati, 2008; Hiskey, 2010). The literature on fiscal federalism, from the economics perspective, has come to the similar conclusion about its uncertain economic efficiency outcomes (Bird and Vaillancourt, 1998; Schou and Hang, 2005). Common to both research streams is an important finding that which way the pendulum swings – whether the benefits of decentralization will be exploited or not – depends on the local political, historical, economic, social and geographical context, as well as on the power relations between the elites on the central and subnational level (Brown, 2008; Rodriguez-Pose and Sandall, 2008; Connerly, Eaton and Smoke, 2010). Brown, for example, states that the impacts of both political decentralization and fiscal federalism are 'mediated by context and other institutional factors' (Brown, 2008: 390). In Bosnia–Herzegovina, the legacy of war, and more specifically that of politicized ethnicity as a backdrop for the political process is paramount for understanding the power relations behind the process of decentralization, and the way in which the outcomes of its political and economic mandate have shaped up (Bojičić-Dželilović, 2003).

Decentralization in its form of extending authority to sub-central jurisdiction has evolved in a politically and administratively complex setting established as part of the peace settlement to end the war in Bosnia–Herzegovina. In the four-tier government structure devised to account for political and ethnic criteria and interests, a weak central state government coexists with two strong entities – the Federation of Bosnia–Herzegovina (FBiH) and Republika Srpska (RS), ten cantons as sub-federal units and the Brcko District, a self-governing unit under the direct jurisdiction of the state of Bosnia–Herzegovina. This asymmetric federal structure further encompasses a total of 141 municipalities – 79 in the FBiH and 62 in the RS, and five cities.[1] Most powers are vested with the two entities and the FBiH cantons, with only limited responsibilities originally entrusted exclusively to the central state. The cantons, of which all but two have clear ethnic majority, exist as de facto mini-states, with fully-fledged legislative and executive structures (EDA, 2005). The primacy of the ethno-territorial criteria behind the political settlement of the 1992–5 conflict has triggered continuing demands for the creation of new municipalities around particular ethnic group boundaries. As a result some 40 new municipalities have been established since the end of the conflict, whose idiosyncratic problems associated with deliberate redrawing of the territorial borders have added more complexity to the ongoing decentralization process.

Historically, motives for decentralization vary and conflict management is one among many (Smoke, Gomez and Peterson, 2006). Bosnia–Herzegovina's case is interesting in that simultaneously, strong international involvement has pushed for decentralization for the reasons of economic efficiency. The main argument put forward in this chapter is that, given the deeply contested structure of the state defined by the Dayton constitution, its renegotiation through decentralization and regionalization has not provided a framework within which the potential 'democratic and allocative virtues' (Bird and Vaillancourt, 1998: 10) of decentralization, and its dividend in terms of development, security and democracy, can be realized. This chapter aims to map the process of decentralization in Bosnia–Herzegovina, to identify its salient aspects, and against this background to highlight implementation challenges and offer some tentative assessment of the outcomes in terms of public service delivery. Part one presents an overview of the decentralization discourse, the actors and institutions in Bosnia–Herzegovina. It highlights how, despite tensions arising from the simultaneous centralization and decentralization under the ongoing reforms of the existing constitutional set-up, substantial progress has been made in modernizing the legislative framework of decentralization, with the international actors in the driving seat. Part two examines the decentralization model, and analyses the key aspects of functional and fiscal decentralization arrangements in the entity legislation and its implementation; it concludes that in reality, progress in decentralization has been limited as a result of a complex set of factors, but most particularly the resistance of the entrenched political interests around the contending centres of power. Based on the fieldwork conducted between February 2010 and February 2011, and recent available studies, part three discusses a number of the core issues pertaining to the position of local units of government, the factors that constrain its work and the consequences for public service delivery outcomes. Part four turns to the issue of regionalization. It reveals its deeply politicized character that has led to a neglect of the regional aspects of development. The last part concludes by identifying the lack of political consensus and commitment as the key challenge to prospects for decentralization in Bosnia–Herzegovina advancing in a way beneficial to democratic governance, development and political stability.

Decentralization: Discourse, actors and institutions

The dysfunctional nature of the complex constitutional arrangement established under the terms of the DPA, and devised primarily to stop the war, became all too clear very early in the post-conflict reconstruction process. The international community has been since the main driving force behind the reform attempts. As a result, two parallel processes have been at play, with repercussions in terms of the direction, patterns and the speed of the decentralization process. On the one hand, the international community, with the most ardent support of the Bosniak political parties, but also a number of other political parties such as the multi-ethnic Social Democratic Party of Bosnia–Herzegovina and segments of the civil society, have put their weight behind reforms aimed to strengthen the central state. On the other hand, efforts to mobilize 'grass-root' pressures for further decentralization have proceeded apace, through engagement of international agencies which see the two dynamics as complementary and indeed essential for establishing a functional and effective system of multi-level government. This has created more ambiguity regarding decentralization itself, which the key political actors at the higher levels of government have approached with caution and reluctance. The main reason is the uncertainty surrounding the pending constitutional reform and its likely repercussions on the position of the intermediate level of government, namely the entities and the cantons, which had effectively taken over many of the prerogatives that the units of self-government had enjoyed in the pre-war period. Thus, in the local political discourse, the strengthening of the position and the role of local government is approached as an issue at the very heart of the contestations over the nature of the Bosnia–Herzegovina state. Consequently, given the ethnically polarized post-war context, decentralization has been consistently framed in an explicitly politicized way through the identity-based discourse (Rodriguez-Pose and Sandall, 2008). For example, the Federation Law on the Principles of Local Government was subjected to the Federation Constitutional Court adjudication after Bosnian Croats claimed that some of its propositions threatened their vital national interest.[2] Similarly, the vital national interest clause by the Bosniaks in the RS parliament delayed the adoption of the new RS Law on Local Self-Government. As a result of the fact that local government is under the entity and cantonal levels mandate, the political coalitions and forces opposed to territorial changes and in favour of only incremental local government reforms have remained strong, particularly in the initial post-war period.[3]

Bosnia–Herzegovina's membership in the Council of Europe in 2002 and obligations under the Stabilisation and Association Process with the European Union have had a decisive impact in prompting legislative change in the area of local government, with some inter-entity variations. In the RS, the Ministry of Administration and Local Self-Government is the key institution in charge of local government alongside the Ministry of Finance. In the FBiH, the primary responsibility for local government rests with the FBiH and cantonal governments.[4] The relations with municipalities differ significantly, depending to a large extent on the political objectives of the incumbent parties and local power dynamic. Although the role of international actors in driving the decentralization agenda in Bosnia–Herzegovina forward has been pivotal, the two-entity Associations of Cities and Municipalities occupy a distinctive place among the local actors actively supporting the decentralization agenda. For example, they participated in 2004 in an initiative spearheaded by the United Nations Development Programme (UNDP) and the Swedish development agency, SIDA, in collaboration with a number of local non-governmental organizations to draft the Bosnia–Herzegovina Strategy for Local Self-Government. The Strategy set in motion a chain of legislative changes that put local governance in Bosnia–Herzegovina on a qualitatively new footing as compared to limited and heavily politicized attempts to steer the process against the backdrop of constitutional reform. This genuinely bottom-up initiative has resulted, among other aspects discussed in greater detail in the subsequent sections of this chapter, in the establishment of a more institutionalized role of the two-entity Associations of Cities and Municipalities within the legislative and regulatory procedures governing the work of the local government.

Functional and fiscal patterns of decentralization

Bosnia–Herzegovina's legal and administrative framework for decentralization is highly fragmented, with governing authority, functions and budgets divided across several layers of government. Prior to 2006, the system of intergovernmental finance suffered from both horizontal and vertical imbalances. As a consequence, the local government was significantly underfunded and the provision of public services was poor. The fiscal position of individual municipalities varied significantly both across as well as within the entities, despite the RS having in place the basic equalization mechanism. In the FBiH, because of its administrative composition, the existence of ten intergovernmental systems at the cantonal level undermined its fiscal coherence and sustainability (Sarajlic-Maglajlic, 2006) while creating a non-transparent and unpredictable pattern of relations between the cantons and municipalities.

Functional decentralization arrangements

The adoption of the new set of local government laws, first in the RS in 2004, and then in the FBiH in 2006, marked a new phase in the evolving local government legal framework. The laws (with some variations) clarified functional assignments to municipalities, their revenue sources, specified the role of local communities as the sub-municipal local-governance structure and made provisos for the participation of the Association of Cities and Municipalities in the legislative and policymaking process in the FBiH (World Bank, 2009: 26). A further related development was the change in the electoral system providing for the direct election of mayors in 2004, which altered the political power balance locally and increased the stake in the local government performance outcomes. The new Federation Law on Public Revenue Allocation and the amendments to the Republika Srpska Budget System Law, adopted in 2006, adjusted the financial framework for local government funding.

The new entity laws were an important step forward in terms of clarifying competences, finance and power of local authority. The role of local government was defined more precisely, and the scope of municipal responsibilities expanded, including the relevant borrowing right, the absence of which had been hitherto a strong barrier to financing local-level capital investment. However, the new legislation stopped short of assigning significant autonomous (mandated) competences to local government. They remained within the traditional remit of exclusive responsibility for waste, water, local roads and sanitation, alongside a number of other policy areas in which the municipality shares competences with the entity and cantons (e.g. education, health, electricity supply and housing). The delegation of tasks to the local government in education and health has, for example, been extremely limited. In the FBiH the most significant spending responsibilities other than preschool education are retained at the cantonal and entity level. Similarly, in the RS, other than some aspects of primary health protection, health and education remain centralized (municipal responsibility is limited to the partial maintenance of secondary school buildings and health care facilities).

Fiscal decentralization arrangements

The introduction of the Value Added Tax and the transfer of the indirect tax revenue collection to the Single Account with the state-level Indirect Taxation Authority in 2006 was a watershed event in the development of fiscal arrangements pertaining to all levels of government in Bosnia–Herzegovina. A Single Account revenue-sharing formula was introduced, assigning specific vertical shares of revenue to each level of government. A predefined percentage of the entity share of the Single Account is allocated to municipalities, FBiH cantons and the entity road funds. Thus municipalities are provided with a more stable, autonomous and predictable source of revenue compared to the derivation-based formula for sales and income tax sharing that had existed under the previous system. Besides introducing a unified and transparent system for securing municipal revenues, and following in the RS footsteps, the formulas for allocating individual cantonal and municipality shares as a rough equalization mechanism have also been introduced in the Federation Law on Public Revenue. The two-entity formulas are similar and take into account the size of the municipal population as the key parameter, combined with the territory and the number of school children. In addition, in the FBiH they include the level of development of the local government unit. The overall system, however, remains centralized, in that locally generated revenue sources are few and the local government has no influence on setting the tax rates upon which the bulk of its revenue depends.

Local governance and public service delivery outcomes

The significant changes in the legal, regulatory and financial framework for local governance, underway since 2004, have normatively improved its position regarding competences, power and available resources. At the same time, there are ongoing challenges in implementing the Federation Law on the Principles of Local Government – particularly the harmonization of cantonal legislation.[5] The adoption of the new RS law on local government, which is expected to further advance functional and fiscal decentralization, has been delayed. Besides, the specific aspects of the local context – namely, the configuration of local government units in terms of their territorial composition, economic profile and specific, war-related problems – make for particularly challenging implementing environment, which is insufficiently reflected in the existing local governance legal and regulatory provisions. One of the consequences of the politically motivated redrawing of Bosnia–Herzegovina's post-war map is the high degree of variation in the size of municipalities, both in terms of territory and population, which impacts on all aspects of public service delivery. Municipal territory ranges from 10.2 square kilometres in Doboj-Jug (in the Federation) to 1232 square kilometres in Banja Luka (in Republika Srpska) (Figure 5.1; Source: FZPR, 2010; MULS, 2010a: 53). Some micro municipalities have no more than around 60 inhabitants compared with 225,123 inhabitants in Banja Luka (MULS, 2010a).

In the RS in particular there is a large number of small municipalities, which are geographically dispersed and in some cases rather isolated due to underdeveloped and inadequate infrastructure (EDA, 2007; MULS, 2010a). The levels of economic development, administrative and fiscal capacity of the local units of government also differ significantly both across and within the entities. Regional disparities are pronounced and, according to some estimates, growing (MULS, 2010a). According to the RS Ministry of Administration and Local Self-Government, around

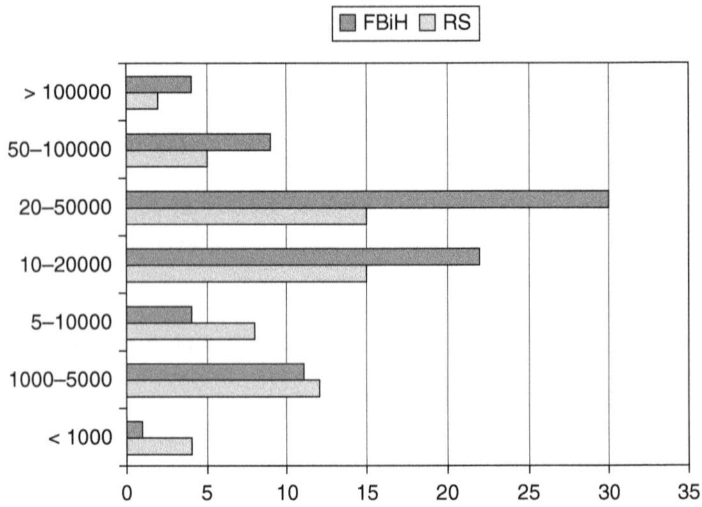

Figure 5.1 Number of municipalities by population*
Note: * Estimate.
Source: MULS (2010a), FZPR (2010).

half of the municipalities were classified as underdeveloped in 2009 (MULS, 2010a: 5) compared to around 40% in the FBiH (FZPR, 2010). Some of Bosnia–Herzegovina's largest municipalities are among the least developed ones, as they tend to cover rural and sparsely populated areas.[6] Hence, the economic context in which many local governments operate limits the potential for improvement in local service delivery outcomes. In some of the new municipalities, established as part of the post-war territorial reorganization of Bosnia–Herzegovina, public administration accounts for as much as 90% of total employment,[7] and in some cases salaries and operating costs take up to 80% of the municipal budget.[8] Furthermore, besides financial constraints, the municipal administration in some cases has no previous experience in local government matters, and hence lacks skills[9] to run public administration.[10] In those municipalities where refugees and displaced people account for a sizable proportion of the local population,[11] the composition of local government expenditures has been affected and the potential for fiscal space improvement squeezed.

The previous short summary highlights some characteristics of the local context within which the legal and regulatory framework for decentralized delivery of public services has evolved and is implemented in Bosnia–Herzegovina. Due to the complex organization of the system of multilevel governance and the entity variations in the decentralization models, the following discussion, aimed at illustrating some of the pertinent shortcomings and limitations of decentralization in Bosnia–Herzegovina and its implications on the public service delivery outcomes, is limited to a few selected issues: competences, funding and local government property status.[12]

Limited and unclear local government competences

Post-war institutional transformation of local governance in Bosnia–Herzegovina has aggravated many a problem besetting the earlier system. The new framework has retained the principle of the monotype municipality, whereby, irrespective of the individual circumstances of local government units, their legal status and responsibilities are the same. Furthermore, the local government remains regulated by a myriad of different legislations, which creates an opaque and unpredictable legal framework.[13] This is particularly problematic in the FBiH where different cantonal legislations cause large variations in the local government operational environment. There is neither a clear nor a transparent separation of responsibilities in discrete policy areas under the local government mandate. The legal framework is made more intricate by a lack of harmonization between the laws regulating intergovernmental functional assignments for public service delivery and sectoral laws. The practice of unfunded mandates, widespread in the earlier system, persists; municipalities are frequently not consulted by higher levels of government regarding the delegation of responsibilities.[14] At the same time, municipalities are in charge of some public services that might be better placed within the remit of the central state. An illustrative case is the provision of social protection services in the RS, where cash benefits are under the local government mandate. This results in huge inter-municipal variations in entitlements – from KM41 per beneficiary in Cajnice to KM200 in Banja Luka.[15] Sometimes, under citizens' pressure, local governments embark on activities that fall within the realm of entity or cantonal government, effectively co-funding the central state at their own budget expense.

The overall range and scope of mandated local government competences remains restricted, which reflects a narrow and archaic view of the local government role as the basic public services provider. It is also indicative of a persistence of strong political interests to cling to the powers concentrated at the entity and the canton level and to control the degree of local government autonomy, which ultimately raises doubts over political authorities' commitment to decentralization.

Uneven fiscal space and resources

Since the new system of indirect tax collection and redistribution was put in place in 2006, the revenue transfers from the Single Account have become the most important source of municipal revenue. Indirect tax revenue accounts for 80% of municipal tax revenue in the RS (not including the municipalities in the Sarajevo canton), and 60% in the FBiH, up from around 50% and 30%, respectively, before 2006.[16] The early results of the equalization mechanisms being phased in since 2006 suggest that some degree of equalization has taken place. In 2006 the indirect tax revenue per capita amounted to around KM21 to KM190 in the FBiH; by 2009 the distribution gap narrowed to KM59 to KM147.[17] However, the overall local government budget envelope rarely matches the responsibilities, which are selectively and partially implemented.

The municipal fiscal position varies significantly in terms of own revenue generation, transfers from higher levels of government, borrowing levels and potential, and expenditure structures (World Bank, 2009: 9).[18] Borrowing rights are in practical terms circumscribed by the existing entity legislation, local economic potential and weak fiscal management capacity. The profile of each municipality in terms of size, location (urban or rural) and level of development determines expenditure composition and the ability to improve the fiscal position, which results in diverse public service outcomes. Generally, since public administration is among the key employers at the local level, the wage bill forms a large and unavoidable share of municipal spending, which results in a chronic shortage of capital investment. Although the borrowing rights have formally softened constraints on capital investment, only a minority of municipal governments have turned to loans to fund long-term investment.

Unresolved local government property status

The legal and regulatory framework in Bosnia–Herzegovina contains provisions regarding municipal property rights over the resources required for the implementation of local government responsibilities. In practice, the legal changes required to reverse the effect of the transformation of the former 'social property' to state property, which took place in 1993, as well as the rescinded local government property rights, have been slow and partial. Consequently, local governments continue to encounter problems of limited jurisdiction over agricultural and construction land, infrastructure, mineral and other resources on their territory. Besides being a barrier to investment, the lack of property rights deprives the municipalities of effective control over delivery of particular services and affects their performance. Furthermore, it also prevents municipalities from exercising their legal right to raise property tax as a source of municipal revenue. The extent to which local government can pursue its role in promoting development—for example, through attracting investment, including concession agreements—is directly affected by its lack of property rights over the resources at its disposal.[19]

Local-level public service delivery outcomes

The organization of public services in Bosnia–Herzegovina is dispersed across different administrative and government levels, involving different degrees of decentralization. For example, the health sector consists of 13 'sub-systems': two entities, ten cantons and the Brcko District. A similar administrative organization also applies to the education system, which operates in an equally fragmented institutional framework of 12 ministries and the Department of Education in the Brcko District. The sheer complexity of the two systems makes the assessment of the outcomes of decentralization in those two sectors rather difficult and outside the scope of this chapter. In the remainder of this section, some of the main findings from the recent (and so far the only) study[20] of local governance performance in public service delivery in Bosnia–Herzegovina are discussed.

The results of the World Bank survey indicate that in many aspects the municipal provision of basic services, such as water, sewerage, heating and local road upkeep has been inadequate and rather poor. Almost a third of the population of Bosnia–Herzegovina has no access to running water or waste removal; about a quarter of the citizens rely on non-asphalted roads; some half a million people lack any sanitary services; and only 65% of households receive their water from the public system (World Bank, 2009: 11). Other studies, which have looked at the particular sectors, including water supply (which is entirely devolved to the local government level) and sewerage, corroborate those findings. In the RS for example, 46% of the population is covered by the municipal water supply system compared to 56% in the FBiH. The coverage in the sewerage sector in the RS is 33%, which is considerably below the EU average of 75%. Although no comparable FBiH-wide data exist, its sewerage system is equally underdeveloped and badly maintained. The World Bank research provides interesting insights into the citizens' level of satisfaction with education, health care and heating services as an important element in the overall assessment of the public service delivery outcomes. According to the study, around 74% of the citizens are satisfied with the state of school buildings and health care facilities whose maintenance is under the local government mandate; 70% are satisfied with the heating and 62% with sanitation facilities (World Bank, 2009: 12). Out of all ten services surveyed by the World Bank, waste has the worst level of satisfaction, while water and health receive the highest score (with approval by about 60% of the population) (World Bank, 2009: 12). The World Bank survey also reveals great unevenness in the access to services, particularly along the rural–urban divide. Other studies show that public services are not necessarily better in urban, typically more developed, municipalities. For example, in the RS the urban sewerage systems cover just over two-thirds of the population, while large cities such as Banja Luka and Doboj are confronted with major sanitation problems. Lastly, the social groups worst affected by the poor access to and low quality of public services in Bosnia–Herzegovina seem to be the most vulnerable and marginalized segments of the rural population, often including a large proportion of returning refugees, and typically from ethnic minorities (World Bank, 2009). Inter-ethnic sensitivities play a role in the under-provision of services with geographical spillovers (World Bank, 2009: 29) while the lack of inter-ethnic trust prevents inter-municipal cooperation across politically determined municipal boundaries. Although the legal framework for local government allows for municipal cooperation in public service delivery, cooperation has been rather limited in practice (Rodic et al., 2008).

Regionalization: Discourse, actors and institutions

The issue of regionalization is subsumed within the broad debates on the modalities of decentralized organization of government in Bosnia–Herzegovina in the context of constitutional reform. It represents the most politically sensitive aspect because a shift towards (re)organizing the country on a regional model usurps the existing distribution of political and economic powers. All major political parties' programmes address regionalization, although it is unclear as to which values and concepts are behind particular preferences. Those proposals have become the key battleground in the political struggle over the direction of the constitutional reforms. Non-governmental organizations, the Catholic Church and the expert community are among some of the most vocal proponents of regionalization, albeit starting from different vantage points in terms of the goals, criteria and proposed regional configurations. Nevertheless, the international community has remained instrumental in championing regionalization, although not in an uncontroversial manner, having followed different criteria depending on the issue. For example, the design of the indirect tax reform system involved defining tax administration regions, as did various police reform proposals – but those regions had no semblance to one another in terms of the geographic areas each of them covered. The European Union Regional Economic Development programme (EURED), a major EU initiative to shift the regionalization discourse towards economic development perspective, failed to gain RS endorsement. The EURED project identified six economic regions, each to host a regional development agency. The main reason for the RS rejecting the proposal was the fear that the regions crisscrossing the inter-entity boundary line would prejudge the outcome of the renegotiation of the Bosnia–Herzegovina constitutional set-up, in that those regions could eventually evolve into administrative-territorial units. The EURED regionalization proposal became a stumbling block in talks on constitutional reforms, and eventually faded from the public agenda.[21]

Subsequently, the international actors' approach towards regionalization in Bosnia–Herzegovina changed. Within the EURED programme itself, the support to the regional development agencies has been gradually phased out, and shifted towards the local community level. The World Bank, which has over the years provided significant support to local and regional development issues, has also shifted its agenda. Likewise, the Stabilisation and Association Progress Reports for Bosnia–Herzegovina no longer mention regional development. This in itself is indicative, since a concern to assist the country to prepare for eventual EU membership, including capacity to access structural funds, drove the EURED initiative in the first place.

Given the controversial nature of regionalization and regional development in the context of local ethno-politics, Bosnia–Herzegovina's strategic development documents – the 'National Development Strategy 2008–2013' – and its predecessor – 'Poverty Reduction Strategy Paper 2004–2007' – do not address regional development in specific terms. The Entities have neither regional development documents nor the institutions with an explicit mandate in that area. In 2009, the Council of Ministers adopted the 'Strategy for the Development of Small and Medium Sized Enterprises in Bosnia–Herzegovina 2009–2011', but its implementation has been slow and fragmentary. The RS government supports local economic development through the Agency for Small and Medium Sized Enterprises. In the FBiH a variety of institutions at the cantonal and entity level are involved in supporting small- and medium-sized enterprises, alongside the international donors and agencies. The five regional development agencies established under the EURED auspices exist in a grey zone, lacking a strategic and/or unified legal framework, although some have managed despite the odds to establish a respectable profile in sectors such as agriculture and wood processing.

Conclusions

Strong political interests to preserve the status quo in terms of relations between central and sub-national levels of governance, and thus cement new territorial and political reality created through war, have been decisive in the evolution of decentralization in Bosnia–Herzegovina, making it an end in itself. The progress has been slow and uneven, and the separation of competences and expenditures across different levels of government more complex and complicated than elsewhere in the Western Balkans. As a result, a fragmented institutional and policy framework has emerged, limiting the potential benefits of decentralized public service delivery. This applies both to the formal legislative process as well as the implementation of respective laws. Despite the formal improvement in the institutional framework for local government, a disrespect for legal provisions, arbitrariness and discretionary handling of local government matters by the ethnic elites at the higher levels of authority have been commonplace. In the context of politically motivated redrawing of territorial borders, massive population displacement and a weak economy, the demands on local governments have been vast. And they have found it by and large difficult to respond adequately. While uneven access to public services has been a general outcome of the way decentralization has been implemented in Bosnia–Herzegovina, its specific feature is that often those communities and individuals worst affected by the impact of war have tended to be at the greatest disadvantage. This is significant in that it speaks of the limitations of the decentralization as implemented in Bosnia–Herzegovina to contribute to conflict mitigation by increasing the well-being of the population as its ultimate goal.

The role of international actors in driving the process of decentralization forward has been decisive in improving the legislative framework for decentralization and promoting to some extent bottom-up demands for decentralization, in contrast to top-down attempts at institutional engineering in the framework of the constitutional reform. At the same time, efforts to shift the decentralization discourse to issues of economic development and improved mobilization of developmental resources (as opposed to the local elites' fixation with guarding ethnic interests through decentralization) by focusing on the regional governance have been controversial. As a result, regionalization as a decentralization track has been suspended despite evidence of growing regional disparity and a need to put in place a framework to address it in a coherent manner. In summary, the defining of an appropriate balance between the local and higher scales of government through locally driven democratic debate – so that decentralization can be made to work towards the internal reintegration of the state, while contributing to the well-being of the nation – remains the biggest challenge in implementing decentralization in the context of Bosnia–Herzegovina's ethnically distorted politics and unfinished state building.

Notes

1. Cities have their own budgets, financed by their own revenues, shared revenues and grants from cantons in the Federation and from entity government in the RS.
2. This was the reason why eventually the Law was adopted as the Law on the Principles rather then the Law on Local Government.
3. The UNDP National Human Development Report claims that 'the absence of [decentralization] strategies has not come about by chance or benign neglect, but as a direct consequence of dominant political forces' implicit opposition to change. It is a depressing prospect but the key obstacle to decentralisation may not be systemic weaknesses but outright political opposition' (UNDP, 2005: 135).
4. The Ministry of Justice and the Ministry of Finance are in charge of overseeing the implementation of the Law on the Principles of Local Self-Government.
5. FBiH cantons were required to harmonize their legislation with the Federation Law on the Principles of Local Self-Government until March 2007. However, the process has been very slow and partial. In October 2010, for example, the Federation Constitutional Court passed a verdict by which Canton Sarajevo had to transfer responsibilities for preschool, primary and secondary education to the City of Sarajevo and municipality Sarajevo Center. The Sarajevo City and Sarajevo Center municipality took the Canton to the court after it changed the legislation to rescind the responsibilities of the City and the municipality in the area of education, just a month after the Law had been passed in July 2006.
6. EDA (2007).
7. Interview, Department of Economics, Sarajevo, 3 March 2010.
8. MULS (2010a: 8).
9. Interview, Department of Economics, Sarajevo, 3 March 2010.
10. The lack of adequate skills remains a general problem at the local government level. This was recognized, for example, in the Republika Srpska Strategy for Local Self-Governance (2009–15), which has been followed by the Strategy for the Training of Local Unit Employees in Republika Srpska (2011–15) (see MULS, 2010b).
11. Refugees and internally displaced population account for 12–46% of municipal population in the Federation and 22–39% in the RS (World Bank, 2009: 22). Among the municipalities with the largest number of internally displaced persons are Sarajevo, Banja Luka, Bijeljina, Tuzla and Prijedor.

12. In the course of the field interviews those three aspects have emerged as being of key concern from the perspective of creating an improved platform for the local government to fulfil its mandate.
13. Interview, Banja Luka City Administration, Banja Luka, 28 January 2011.
14. Interview, Banja Luka City Administration, Banja Luka, 28 January 2011.
15. Interview, Banja Luka City Administration, Banja Luka, 28 January 2011.
16. Uprava za indirektno oporezivanje, Bulletin No. 52/53, November/December 2009 and Bulletin 28/29 December 2007.
17. Uprava za indirektno oporezivanje, Bulletin No. 52/53, November/December 2009, p. 6.
18. The report provides detailed overview of the differences in the municipal expenditure structure.
19. In the RS the law on transferring property rights over communal infrastructure to municipalities is under preparation.
20. The World Bank conducted a survey of 2000 households in 20 Bosnia–Herzegovina municipalities looking at the performance in the delivery of ten services, both mandated and the devolved ones, which are the responsibility of local government (World Bank, 2009).
21. Expert community was also critical of the proposal arguing that it sidestepped a historic experience of regionalization in Bosnia–Herzegovina, where the distinct regions had formed along functional-gravitational lines, which were disturbed by the political redrawing of the border (see, for example, Osmankovic and Pejanovic, 2006).

References

Bird, R. M. and Vaillancourt, F. (1998) *Fiscal Decentralisation in Developing Countries*, Cambridge: Cambridge University Press.

Bojičić-Dželilović, V. (2003) 'Managing ethnic conflicts: Decentralisation in Bosnia–Herzegovina', in R. Luckham and S. Bastian (eds) *Can Democracy be Designed? The Politics of Institutional Choice in Conflict-Torn Societies*, London; New York: Zed Books, pp. 277–303.

Brancati, D. (2008) *Peace by Design: Managing Intra-State Conflict through Decentralisation*, Oxford: Oxford University Press.

Brown, G. K. (2008) 'Decentralisation and conflict: Introduction and overview', *Conflict, Security and Development*, 8(4): 387–92.

Connerley, E., Eaton, K. and Smoke, P. (eds) (2010) *Making Decentralisation Work: Democracy, Development and Security*, Boulder, CO: Lynne Rienner.

EDA (2005) *Analiza stanja lokalne uprave i samouprave u Bosni i Hercegovini*, Banja Luka: Razvojna agencija EDA.

EDA (2007) *Kocka do kocke – dobro je dobro graditi – modeli organizacije lokalne samouprave*, Banja Luka: Razvojna agencija EDA.

FZPR (2010) *Socioekonomski podaci po opcinama Federacije Bosne i Hercegovine u 2009 godini*, Sarajevo: Federalni zavod za programiranje razvoja.

Hiskey, J. T. (2010) 'The promise of decentralised democratic governance' in E. Connerley, K. Eaton and P. Smoke (eds) *Making Decentralisation Work: Democracy, Development and Security*, Boulder, CO: Lynne Rienner, pp. 25–47.

MULS (2010a) *Strategija razvoja lokalne samouprave u Republici Srpskoj*, Banja Luka: Ministarstvo uprave i lokalne samouprave.

MULS (2010b) *Strategija obuke za jedinice lokalne samouprave u Republici Srpskoj (2011–2015)*, Banja Luka: Ministarstvo uprave i lokalne samouprave.

Osmankovic, J. and Pejanovic, M. (2006) *Euroregije i Bosna i Hercegovina*, Sarajevo: Fakultet politickih nauka.

Rodic, D., Simic, A., Milak, V., Djukic, J., Secerovic, R. and Mrsic, D. (2008) *Kreiranje i uvodjenje modela raspolaganja i vlasnistva nad lokalnim resursima u Bosni i Hercegovini*, Banja Luka: Ekonomski Institut.

Rodriguez-Pose, A. and Sandall, R. (2008) 'From identity to the economy: Analysing the evolution of the decentralisation discourse', *Environment and Planning C: Government and Policy*, 26(1): 54–72.

Roeder, P. G. and Rothchild, D. (eds) (2005) *Sustainable Peace: Power and Democracy after Civil Wars*, Ithaca: Cornell University Press.

Sarajlic-Maglajlic, D. (2006) 'Process management and finances: The case of Bosnia and Herzegovina', Paper presented at the conference *Decentralisation between Regionalism and Federalism in the Stability Pact Countries of the Western Balkans'*, Tirana.

Schou, A. and Hang, M. (2005) 'Decentralisation in conflict and post-conflict situations', *Working Paper No. 139*, Oslo: Norwegian Institute for Urban and Regional Research.

Smoke, P., Gomez, E. J. and Peterson, G. E. (eds) (2006) *Decentralisation in Asia and Latin America: Towards a Comparative and Interdisciplinary Perspective*, Cheltenham: Edward Elgar.

UNDP (2005) *Bosnia–Herzegovina National Human Development Report 2005: Better Local Governance in Bosnia and Herzegovina*, Sarajevo: United Nations Development Programme.

World Bank (2009) *From Stability to Performance: Local Governance and Service Delivery in Bosnia and Herzegovina*, Washington, DC: The World Bank.

6

Decentralization in Kosovo: Defusing Ethnic Tensions or Furthering Ethnic Isolation?

Lars Burema[1]

Introduction

Advocates of decentralization have long maintained that it can be used as a mechanism for defusing inter-ethnic tension. Where successful, it creates cohesive multi-ethnic societies by giving communities extensive rights over the issues affecting their daily lives – for example, language, education, local administration – but avoids the disintegrative effects of separatism by allowing the state to retain control over national questions such as security and foreign affairs (Lijphart, 1977, 1996; Tsebelis, 1990; Horowitz, 1991a; Kaufman, 1996; Stepan, 1999; Gurr, 2000; Lustik, Miodownik and Eidelson, 2004). For example, Finland's Åland Islands have experienced a large degree of autonomy since 1920, successfully balancing the demands for minority rights of the Åland Islands' mostly Swedish population and the interests of the Finnish state.[2]

By contrast, its detractors point to cases where the formalization of ethnic cleavage through decentralization has in fact exacerbated tensions and, at worst, fuelled calls for secession (Nordlinger, 1972; Horowitz, 1991a; Roeder, 1991; Hardgrave, 1994; Kymlicka, 1998; Leff, 1999; Snyder, 2000). In Spain, for example, the process of devolution after the transition to democracy in 1979 treated 17 'autonomous communities', each with advanced rights of local self-governance. However, while this successfully mollified separatist tendencies in most states, Catalunya and the Basque country have continued to call for secession, in the latter case through terrorist violence.[3]

This chapter will consider both views of decentralization and, through an assessment of Kosovo's socio-political circumstances, will assess the potential for decentralization as a mechanism for defusing inter-ethnic tensions at the local level and increasing the participation of the Kosovo Serb community in southern Kosovo in local structures. The assessment will contrast the consociationalist approach to managing diversity, centred on power sharing and group autonomy (Lijphart, 2004: 97), with the integrationist approach, which focuses on the creation of a multi-ethnic identity through shared political, social and civil institutions (Horowitz, 1991b: 471).

Of course, decentralization in Kosovo also affects communities other than the Kosovo Serbs and is relevant to northern Kosovo. However, this chapter chooses to focus on the Kosovo Serb community, as they are the largest and politically most important minority community in Kosovo, and the community most affected by the decentralization process. It will exclude northern Kosovo, where the situation is fundamentally distinct and requires a separate approach. The status of northern Kosovo (Mitrovica/Mitrovicë North, Leposavic/Leposaviq, Zubin Potok and Zvecan/Zveçan)[4] will play an important role in any eventual agreement between Serbia, Kosovo and the Kosovo Serb community. However, while Serb enclaves in southern Kosovo are surrounded by the reality of a de facto independent Kosovo, in the Serb-dominated north the Kosovo Albanian community faces the different circumstance of a significant and visible influence of the Serbian government and the nearly negligible influence of Kosovo institutions and international organizations. The Kosovo government may consider northern Kosovo as an indisputable part of Kosovo but that has not prevented Serbian institutions from operating 'pretty much as if in Serbia' (ICG, 2011: 2). Furthermore, decentralization requires at least minimal acceptance from local citizens, which is present in the south but not in the north (KIPRED, 2008). Moreover, any analysis of decentralization in northern Kosovo – currently at the centre of ongoing disagreements between Kosovo and Serbia (ICG, 2011) – would shift the focus of analysis from decentralization as a mechanism for defusing ethnic tensions at the local level, to decentralization as an integrative tool of ethnic conflict settlement (Weller, 2010), which is expressly not the focus of this chapter.

This chapter will provide a summary of the historical context and technical details of decentralization in Kosovo. The main substantive section will then assess the potential dangers of decentralization against its positive effects on levels of participation and integration among the Serb community. Recognizing that it is too early to form a definitive judgement, the concluding section will highlight some of the key factors that are likely to have a decisive impact on the overall success of decentralization as a mechanism for improving inter-ethnic relations.

Decentralization in Kosovo: The context

In the European context, Kosovo is one of the regions with the most troubling inter-ethnic relations. Although its history has been marked by long periods of inter-ethnic cooperation, the last few decades have been scarred by ethnic antagonism, mainly between the Serb and Albanian communities, which in 1999 resulted with a massive displacement of ethnic Albanians and a military intervention by NATO forces.[5] After almost a decade as an international protectorate, Kosovo unilaterally declared independence on 17 February 2008 and, under international pressure, embraced decentralization as one of the main mechanisms for defusing inter-ethnic tensions and improving Serb participation in Kosovo's socio-political environment.[6]

Decentralization had been long discussed as a potential mechanism for resolving some of Kosovo's ethnic differences. In October 2002, UN Special Representative of the Secretary General (SRSG), Michael Steiner (2002) proposed decentralization as a solution to the problem of the divided nature of the city of Mitrovica/Mitrovicë North. The plan was never implemented, but decentralization has been high on the international agenda ever since.

Although decentralization and the creation of two Serb-majority municipalities was proposed in 2005 by the then minister of local self-government, Lutfi Haziri (Framework Document on the Reform of Local Government), it was rejected by the Serb community. However, it was put back on the table in 2006 at the status negotiations in Vienna, led by UN SRSG, Martti Ahtisaari. It became a key chapter in Ahtisaari's Comprehensive Proposal for the Kosovo Status Settlement (henceforth 'Ahtisaari Proposal') and as such was regarded as one of the central mechanisms for ensuring the protection of minority rights and interests under Kosovo's 'supervised independence'. Although the Ahtisaari Proposal was rejected by Serbia, it was adopted by Kosovo with its unilateral declaration of independence. Moreover, the decentralization process as laid out in the Ahtisaari Proposal was incorporated into the Law on Local Self-Government that was passed by the assembly of Kosovo on 20 February 2008, and on 3 April 2008 the 'Action Plan on the Implementation of Decentralization' (2008) was adopted by the government of Kosovo. The Ministry for Local Government Administration (MLGA) was assigned with the leading role in implementing the decentralization plan while the International Civilian Office (ICO), under the leadership of EU Special Representative, Pieter Feith, was given the responsibility of supervising its implementation.

The decentralization process, as applied in Kosovo, foresees both administrative decentralization – the transfer of competences from the central to the municipal level – and political decentralization – the creation of eight new municipalities, including two Albanian-majority municipalities, one Turkish-majority municipality and five new municipalities in which the Serb community will constitute a majority (see Table 6.1).

All municipalities in Kosovo have competences covering a wide range of issues, from local economic development to primary health care and education up to secondary level. Serb-majority municipalities are awarded 'enhanced competences' giving them additional responsibilities in comparison to other municipalities. All Serb-majority municipalities are given enhanced competences in the area of cultural heritage, and participatory rights in the appointment of the police station commander. Selected Serb-majority municipalities are awarded enhanced competences in secondary health care,[8] while the municipality of Mitrovica/Mitrovicë North is also given enhanced competences in university education (Law on Local Self-Government, Ch. III). This means

Table 6.1 New municipalities in Kosovo

New municipality	Total population	Ethnic balance
Mamuşa/Mamushë/ Mamuša	6007	Turkish majority (97%), Albanian and Roma Minorities
Hani i Elezit/Đeneral Janković	10,029	Albanian majority (99,7%), Bosniak minority
Junik	10,000	Mono-ethnic Albanian
Gračanica/Graçanicë	18,392	Serb majority (85.7%), Albanian and Roma minorities
Klokot/Kllokot	5145	Serb majority (72%), Albanian and Roma minorities
Parteš/Partesh	–	–
Ranilug/Ranillug	5150	Serb majority (99%), Albanian minority
Mitrovica/Mitrovicë North	Not yet established	
Novo Brdo/Novobërdë[7]	9670	Serb majority (73%), Albanian and Roma Minorities

Source: Data collected from the Ethnopolitical map of Kosovo (www.ecmi-map.com). These are estimates by the municipal administrations. No official data are available until the results of the 2011 census become available. Unfortunately, no official data was available for Parteš/Partesh.

that although the relevant municipalities have to comply with national legislation and policy, they have far-reaching autonomy in the areas described previously. Also, the Law on Local Self-Government (Art. 30) established the right of municipalities 'to cooperate, within the areas of their own competences, with municipalities and institutions, including government agencies, in the Republic of Serbia'. Moreover, all municipalities are allowed to raise their own revenue through local taxes, services and donations, while the law states specifically that any municipality can request financial and technical assistance from the Republic of Serbia (Law on Local Self-Government, Art. 30). Finally, it should be mentioned that all the legislation concerning the competences and boundaries of municipalities in Kosovo is considered 'legislation of vital interest' and therefore cannot be changed without both a general majority in the Kosovo assembly and a majority of the deputies in the assembly holding seats guaranteed for representatives of minority communities (Constitution of the Republic of Kosovo, Art. 81, 2008).

So far, with the exception of Mitrovica/Mitrovicë North, all planned new municipalities have been established and are fully operational, and the municipality of Novo Brdo/Novobërdë has been expanded to transform it into a Serb-majority municipality. Three of the Serb-majority municipalities were established through the municipal elections of 15 November 2009, while the municipal elections for Parteš/Partesh were delayed until 20 June 2010, as conditions were not judged ready before then (KIPRED, 2009). No date has yet been set for the establishment of the municipality of Mitrovica/Mitrovicë North, although a Municipal Preparation Team has been established to prepare conditions for the creation of this municipality (ICG, 2011).

The pros and cons of decentralization

In the years immediately before the November 2009 elections, Serb participation in southern Kosovo was in decline. The 2007 local and general elections had been successfully boycotted by most of the Serb community (OSCE Kosovo, 2008). Following the 12 February 2008 unilateral declaration of independence, many Serb community members had withdrawn from the Kosovo administration, including from the Kosovo police service (OSCE Kosovo, 2008). In fact, since the 1999 conflict and the 2004 riots, the Serb community had existed as 'islands' (Judah, 2008: 147) – geographically, socially, politically and economically isolated from the Albanian majority community, making use of 'parallel' systems in everything from health care to telephone providers

(OSCE Kosovo, 2008).[9] The decentralization process aimed to address this situation and improve the integration of the Serb community into Kosovo's institutional framework. This chapter will assess the potential positive and negative effects of decentralization on the integration of the Serb community in southern Kosovo.

The benefits of decentralization

Kosovo's decentralization process, in its most basic form, is an attempt to engage the Serb community in the Kosovo institutional system through an offer of local autonomy. The power of this offer lies in the fact that it addresses the most important problems related to Kosovo's legislative and institutional framework for the protection of its minority communities, including its slow and uneven implementation and the lack of decision-making powers for minority communities within this system. Decentralization creates municipal institutions that, requiring only limited Serb participation in municipal elections, are led by representatives directly elected by the Serb community and with significant autonomy from other institutions to take decisions on important matters of everyday life, such as health care, education, infrastructure and economy.

However, the Serb community has raised strong objections to the link between decentralization, the Ahtisaari Proposal and Kosovo's unilateral declaration of independence, which is strongly opposed by the Serb community. Nonetheless, there are several reasons to believe that the offer of local autonomy, regardless of these objections, might be accepted by the Serb community in southern Kosovo for three main reasons. First, the Serb community in southern Kosovo has been increasingly disillusioned by the 'parallel' institutions, as was evident in the low turnout for the parallel municipal elections organized by Serbia in August 2009 (KIPRED, 2009). Second, this community has received several important signs that, at some level, the Serbian state has accepted that Kosovo is no longer fundamentally a part of its territory, notably through the signing by Serbia of the Stabilisation and Association Agreement with the EU on 29 April 2008, which did not include Kosovo and, similarly, through the exclusion of Kosovo in Serbia's agreement with the EU for visa-free travel within the Schengen zone.[10] Finally, the Serb community in southern Kosovo is confronted, on a daily basis, by the unavoidable de facto reality of an independent Kosovo, as they are living in small enclaves surrounded by Albanian-majority municipalities and strong and visible local and national Kosovo institutions. Although these factors will do little to change the

Kosovo Serbs opposition to Kosovo's independence, they do increase the likelihood that the Serb community in southern Kosovo will take a pragmatic approach to engagement with Kosovo institutions and the new municipalities in particular.

So far the first indicators of Serb participation seem to support the theory set out earlier, in particular the significant increase in Serb turnout in both municipal and local elections following the establishment of the new municipalities is a strong sign of increased political participation. Although exact percentages for Serb participation are unavailable, a rough estimate can be made by looking at the number of votes cast for Serb political parties. In the municipal elections of 2007, the largest Serb party in the municipality of Prishtinë/Priština – with an estimated Serb community of around 12,510 members (OSCE Kosovo, 2008) and covering most of the new municipality Gračanica/Graçanicë – received 92 votes.[11] In the municipal elections of 2009 the largest Serb party in the municipality of Gračanica/Graçanicë received 2139 votes. While this represented a voter turnout of only 24% (KIPRED, 2009), it was a huge increase on the previous showing nonetheless. In all Serb-majority municipalities in southern Kosovo similar increases in voter turnout were visible, albeit of differing magnitudes.[12]

The results of the 2010 general elections presented a further opportunity to assess whether the increase in Serb participation could be sustained over time and carried over to the central level. In the 2007 general elections the largest Serb political party received a total of 855 votes and all Serb parties combined received a total of 3038 votes. In the 2010 general elections the largest Serb party received 14,352 votes and all Serb parties combined received a total of 23,389 votes.

Clearly, between the 2007 elections and the 2010 elections there was a significant increase in Serb political participation in southern Kosovo. Importantly, these results were achieved despite official calls from Belgrade for a boycott. Therefore, it is safe to say that decentralization has contributed to an increase in the involvement of both Kosovo Serb community members and political parties in Kosovo's political process and a reorientation of at least a part of the Kosovo Serb community away from Belgrade.

The dangers of decentralization

Although Serb political participation has increased, at least in the short term, this will not necessarily lead to the integration of the Serb community in other aspects of life, particularly considering the dangers associated with the decentralization processes. Many authors are sceptical about decentralization as a conflict management tool, suggesting that rather than promoting participation and integration, decentralization may by its very nature exacerbate ethnic tensions.[13] Dawn Brancati (2006: 1) identified three main ways in which scholars argue that decentralization can adversely affect ethnic relations: it may provide an institutional base for secessionist movements, it may advance discrimination against regional minorities, and it may reinforce ethnic and regional identities. Each of these will be discussed in the context of Kosovo next.

Secessionism

The most commonly acknowledged danger of decentralization is that it can strengthen secessionist movements, by providing strong regional or ethnic groups with an institutional base from which to pursue secessionist goals.[14] This was also the main argument of Albin Kurti – leader of the political party 'VETËVENDOSJE!' – who believes that decentralization will lead to secession because it will 'obstruct cooperation with Prishtina and disconnect these municipalities from the rest of Kosova'.[15] In other words, he believes that the new Serb-majority municipalities will be hijacked by Serb political parties willing to participate in the elections but unwilling to form any constructive cooperation with Kosovo institutions.

However, opponents of this view argue that group autonomy is in fact key to the 'successful establishment of democratic government in divided societies' (Lijphart, 2004: 97). Applying this perspective, decentralization is more likely to strengthen the unity of southern Kosovo than to lead to further division, particularly taking into consideration the presence of three strong factors decreasing the chance for secessionism through the southern Serb-majority municipalities. First, there is strong international support for the territorial integrity of southern Kosovo and for the new municipalities in particular; the US has specifically condemned any moves towards partition[16] and most European Union member states support the International Civilian Office, which supports the Ahtisaari Proposal and subsequently the decentralization process.[17] Second, the new Serb-majority municipalities are not geographically linked, nor (with one exception) do they border Serbia.[18] Third, they are small in size, not exceeding 25,000 inhabitants.[19]

It is therefore not surprising that, so far, no moves towards secessionism have been reported. Instead, the new Serb-majority municipalities seem intent on establishing administrations in accordance with Kosovo legislation and as part of the Kosovo institutional system (KIPRED, 2010).

Promoting discrimination against regional minorities

The second identified danger of decentralization is that it can promote discrimination against regional minorities, increasing inter-ethnic tensions. This is certainly a relevant concern in the case of Kosovo as Albanian communities of varying size reside in all but one of the new Serb-majority municipalities.[20] Although Albanian communities in the new Serb-majority municipalities are protected by the same comprehensive legislative framework that protects minority communities throughout Kosovo, they are also affected by the same deficiencies in the application of these rights.

However, the central level is likely to be much more sensitive to the plight of local Albanian minority communities than it is to that of other communities. This is mainly due to the fact that the Albanian representatives in the new Serb-majority municipalities are members of national parties, giving them a direct link to the central level and consequently the ability to exert significant pressure on the municipality.[21]

It is possible to provide an early assessment of the new Serb-majority municipalities' attitudes towards their minorities by observing the inclusion of minorities in their municipal administrations. So far most new Serb-majority municipalities have complied with the requirement that any municipality with a minority community of at least 10% of the total population must appoint a deputy chairperson of the municipal assembly and a deputy mayor for communities (Law on Local Self-Government, Art. 54 and 61). Only the municipality of Gračanica/Graçanicë has failed to appoint a deputy mayor for communities (OSCE Kosovo, 2010: 15) due to a conflict between the Albanian and the Roma communities. The reason why the deputy mayor has not been appointed is that since the Roma community is by far the largest minority community in Gračanica/Graçanicë, it is implicitly understood that it will supply the deputy mayor for communities, particularly since the Albanian community already supplies the deputy chairperson of the municipal assembly for communities. However, according to the Law on Local Self-government (Art. 61.3), the election of the deputy mayor for communities requires the majority vote of the municipal assembly members representing minority communities. Because the Roma community is not represented in the municipal assembly, the Albanian community has a de facto veto in the appointment of a Roma deputy mayor and has blocked such an appointment. As such this situation is perhaps less the fault of the decentralization process than a consequence of a system that recognizes and promotes participation through ethnic groups rather than through inter-ethnic coalitions.

Evidently, the appointment of community representatives to positions which they are legally entitled to is hardly a conclusive sign of strong respect for minority rights. However, considering the huge problems faced throughout Kosovo in the implementation of legislation it suggests that fears of the emergence of discriminatory practises towards local minorities have not yet materialized.

Strengthening regional and ethnic identities

The third potential danger is that decentralization, by entrenching ethnic difference and promoting ethnicity-based politics, can reinforce ethnic and regional identities, creating tensions between the Albanian- and the Serbian-led institutions. This is also part of Albin Kurti's platform against the Kosovo decentralization process (14 June 2010).

This is probably the strongest argument against decentralization in Kosovo, since the process undoubtedly institutionalizes ethnic difference. Not only does it recognize that Kosovo's minority communities and the Serb community in particular have retreated into isolated enclaves since the 1999 war, but it also expressly separates those enclaves from the majority population. Advocates of an integrationist understanding of multi-ethnicity would argue that a better approach would be to foster a common sense of 'Kosovo identity' through shared political, social and civil institutions.[22]

Alternatively, proponents of a consociational approach argue that the recognition of ethnic difference promotes allegiance to the state precisely because it recognizes their distinct identity (Kymlicka, 1995: 13, 189). Although the integrationist approach might be a viable strategy in the long term, it is simply not applicable to the realities of community relations in Kosovo today due to the lack of overarching Kosovo identity and the strong consociational tendencies in Kosovo's wider institutional and legislative system. Therefore, the consociational approach inherent in decentralization is preferable since it builds on the existing institutional and legislative framework and is sufficiently flexible to allow for a more multi-ethnic construct in the medium to long term.

Currently, no common narrative exists that could unite the Albanian and Serb communities. In fact there are serious obstacles to the creation of a Kosovo identity, the most important being that the majority of the Serb community rejects the proclaimed independence of the Kosovo state (ICG, 2009: 1) and consequently any identity formed around this state. It is also worth mentioning that most Albanian community members still consider themselves to be Albanian before they consider themselves to be Kosovar.[23] It can therefore be reasonably assumed that the Serb community will not, in the short to medium term, subscribe to a Kosovo identity and that such an identity is therefore not an appropriate foundation upon which to build a strategy for Serb integration.

Moreover, decentralization is an additional acknowledgement of ethnic difference; the Constitution of Kosovo explicitly recognizes that Kosovo is made up of different communities (Art. 3), protects them from assimilation (Art. 58.6) and assigns a wide range of rights and protective measures to them.[24] Therefore, the recognition of ethnic difference through decentralization should be seen as part of a wider system that explicitly recognizes ethnic difference and aims to protect it.[25]

However, the institutional and legislative framework for the protection of minority rights – in place long before the November 2009 elections – failed to promote the integration of the Serb community as for the most part it did little to address the participation of the Serb and Albanian communities in two separate institutional systems, with no visible movement towards their integration (ICG, 2008: 6–10).

In this context, decentralization expands and improves on the consociational elements of Kosovo's political system by providing minority communities in Kosovo with the legal, political and financial space to attend to their own needs and develop their own identity, while ensuring that this takes place within the overarching framework of Kosovo institutions under strong international scrutiny and not within a parallel institutional system outside the Kosovo constitutional framework. If properly managed, decentralization might not only address the needs and interests of minority communities, but might also gradually erode kin-state loyalties as members of communities begin to feel a growing sense of ownership over the laws and policies that affect their lives and are drawn deeper into the political, civic and social institutions of a multi-ethnic Kosovo.

The design of Kosovo's decentralization process expressly leaves room for such medium- to long-term developments by not assigning veto or blocking powers to the Serb community.[26] Decentralization provides privileges to the Serb community by creating municipalities with enhanced competences in areas where they are the majority. However, in all other aspects the Serb-majority municipalities function in the same way as a normal Kosovo municipality: they function within the Kosovo legislative framework, with the same general procedures for municipal decision-making and no specific privileges are assigned to the Serb community (Law on Local Self-Government). This institutionalizes a situation in which the Serb community has neither blocking nor veto powers to prevent possible future changes in demographics or politics from being reflected in municipal institutions. The flexibility of the system is exemplified by the current situation in the municipality of Novo Brdo/Novobërdë, where the Serb voter turnout, although significantly increased from the previous elections, was insufficient to win either the mayoral or municipal assembly elections. Although the Serb minority in the municipal assembly was not able to block the decision-making process, it was also not marginalized. In fact the winner of the elections, the ethnic Albanian Democratic League of Kosovo (LDK), entered into a coalition with two Serb political parties rather than with the other ethnic Albanian political parties.

There are currently two main indicators that can shed some light on the effects of decentralization on the reinforcement of ethnic and regional identity: first, the emergence of regional political parties; and second, but related, the development of tensions between Serb- and Albanian-led institutions.

Brancati (2006: 11) observes that the emergence of regional parties that reflect an enhanced regional identity may undermine the potential benefits of decentralization and promote ethnic conflict. However, in Kosovo there is little evidence to suggest the emergence of strong regional parties. The Serb political parties that have emerged to date are mostly Kosovo-wide parties with a firm commitment to working for the Serb community in Kosovo through Kosovo institutions. The biggest Serb political party at both the central and municipal level is now the Serb Liberal Party (SLS), a Kosovo-wide party that is part of the ruling coalition at the central level.[27]

Although there have been disagreements between Albanian- and Serb-led institutions, two main factors have mediated their potentially disintegrative effects. First, because the SLS is in power at both the municipal and central level and is leading the MLGA,[28] it has considerable ability to protect the interests of Serb-majority municipalities and provide assistance in communication and cooperation between the central and municipal level. Second, significant autonomy is assigned to municipalities in Kosovo, and to the Serb-majority municipalities in particular, limiting the power of the central level in its relations with the municipalities; with regard to most competences of the municipality, including enhanced competences, central authority is limited to a review of legality (Law on Local Self-Government, Art. 79). Moreover, the majority of the funds received by the municipalities from the central government are calculated according to a precise formula set out in the Law on Local Government Finance (Part III and IV), which leaves limited room for negotiation.[29]

In summary, this chapter has argued that decentralization, although recognizing ethnic difference, has proven itself to be more successful in improving the integration of the Serb community than the legislative and institutional protections in place prior to the process' implementation; it has increased Serb political participation without leading to secessionist movements or substantial mistreatment of local minorities.

Decentralization's future: Key areas of importance

It is still too early to provide a conclusive assessment of the success of the decentralization process in Kosovo. While it might have increased political participation, there is no certainty that these results will be sustained. Nor is it guaranteed that political participation will lead to social and/or economic integration, as this would require abandonment by the Serb community of all parallel institutions, which in turn would require that the new Serb-majority municipalities convince their Serb residents that they offer a better vision of a sustainable future in Kosovo than the government of Serbia.

Therefore, the new Serb-majority municipalities will have to address the most important problems faced by their inhabitants. In the UN Development Programme's 2009 'Kosovo Mosaic Survey', Serb respondents most commonly identified the following three issues as important both at the municipal and the central level: poverty and a low standard of living, limited freedom of movement, and unemployment. Of these, freedom of movement is not an issue that can realistically be addressed at the municipal level; it mostly concerns travel outside of the Serb-majority municipalities. However, municipalities can have an important impact on the other two areas, and it can therefore reasonably be expected that these are the issues on which they will be judged in the next elections.

Unemployment is a Kosovo-wide, even regional, problem.[30] As such it is unrealistic to expect major changes in the employment situation. However, considering the small size of the new municipalities, the new Serb-majority municipalities can make a small, but immediate and significant improvement in the employment situation. At the most basic level, an impact can be expected solely through the establishment of the new institutions, which will require a civil service to run it. On a second level, some employment may be generated by projects run or financed by the municipalities. Finally, and most importantly in the medium to long term, the municipalities will need to make significant progress in local economic development.

Improvements in the unemployment situation will also lessen levels of poverty and improve standards of living. However, the easiest and most visible way to improve the living standards is likely to be through infrastructure development. Through such development as, for example, asphalting roads, fixing sewage systems and improving water delivery systems the new Serb-majority municipalities can have a quick and tangible positive influence on people's lives.

Currently, signs are mixed. Improvements in infrastructure are already visible and more developments are expected.[31] However, particularly in the smaller new municipalities, there are significant difficulties in finding qualified staff, and civil society actors have also expressed dissatisfaction with the transparency of the new municipalities in their decision-making and hiring processes.[32] This could be a significant obstacle to the success of the decentralization process, which is ultimately a trust-building exercise: developing confidence between institutions and citizens is about more than building roads and creating jobs. It is about listening to the needs of citizens and explaining, why, how and for whom these things are being done. Any impact from improvements in these areas will be lessened if they are not achieved alongside effective communication with the local citizens.

Conclusions

There is good reason for a cautious optimism regarding decentralization as a viable mechanism for defusing ethnic tensions at the local level and increasing the participation of the Serb community in southern Kosovo. Many of the typical pitfalls of decentralization either do not apply to the case of Kosovo or have been avoided. Kosovo has significant international backing and the decentralized units are too small, too far away from Serbia, and too fragmented to form a strong movement for secession. Moreover, decentralization has the potential to solve some of the problems of the legislative and institutional mechanisms for minority protection in Kosovo, in place prior to the decentralization process. It enables a fundamental shift from a situation in which the Serb community was mostly dependent on the Albanian community for the implementation of policies and legislation affecting them, to a situation where their own representatives have the competences and financial means to affect change in areas vital to their community, such as economic development, health care and education. This positive assessment is supported by some of the available early indicators. Decentralization has led to a significant increase in participation in elections and the political parties that have been elected are focused towards the Serb community in Kosovo and are willing to cooperate with Kosovo institutions. Furthermore, early indicators show that the institutions in Kosovo and the international community are willing to support the new Serb-majority municipalities.

Naturally, these optimistic signs have to be balanced by caution. Although participation in the elections increased, it was still low, just as political competition in some municipalities was extremely limited. The Serb community has shown some willingness to redirect itself towards the political institutions in Kosovo, but this willingness is based on a fragile trust that can easily be lost. In order for the early successes of decentralization to be sustained and built on the new Serb-majority municipalities, supported by Kosovo institutions and the international community, there will have to be sustained progress. In particular, there are three key areas in which quick and visible advancements need to be made: employment opportunities need to be increased, infrastructure needs to be developed and this progress needs to be achieved in close consultation with the local community.

Finally, even though Kosovo's decentralization programme is well designed and may potentially exercise a significant positive influence, this is not likely to be enough in itself to create a Kosovo that is acceptable to the Kosovo Serb community. This also depends on developments in other areas: for example, the creation of Kosovo-wide Serbian language media, the development of a Serbian language curriculum and significant improvements in the representation of minority communities in Kosovo institutions. Only with improvements across the board in the protection and promotion of the rights and interests of minority communities in Kosovo can the progress made so far through decentralization be consolidated in the future.

Notes

1. The author would like to thank Ms Katherine Nobbs for advice and editing.
2. For an analysis of Åland's autonomy arrangements, see, for example, Scarpulla (2002).
3. For analysis of Spain's autonomy arrangements, see, for example, Conversi (1998).
4. All Kosovo municipalities mentioned in this chapter will be referred to by both their Serbian and Albanian names, quoted in the order which reflects the majority community in a particular municipality.
5. For a general history of Kosovo, see Malcolm (1999).
6. All references to Kosovo in this text, whether to the territory, institutions or population, should be understood in full compliance with the United Nations Security Council Resolution 1244 and without prejudice to the status of Kosovo.
7. Although this is not a new municipality, its territory was expanded through the decentralization process causing a significant shift in the ethnic balance.
8. Gračanica/Graçanicë, Mitrovica/Mitrovicë North and Štrpce/Shtërpcë.

9. 'Parallel institutions' is a term used when referring to institutions and organizations in Kosovo working under institutional and legislative system of the Republic of Serbia. For example, there are numerous municipal administrations, functioning within the institutional system of Serbia, operating parallel to Kosovo municipalities.
10. *The Economist*, 2 June 2011.
11. All election results cited in this chapter are based on the statistics presented by the central election commission of Kosovo on its official website: http://www.kqz-ks.org/
12. Both the 2009 and 2010 elections were boycotted almost completely by the Serb community in northern Kosovo.
13. See, for example, Monteux (2006).
14. Carol Skalnik Leff (1999), for example, applies this reasoning to explain the cases of post-communist state dissolution.
15. Kurti, A. (14 June 2010) *Objection against the Panel*, available at http://www.vetevendosje.org/?cid=2,2,1654
16. Voice of America (18 June 2011) *US Envoy Condemns Kosovo Partition Plans, Ethnic Tensions*, available at http://www.voanews.com/english/news/US-Envoy-Condemns-Kosovo-Partition-Plans-Ethnic-Tensions--124118989.html (accessed on 16 June 2011).
17. The full list of member states of the International Steering Group overseeing the International Civilian Office can be found at http://www.ico-kos.org/ico/?id=10
18. The only Serb-majority municipality in southern Kosovo bordering Serbia is Ranilug/Ranillug
19. See www.ecmi-map.com
20. The only Serb-majority municipality with no Albanian minority is the municipality of Parteš/Partesh.
21. Several ethnic Albanian parties, also represented at the central level, have been elected in the Municipal Assemblies of the new municipalities. The exact results can be found on the website of the Central Election Commission of Kosovo: http://www.kqz-ks.org/
22. Donald L. Horowitz (1991b), for example, provides a strong argument for the integrationist approach.
23. See L'Humanité (18 February 2008) 'Kosovar ou Albanais, questions d'identité' and *The New York Times* (17 December 2007) 'Kosovo Struggles to Forge an Identity', http://www.humanite.fr/node/60292 and http://www.nytimes.com/2007/12/17/world/europe/17kosovo.html?ref=world
24. Examples of these rights are these assembly seats set aside for political parties representing communities, their representation of communities through the consultative council for communities and their equitable representation in employment in public institutions.
25. Kosovo's institutional and legislative system is consociational at heart, as it adheres to its basic principles, as identified by Lijphart (1996: 258): '(1) grand coalition governments that include representatives of all major linguistic and religious groups, (2) cultural autonomy for these groups, (3) proportionality in political representation and civil service appointments, and (4) a minority veto with regard to vital minority rights and autonomy.'
26. This in contrast to community protection mechanisms at the central level, where legislation covering certain community sensitive issues is considered 'legislation of vital interest' and requires a double majority, both from the

full assembly and from the deputies for its adoption, amendment or repeal (Constitution of Kosovo, Art. 81).

27. The SLS is currently the largest political party in three of the Serb-majority municipalities: Štrpce/Shtërpcë, Gračanica/Graçanicë, and Klokot/Kllokot.
28. The ministry for local government administration is currently led by minister Slobodan Petrovic, member of the SLS (http://mapl.rks-gov.net/?cid=2,238,552).
29. Law on Local Government finance, 2008/03-L049, Republic of Kosovo.
30. According to the World Bank (2010), Kosovo has an unemployment rate of 47%.
31. Already several international donors have pledged to support the new municipalities, while the Government of Kosovo has allocated funds for the construction of two new hospitals (KIPRED, 2010: 10).
32. An interesting example of such dissatisfaction is the petition for the dismissal of the Mayor of the new municipality of Klokot/Kllokot, signed by 617 of the municipality's residents (*Koha Ditore*, 22 June 2011). On the one hand this reflects a significant lack of faith in the current municipal leadership, while on the other hand it also shows a willingness to attempt to address their dissatisfaction through the Kosovo institutional system.

References

Brancati, D. (2006) 'Fuelling the fire or dampening the flames: The impact of political decentralisation on ethnic conflict and secessionism', *International Organization*, 60(3): 651–85.

Conversi, D. (1998) 'The Spanish federalist tradition and the 1978 Constitution', *Telos*, 112: 125–44.

Gurr, T. R. (2000) *Peoples Versus States: Minorities at Risk in the New Century*, Washington, DC: United States Institute of Peace Press.

Hardgrave, R. Jr (1994) 'India: The dilemmas of diversity', in L. Diamond and M. F. Plattner (eds) *Nationalism, Ethnic Conflict and Democracy*, Baltimore: The John Hopkins University Press, pp. 71–85.

Horowitz, D. L. (1991a) *A Democratic South Africa? Constitutional Engineering in a Divided Society*, Berkeley: University of California Press.

Horowitz, D. L. (1991b) 'Making moderation pay: The comparative politics of ethnic conflict management', in J. V. Montville (ed.) *Conflict and Peacemaking in Multiethnic Societies*, New York: Lexington Books, pp. 451–75.

ICG (2008) 'Kosovo's first month', *Europe Briefing*, No. 47, Brussels: International Crisis Group.

ICG (2009) 'Serb integration in Kosovo: Taking the plunge', *Europe Report*, No. 200, Brussels: International Crisis Group.

ICG (2011) 'North Kosovo: Dual sovereignty in practice', *Europe Report*, No. 211, Brussels: International Crisis Group.

Judah, T. (2008) *Kosovo: What Everyone Needs to Know*, New York: Oxford University Press.

Kaufman, C. (1996) 'Possible and impossible solutions to ethnic civil wars' *International Security*, 20(4): 133–75.

KIPRED (2008) *Looking Beyond Mitrovica Bridge: An Ahtisaari Plus Package Proposal*, Pristina: Kosovar Institute for Policy Research and Development.

KIPRED (2009) *Decentralisation in Kosovo: Municipal Elections and the Serb Participation*, Pristina: Kosovar Institute for Policy Research and Development.
KIPRED (2010) *Review of Decentralisation – Functioning of Serb Majority Municipalities*, Pristina: Kosovar Institute for Policy Research and Development.
Kymlicka, W. (1995) *Multicultural Citizenship: A Liberal Theory of Minority Rights*, Oxford: Clarendon Press.
Kymlicka, W. (1998) 'Is federalism a viable alternative to secessionism?' in P. B. Lehning (ed.) *Theories of Secessionism*, London: Routledge, pp. 109–48.
Leff, C. S. (1999) 'Democratization and disintegration in multi-national states: The breakup of the communist federations', *World Politics*, 51(2): 205–35.
Lijphart, A. (1977) *Democracy in Plural Societies: A Comparative Exploration*, New Haven: Yale University Press.
Lijphart, A. (1996) 'The puzzle of Indian democracy: A consociational interpretation', *American Political Science Review*, 90(2): 258–68.
Lijphart, A. (2004) 'Constitutional design for divided societies', *Journal of Democracy*, 15(20): 96–109.
Lustik, I. S., Miodownik, D. and Eidelson, R. J. (2004) 'Secessionism in multicultural states: Does sharing power prevent or encourage it?' *American Political Science Review*, 98(2): 209–29.
Malcolm, N. (1999) *Kosovo: A Short History*, New York: New York University Press.
Monteux, C. (2006) 'Decentralisation: The new delusion of ethnic conflict regulation?' *International Journal on Multicultural Societies*, 8(2): 162–82.
Nordlinger, E. (1972) *Conflict Regulation in Divided Societies*, Cambridge: Harvard University Center for International Affairs.
OSCE Kosovo (2008) *Municipal Profile: Prishtinë/Priština*, Pristina: OSCE Mission in Kosovo.
OSCE Kosovo (2010) *Communities Rights Assessment Report: Second Edition*, Pristina: OSCE Mission in Kosovo.
Roeder, P. G. (1991) 'Soviet federalism and ethnic mobilization', *World Politics*, 43(2): 196–232.
Scarpulla, C. (2002) *The Constitutional Framework for the Autonomy of Åland: A Survey of the Status of an Autonomous Region in the Throes of European Integration*, Mariehamn: Ålands högskola.
Snyder, J. (2000) *From Voting to Violence: Democratization and Nationalist Conflict*, New York: W. W. Norton and Company.
Steiner, M. (2002) *A Choice for Mitrovica – The Seven Point Plan*, UNMIK/PR/837.
Stepan, A. (1999) 'Federalism and democracy: Beyond the US model.' *Journal of Democracy*, 10(4): 19–34.
Tsebelis, G. (1990) 'Elite interaction and constitution building in consociational societies.' *Journal of Theoretical Politics*, 2(1): 5–29.
Weller, M. (2010) 'Introduction', in M. Weller and K. Nobbs (eds) *Asymmetrical Autonomy and the Settlement of Ethnic Conflict*, Philadelphia: University of Pennsylvania Press, pp. 1–14.
World Bank (2010) *Kosovo Country Brief 2010*, Washington DC: The World Bank.

7
Decentralization as an Effective Tool of State-Building? The Cases of Bosnia and Herzegovina and Kosovo

Lana Srzić

Introduction

Decentralization has appeared as the only option of governance in internationally led state-building projects in South East Europe. Post-Dayton Bosnia and Herzegovina has been the prime example, with its complex multilayered institutional arrangements, consisting of a weak central government, and two ethnically based entities: the Federation of Bosnia and Herzegovina inhabited predominantly by Bosnian Muslims and Bosnian Croats, and Republika Srpska inhabited mainly by Bosnian Serbs. The experience of post-Dayton Bosnia poses the question of whether decentralization inevitably reflects and perpetuates ethnic divisions. Despite the commonly cited shortcomings of the decentralized form of government, including its failure to transform Bosnia and Herzegovina into a viable state and, in particular, a viable economy, post-Dayton decentralization can be defended as a last resort measure, and the only possibility of preserving and governing the country given its recent history. The Bosnian case provides many parallels to the post-independent Kosovo, where calls for municipal decentralization were justified as a means of providing the Serbian minority with a participatory role in the new state.

This chapter will examine the experience of Bosnia and Herzegovina, its institutional arrangements and its particular model of decentralization, in comparison to that of the post-independence Kosovo. The role of the international community, present in both cases of state-building and able to determine particular models of decentralization, will be taken into account, as well as the inherent differences of the two cases due to their particular ethnic composition. Moreover, the possibility of alternative models of decentralization, based on regional rather than ethnic units will be examined. Finally, we will look at the ability of the existing models of decentralization to provide political stability and a basis for viable economic development.

Theoretical framework

Attempts to manage ethnically diverse and divided post-war societies include various forms of group autonomy and power-sharing mechanisms. Decentralization, in its different varieties, has become one of the main tools of international post-war reconciliation of divided societies, as well as the only alternative once a more unitary state structure is excluded due to ethnic divisions and legacies of the conflict. The two main theoretical directions include the 'consociational' approach, associated with theories of Arend Lijphard, and Donald Horowitz's 'integrative' approach (Lijphard, 1977; Horowitz, 1985). The 'consociational' approach assumes that ethnic groups are the starting units of cooperation and calls for cooperation among ethnic elites, while explicitly accepting and institutionalizing ethnic divisions. At the central level, the government is marked by attributes of power sharing, minority veto and ethnic proportionality. The system's potential shortcomings include 'deadlock and immobility', while also institutionalizing and entrenching potentially fluid ethnic divisions.

The 'integrative' approach's starting assumption is a fluidity of identities. It proposes a model of federalism based on ethnically heterogeneous political units, with an electoral system in which political parties, in order to win, need to attract votes from other ethnic groups, thus diminishing the ethnic principle as the main determining factor in elections. As argued by Caspersen (2004), the main problem of the model is in gaining its acceptance from the nationalist parties in power, and in the lack of adequate mechanisms for the protection of minorities in a majoritarian system.

The aforementioned models provide two poles against which individual institutional cases can be situated and reflect the main ideological division within institutional arrangements in post-conflict multi-ethnic societies. The consociational approach accepts the institutionalization of ethnicity as being necessary to achieve consensus among the political elites and legitimacy of the system among its populations. In contrast, the integrative approach claims that institutionalizing ethnicity as the central political category perpetuates the thinking behind the ethnic conflict and 'freezes it', preventing the possibility of a gradual transformation of ethnicity. This theoretical debate is highly relevant to the cases of Bosnia and Herzegovina and Kosovo, while it is also important to take into account their individual particularities, including variables such as demographic balance between groups, intergroup attitudes, regional political factors and levels of international involvement.

Decentralization in Bosnia and Herzegovina

The institutional complexity of Bosnia and Herzegovina (hereafter Bosnia) represents a special case of a state formed by international agreement that institutionalized ethnic divisions. It provided institutional recognition to ethnically based groups and political power and legitimacy to their leaders, while at the same time trying to promote their cooperation and preserve the unity of the state. Moreover, the Bosnian case unites various aspects of political theory dealing with institutional arrangements in a divided society, as its multiple levels of state organization based on diverse arrangements include various elements of the aforementioned approaches.

The Bosnian institutional structure emerged from the General Framework Agreement for Peace in Bosnia and Herzegovina of December 1995, established by the Dayton Agreement, which created a multilevel decentralized structure, and territorially entrenched post-conflict ethnic divisions. Regarding the international dimension, the powers of the Office of the High Representative (OHR) were expanded in 1997 through the so-called Bonn Powers granted by the Peace Implementation Council and including wide-reaching executive power to impose policy and remove recalcitrant politicians. The activities of the OHR failed to create functional government, mainly due to a lack of consensus at either the domestic or the international level.

The Bosnian state was divided between two Entities, the Federation of Bosnia–Herzegovina and the Republika Srpska, while the autonomous district of Brčko was created as a distinct territorial unit through international agreement. The Federation, inhabited by Bosniaks and Croats, consists of ten cantons determined largely on the basis of ethnicity, which consist of five predominantly Bosniak cantons, three Croat and two mixed. The central state government is composed of three main bodies: the presidency, the parliamentary assembly and the constitutional court. The political institutions of the central state strictly follow consociational principles. For example, the parliamentary assembly's House of People includes 15 delegates, composed of five from each ethnic group, while the House of Representatives has two-thirds of its members from the Federation and one-third from Republika Srpska. Each Entity has autonomy over taxation, commerce and general legislation, while the central state has authority over foreign policy, external trade, customs, monetary policy, and international and inter-Entity criminal law enforcement (Szewczyk, 2010).

Significant power and independence were given to the two Entities short of their becoming independent and sovereign units. Moreover, one of the main features of the system is consociational power sharing at both the level of the central state and at other levels of government. Thus, within the Federation there is a similar complex system of power sharing, including 'minority veto, parity of representation and considerable autonomy for homogenous cantons and municipalities' (Caspersen, 2004). The complex structure of government is based on asymmetric organization, decentralization and a combination of exclusive and shared competences between different levels of government, and a transfer of competences between different levels.

The two Entities and the autonomous district of Brčko each have distinct governing structures. The internal organization of the Federation is highly decentralized, as this was a necessary precondition for the Croat participation in state institutions. The federative units are the cantons, named after their respective capitals or geographical features, exclude any names of national connotation even where their ethnic bases are entrenched and evident (Bose, 2002).[1] Within each canton, government responsibility is further shared with numerous municipalities. In contrast, the Republika Srpska is organized on a centralized basis in which the responsibilities of government are divided directly between the Entity and municipality levels.

In practice, there has been a lack of clear hierarchy between different levels of government as the Entity administrations are not obliged to implement the decisions of the Council of Ministers of Bosnia and Herzegovina, being directly accountable towards the Entity rather than the state-level authorities. This inevitably reduces the effectiveness of the central state whose institutions have not been able to implement required reforms at lower state levels. The multiplicity of power levels has created confusion and overlap with regards to the separation of competences between the municipalities and the cantons, the cantons and the Federation, as well as the Entities and the state (Bieber, 2006a). Furthermore, the veto powers conferred to each ethnic group have the potential to paralyse the central administration. International organizations and in particular the Office of the High Representative, charged with implementing the Dayton Agreement, have applied constant pressure to introduce economic and social reforms. In response, the principal strategy used by political actors has been to delay or obstruct the implementation of proposed laws, in particular by the officials from the Republika Srpska with regards to decision-making which threatens the autonomy of their Entity.

The sub-state levels of governments, including the Republika Srpska and the cantons, have held a greater legitimacy than the state due to their ethnic homogeneity, while the central state has been weakened by the veto power and other constitutional mechanisms used by individual ethnic groups to preserve the autonomy and power of their ethnic units of government. Moreover, the extent to which the central government has been supported has varied greatly among different ethnicities; Bosniaks have tended to identify with the central state more than Serbs and Croats. This asymmetrical commitment was addressed in 2002 through constitutional reforms imposed by the Office of the High Representative by granting all three constituent ethnic groups the right of veto at the Entity and cantonal level, with the practical result of further complicating and slowing down the decision-making process.

Although the Dayton agreement included both 'consociational' and 'integrative' factors, as evident from the previous discussion, the 'consociational' aspects have been considerably more prominent. However, parallel to the main 'consociational' features of the system, there is some room for more 'integrative' developments, including the potential of refugee returns to change the ethnic balance within local units, and to create multi-ethnic municipalities. Furthermore, several central state institutions have the potential to foster the integrative approach. For example, the Constitutional Court, the Central Bank, the Commission for Displaced Persons and Refugees, while being based on ethnic parity, lack veto powers and operate on the basis of a simple majority. Such central state institutions going beyond ethnic divisions hold the potential for creating a sense of supranational identification with the state of Bosnia.

However, despite some elements of a unified state structure, ethnic divisions remain central. Political parties based on ethnicity have been one of the key features of the political life in Bosnia, with the post-Dayton dominance of the Bosniak Party of Democratic Action (SDA), the Serbian Democratic Party (SDS) and the Croatian National Community of Bosnia and Herzegovina (HDZ BiH). The nationalist parties have enjoyed stable support among their respective ethnic audiences, with limited cross-ethnic voting. Ethnic issues have dominated the political agenda, and have not allowed political allegiances to develop along alternative social or economic cleavages.

Constitutional change and alternative models of decentralization

Constitutional reform has been an ongoing idea in Bosnia since the Dayton Agreement, shared by both the international and domestic political actors preoccupied with the previously described problems as well as with the ineffectiveness of the institutional system and the continuous demands of each ethnic group to secure a constitutional framework more favourable to their constituencies. Whereas the dominant view from the part of the Federation is that abolishing the Republika Srpska should be the starting point for further reforms, the politicians in Republika Srpska have based their policies on preserving and strengthening their Entity. The third and smallest constituent group, the Croats, have in turn been preoccupied with preserving their status through promoting the idea of establishing a third entity as a way of protecting and entrenching their status in relation to the other two ethnic groups.

The proposals for constitutional reform have ranged from a radical revision of the Dayton Agreement to more moderate changes. In 2000 the Party for Bosnia–Herzegovina of the former Prime Minister Haris Silajdžić made the first significant attempt at complete revision of the Dayton Agreement, with the electoral slogan of 'Bosnia without Entities' (Bieber, 2006a). Moreover, following the 2002 electoral success of the nationalist parties, there were proposals for the territorial reorganization of the state that would abandon ethnic lines and instead establish alternative lines of division between units, along with a strengthening of the central state. For example, the proposal of the European Stability Initiative to abolish the Federation and create a simplified structure which would include the existing ten cantons, Republika Srpska and the District of Brčko – thereby proposing a simplified structure based on 12 units – provoked strong reactions.[2]

In response to the proposal, some political parties, such as the Social Democratic Party of Bosnia and Herzegovina and the Croatian National Community of Bosnia and Herzegovina were in favour of further decentralization based on an entirely new regional structure.[3] This raised several questions concerning (i) which economic or historical principles would be followed in setting up the new regions in order to avoid further ethnic divisions; (ii) the power of the new decentralized units and whether they would be 'constituent parts of a genuine federation, with their own elected governments and parliaments, or mere administrative units of a centralized state';[4] and (iii) whether such new multi-ethnic units could lead to more effective governance or only maintain the dysfunctional system for which the current institutions are being criticized.

Possible constitutional change continues to be a pressing issue in Bosnia, as well as a necessity to create a more effective and functional state. For example, in January 2009, the leaders of the three dominant parties, Sulejman Tihić of the Party of Democratic Action, Milorad Dodik of The Alliance of Independent Social Democrats and Dragan Čović of the Croatian National Community announced that they had reached a general agreement calling for constitutional change which would divide the state into four territorial and administrative units. Bosnia would become a decentralized state with three levels of government, of which the second level would be divided into four territorial units each with its own legislative, executive and judicial powers. The idea, however, soon provoked conflict and confusion in interpretation and led nowhere.

Overall, the factors of ethnic division, dysfunctionality of the state, and the international presence and its parallel and overriding decision-making power in relation to Bosnian institutions all need to be taken into account when considering alternative proposals for the decentralization of Bosnia. The new and improved decentralized power structure would have to lead to economic development, grass-root democracy and inter-ethnic cooperation, rather than solely perpetuating and replicating the national ethnic politics model on the local level.

Decentralization in Kosovo

Despite the rupture in inter-ethnic relations in Bosnia due to the conflicts of the early 1990s, the constituent national groups in Bosnia share a legacy of cooperation and coexistence, with linguistic and cultural factors presenting a potential for cooperation. In the case of Kosovo, the division between the Albanian majority and the Serbian minority needs to be taken into account when trying to transpose any of the lessons from the Bosnian case. Indeed, a long-lasting legacy of conflict and cultural separation underpin and accentuate the existing problems of opposing perceptions of the common state, its legitimacy and status.

Instead of specifying the internal organization of the province, the principal aim of the proposed and unsuccessful Rambouillet Agreement's was to end the fighting in the province in early 1999. Following the end of the 1999 war, the United Nations Security Council Resolution 1244 established a UN mandate under international protection. Following the first local elections in Kosovo in October 2000, the United Nations Mission in Kosovo developed a constitutional framework that established provisional institutions of self-government for the province. The institutional structure was entirely created by the international administration, rather than reflecting any agreement with the demands of the local actors.

The idea of decentralization of Kosovo was first proposed in 2002 by the Special Representative of the Secretary General Michael Steiner. His proposal was to institutionalize an ethnically based self-government in the municipality of Mitrovica as a way of convincing the Serb population of North Mitrovica to accept the local institutions. However, for Albanians, such an institutionalization of the Serb status led to the fear of eventual secession, and the plan was rejected. The issue of decentralization and local self-government became sidelined and only re-emerged in relation to the discussions on the constitutional status of the province following the ethnic disturbances of 2004. The international community continued dealing with the question of self-government with the establishment of the Working Group on Local Government in 2004, and the production of document on 'Reform of Local Self-Government in Kosovo'.[5]

The Serbian response to international initiatives was the creation of parallel structures, with the 'Union of Serb Municipalities' being supported by the Coordination Centre for Kosovo and Metohija. Parallel structures have included those Serbian state institutions that have been operational in Kosovo after 10 June 1999 and are not mandated for under the United Nations Security Council Resolution 1244. These institutions have mostly operated 'under the de facto authority of the Serbian government', asserting jurisdiction over Kosovo from Serbia proper, or operating in the territory of Kosovo.[6] Mostly present in the north of Kosovo, they have included parallel courts, parallel security structures, parallel administrative structures related to property issues, parallel schools and parallel health care facilities.

Following Kosovo's declaration of independence in February 2008, decentralization has become a topic high on the agenda. Following the entry into force of the Kosovo Constitution on 15 June 2008, the Law of Local Self-Government was adopted which provides municipalities with competences over health care, education, social services and local economic development. With regards to the implementation of the new legal framework, the establishment of new municipalities in Serb-inhabited areas has been a particular problem (Tahiri, 2009). Decentralization has given Serbian municipalities a significant level of autonomy, while also allowing 'Belgrade to exercise its legitimate interest in supporting and financing Kosovo Serb institutions and activities without destructively isolating Serbs from their Kosovo surroundings'.[7] The aims of the international administration have included the formation of the municipality of Northern Mitrovica and the organization of elections in three municipalities in the north of Kosovo – Zvečan, Leposavić and Zubin Potok. The involvement of the Serbian government in Belgrade was envisaged in the decentralization plans and has been carried out in cooperation with Kosovo's Ministry of Local Government Administration.

However, the small number of ethnic Serbs participating in elections organized by the Kosovo government in Priština has revealed the limited acceptance of the central government by the Kosovo Serbs living in the north. Moreover, the response of the Serbian government has been to continue to support the Serbian parallel institutions, coordinated through the Ministry for Kosovo and Metohija. In the words of the Minister for Kosovo and Metohija, Goran Bogdanović, 'Belgrade is not planning to give up its institutions in Kosovo ... In the same way that a part of the international community calls our institutions parallel, we, as well as the other part of the international community, have the same attitude towards institutions that are not in accordance with the Resolution 1244.'[8]

Decentralization has offered the Serbian community a high level of competences, with plans for additional municipalities to be established with Serbs in the majority. However, despite its practical benefits, the acceptance of the local institutions has become implicitly linked to the Kosovo Serbs' acceptance of the central governing structures as legitimate, thus 'politicizing' the Serbian acceptance of decentralization (Tahiri, 2009). Kosovo Serbs view decentralization with suspicion as they associate it with the Ahtisaari plan[9] for the independence of Kosovo, while also viewing unfavourably the International Civilian Office, created according to the Ahtisaari plan. The lack of support is particularly evident in the north, with a very limited presence of the Kosovo and instead parallel institutions operate most effectively in the municipalities of Zvečan, Leposavić, Zubin Potok and North Mitrovica, contrary to the efforts of the international administration to integrate the area into Kosovo's institutions.[10]

Moreover, Kosovo's ethnic Serbian community has not been acting as a unified community. The interests of Serbs within Kosovo depends on whether they live in municipalities adjacent to Serbia or in scattered enclaves south of the Ibar river, with the two groups having different responses to the problems of integration in the new state and its institutions (Bieber, 2004). The Kosovo Serb political elite has been further divided by its support for different political parties from Belgrade, while the level of participation in Kosovo Albanian institutions was another point of contention among the Kosovo Serbs. According to the Kosovo Serb politician Rada Trajković, a community of Serb municipalities should be encouraged, which would allow Serbs to be represented at the international level where they could present their grievances, which is not possible as long as the Serb community continues to boycott the Kosovo Albanian institutions.[11]

The concept of decentralization has also become politicized on the Albanian side due to the belief that the creation of the Serb municipalities goes against Kosovo's sovereignty, building on earlier fears that the decentralized northern municipalities might call for secession. Regardless of the ethnic problems, the passing of competences to the local level has also faced problems of inadequate funding, lack of qualified staff and a lack of cooperation between the different levels of government.

Comparison of the two case studies

In the situations of fragile statehoods of Bosnia and Kosovo, decentralization has served as a last result measure to ensure the preservation of the state through creating a compromise among its ethnic groups. In theory, the role of decentralization should go beyond simple state preservation and should lead to strengthening democracy and local governance, and promoting local economic development and public services responsive to local needs. However, in the two cases, instead of being a central component of the potential response to the highly unfavourable economic and social situation and an instrument to bring the state services closer to the population, decentralization, serving as a tool in creating a compromise between hostile ethnic groups, was established at the expense of functionality and other aims such as economic development. Thus, while serving well the basic function of preserving the state, the decentralized structures have failed to contribute to the other key aims needed for the effective functioning of the two states. In the Bosnian case, as argued previously, decentralization has been closely linked to ethnic separation, while in Kosovo, decentralization has been imposed by the international community, and as a result, mistrusted by both the Kosovo Albanian majority and the Serb minority.

In Bosnia, as we have seen before, the current decentralized system has been placed in the service of the county's ethnic elites. For example, the administrative units of cantons in the Federation have been mostly ethno-national territories, as the presence of ethnic minorities is limited to nominal freedom of confession and cultural–educational institutions. For this reason, this level of government has not been acting as a link between federal level government and municipalities. Instead, the cantons have been used to entrench and reproduce ethnic power at local level. This entrenchment of ethnicity as the central political category, and the primacy of ethnic identities has not allowed for any move towards 'integrative' politics and shared loyalty towards the common state of Bosnia. Moreover, no alternative identity has proved strong enough to compete with and counterbalance the ethnic divisions.

At the same time, the complex decentralized structure in Bosnia has provided a serious obstacle to economic development. The disparities in financial, tax and economic systems between the two entities have been detrimental to much-needed investment. The limited powers at the state level do not allow for coordination between the entities and other levels of local government. Instead of constructive and practical debate on harmonization of legislation, greater efficiency of the system and communication between different levels of government, the institutional structure has been used to promote the interests of separate ethnic groups, excluding consideration for the common benefit of state-level economic development.

Moreover, the aforementioned lack of clear hierarchy among institutional units is a further obstacle to the implementation of economic reforms. Therefore, rather than empowering local units, and allowing for economic development, the current structures have led to a deadlock, lack of accountability and constant power struggle justified by ethnicity. Bosnia has been facing a paradox as the complex consociational system which allowed for its survival as a state has also become an obstacle to the state's normal functioning.

The failure of the consociational system in Bosnia based on power sharing between territorially separated communities to bridge the divide between ethnic groups has provided a strong lesson for the international community designing the institutional set-up in Kosovo. Consequently, decentralization in Kosovo has not followed the Bosnian model based on the creation of ethnically based cantons. This has led to a paradoxical situation in which a rigid system that enshrines ethnic divisions has been established to a greater extent in Bosnia than in Kosovo, where ethnic divisions have historically been deeper (Bieber, 2004).

However, in Kosovo as in Bosnia, the centrality of ethnicity has been detrimental to establishing a functional state. Decentralization is seen within the ethnic prism, either as an instrument to improve the relative position of one's ethnic group, or with mistrust as an internationally imposed structure potentially harmful to ethnic interests. Whereas the Serb minority has associated decentralization with acceptance of the existing Kosovo Albanian political structure, for the Kosovo Albanian majority allowing for decentralization and Serb-dominated municipalities has been linked to the possibility of secession of the Serb-dominated north. Moreover, moving towards practical issues of economic development is difficult in the context of continuous disagreements over sovereignty. This has especially been the case with respect to the north of Kosovo, given the local Serb inhabitants' unwillingness to recognize the authority of the Kosovo state. In such a context of disputed sovereignty, as was the case in the post-1995 Bosnia, decentralized institutional design serves again as the last resort of state preservation, being inevitably closely tied to inter-ethnic relations, at the expense of other key issues of development and democracy.

Apart from the close links between ethnicity and decentralization which has been detrimental to effective functioning of the two states, Bosnia and Kosovo also share particular regional and international elements, which have the potential to perpetuate the centrality of ethnicity, challenge state sovereignty and make the local institutions appear imposed from above and lacking accountability. The international community has had a prominent role in setting up and maintaining local governing institutions. On the positive side, this has allowed for a degree of self-government in decentralized governing units. On the negative side, this has prevented the development of a culture of local accountability. The problematic long-term sustainability of the system has been the core focus of debates on future constitutional changes, especially in preparation for the expected future reduction of the level of involvement by the international community.

Moreover, the regional context provides external ethnic homelands for the Serb and Croat ethnic groups in Bosnia, and for the Albanian and Serb ethnic group in Kosovo, which to varying extents have influenced the development of national groups within both countries, as well as their limited acceptance of participation in their respective multi-ethnic states. This is currently more striking in the case of Kosovo, even though Bosnia's problems also include serious centrifugal tendencies and the persistent separation of the three ethnic groups.

Conclusion

Beyond preserving the state unity, the existing political systems in Bosnia and Kosovo have not allowed for other crucial elements of state-building, namely providing the basis for viable economic development, and promoting democracy and cooperation beyond ethnic lines. In the midst of a highly unfavourable situation in the region, any potential reform of the governance systems should try to combine ethnic compromise with a degree of effectiveness and pragmatism in the design of decentralized governance structures that would be needed to bring about economic development. Rather than being a tool in bargaining between the ethnic elites, international organizations and other regional states, decentralization could then facilitate the development of local communities. At the same time, in place of continuous ethnic divisions, a gradual development of loyalties at the state, regional or local level, as well as some progress beyond the current preoccupation with ethnic self-identities remains the main hope for a more effective future functioning of the two states.

Both Kosovo and Bosnia are faced with the challenge of developing an institutional structure that could create some unity at the central level, while promoting active citizen participation at the local level, thus strengthening the common state as well as allowing for local democracy. In Bosnia, a possibility for such development would include strengthening some competences of the common state, while at the same time increasing the power of municipalities. In Kosovo, drawing from the Bosnian lessons, the last-resort measure of ethnically based municipalities could also further entrench ethic divisions. Whereas both the majority and the minority view decentralization with mistrust and in terms of potential disadvantages for their ethnic group, the decentralization plan governed by the international community should link decentralization to the most crucial issues such as poverty, under-development and unemployment, and demonstrate the potential benefits of decentralization when it comes to economic development and greater government accountability. This could allow the new institutional structure to go beyond solely preserving the state unity, and instead serve as the central element of effective state-building.

Notes

1. Regarding the division of powers between the Entity and the canton level, the Entity competences are limited to a vague provision of defence and economic policy, among others.

2. 'Waiting for a Miracle? The Politics of Constitutional Change in Bosnia and Herzegovina', European Stability Initiative, 3 February 2004.
3. Ibid.
4. Ibid.
5. Available at http://lgi.osi.hu/country_datasheet.php?id=203
6. OSCE Mission in Kosovo, Department of Human Rights, Decentralisation and Communities, 'Parallel structures in Kosovo'.
7. 'Serb Integration in Kosovo: Taking the plunge', International Crisis Group Europe Report, 12 May 2009.
8. 'Priština Srbima ne nudi ništa sem iluzija', Interview with Goran Bogdanović, *Nova srpska politička misao*, 21 April 2010, available at http://www.nspm.rs/kosovo-i-metohija/pristina-srbima-ne-nudi-nista-sem-iluzija.html
9. Ahtisaari plan is a proposal for the Kosovo status settlement, created by the UN Special Envoy Martti Ahtisaari dealing with a range of issues relevant to the process. It includes the establishment of the International Civilian Office led by the International Civilian Representative, with aims to ensure full implementation of the status settlement proposal by the government of Kosovo, and support Kosovo's European integration.
10. 'Serb integration in Kosovo: Taking the plunge', International Crisis Group Europe Report, 12 May 2009.
11. 'Neophodan kontakt između Beograda i Prištine', Interview with Rada Trajković, *Nova srpska politička misao*, 28 April 2010.

References

Bieber, F. (2004) 'The legal framework for post-war Kosovo and the myth of multiethnicity', in N. Dimitrijević and P. Kovacs (eds) *Managing Hatred and Distrust: The Prognosis for Post-Conflict Settlement in Multiethnic Communities in the Former Yugoslavia*, Budapest: Open Society Institute, pp. 115–35.

Bieber, F. (2006a) 'After Dayton, Dayton? The evolution of an unpopular peace', *Ethnopolitics*, 5(1): 15–31.

Bieber, F. (2006b) 'Bosnia–Herzegovina: Slow progress towards a functional state', *Southeast European and Black Sea Studies*, 6(1): 43–64.

Bose, S. (2002) *Bosnia after Dayton: National Partition and International Intervention*, London: Hurst and Company.

Caspersen, N. (2004) 'Good fences make good neighbours? A comparison of conflict-regulation strategies in postwar Bosnia', *Journal of Peace Research*, 41(5): 569–88.

Horowitz, D. (1985) *Ethnic Groups in Conflict*, Berkeley, CA: University of California Press.

Lijphart, A. (1977) *Democracy in Plural Societies*, New Haven, CT: Yale University Press.

Szewczyk, B. M. (2010) 'The EU in Bosnia and Herzegovina: Powers, decisions and legitimacy', *Occasional Paper 83*, Paris: European Institute for Security Studies.

Tahiri, B. (2009) *Implementing Decentralisation in Kosovo: One Year On*, Pristina: Kosovo Local Government Initiative.

Part IV
Implementation Deficits – Case Studies

8

Decentralization and Regional Policy in Romania and Bulgaria

Cristina Matiuta

The concept of decentralization

The concept of decentralization is generally understood as the transfer of power, responsibility and resources from central to regional and local governments. It covers a broad range of meanings, being a complex process that modifies the fundamental structure of state power. According to the World Bank Institute (Litvack and Seddon, 1999), decentralization has three main dimensions – *political, administrative* and *fiscal* – each of which has different characteristics, policy implications and conditions for success.

Political decentralization aims to give citizens and their elected representatives more power in public decision-making, in formulating and implementing policies. This type involves the transfer of political authority to the local level (often as part of a democratization process) and requires democratic reforms (electoral reform, development of pluralistic political parties and the authorization of participatory process).

Administrative decentralization means the full or partial transfer of responsibility for planning, financing and managing certain public services (such as health care service, the management of schools, the building and maintenance of roads, and garbage collection) from central government to subordinate units or levels of government.[1]

Fiscal decentralization implies the provision of adequate revenues for local governments (raised locally or transferred from the central government), as well as the authority to make expenditure decisions.

Many scholars point out that many factors influence the process of decentralization, covering a wide range of elements, such as the legal tradition of the country, institutional design or its economic background (Basta Fleiner, 1999). For instance, the extent to which a unitary state is decentralized depends on the existence of a second chamber of parliament, composed by the representatives of local/regional communities and meant to promote the local interest within the legislature. In this respect, the electoral system also gains major relevance because, if the electoral districts correspond to decentralized units and if the local political parties can choose the candidates within these electoral districts to run the elections they will defend better the local interests within the second chamber and will contribute to the advancement of decentralization.

However, the real effects of decentralization, besides the constitutional framework, depend on two other very important factors: 'first, the authority in question must have a decision-making competence; second, the authority in question should dispose of necessary measures to accomplish its tasks' (Basta Fleiner, 1999: 33). In other words, decentralization can work only when substantial tasks and powers are transferred together with the staff and financial means to match.

In the literature that analyses the process of transition to democracy in former communist countries, decentralization is seen as a very important factor for development and democratic consolidation.[2] Because power was extremely centralized during the communist regimes, local authorities being simply administrative agents of central power, the dispersion of power after the regimes fell was considered to be an important factor for democratization. Decentralization was seen as a key factor in building democracy and state legitimacy from the bottom-up.

But decentralization is not always a 'success story'; as well as having positive effects it may also have negative ones. A study on decentralization and local governance in the Western Balkans emphasizes several challenges specific to the region (Byrne, 2005). Summarizing, these challenges are related to the following factors:

- An unclear distribution of responsibilities between central, regional and local governments
- Inadequate capacities of the local levels to deal with the responsibilities they have
- Inadequate decentralization of functions related to policy implementation at the local level
- An uneven implementation of legislation
- A lack of institutional dialogue and the insufficient recognition of local government as partner
- A low level of citizens participation in decision-making process
- The size of municipalities (if they are too small, they are not sustainable in terms of demographic structure, economic viability and

organizational capacity; if they are too large by population or territory, the relations between their inhabitants and local authorities may be rather distant)

- The risk of elite, interest-group or political-party capture at the local level (decentralization could contribute to the concentration of power to smaller circles of unaccountable local leaders, economic or political oligarchies or organized crime structures)
- The risk of uneven allocation of resources in ethnically divided communities and, more than that, of turning the 'minority question' into a 'territorial question' (by minorities who feel more secure in an 'ethnically pure' political environment)

This chapter sets out the key elements of the legal framework for decentralization in Bulgaria and Romania before going on to assess whether and how these challenges are applicable in each case, with a focus on the lack of administrative capacity, the extent of corruption and central political interference in the activities of local public administration.

The legal framework for decentralization and regional policy

Concerning the legal framework of decentralization in Romania and Bulgaria, the Constitutions of both countries enunciate the basic principles regarding the form of government and the relationship between central and local public authorities. According to its Constitution, Romania is a 'sovereign, independent, unitary and indivisible National State'; the territory of the country is organized administratively into communes, towns/municipalities and counties.[3] The public administration in territorial-administrative units 'shall be based on the principles of decentralization, local autonomy and deconcentration of public services' (Art. 120, §1). The government representative at the local level (in each county) is the prefect, who shall direct the decentralized public services of ministers and other bodies of the central public administration in the territorial-administrative units. Among the prefects, the local councils and the mayors, as well as the county councils and their presidents, there are collaborative relations rather than relations of subordination. Romania's Constitution does not recognize the existence of an intermediary regional level or the possibility to create other administrative territorial units.

Regarding Bulgaria, the Constitution defines it as 'a unitary state with local self-government'.[4] The territorial integrity of the country is inviolable and no autonomous territorial formations shall exist. The territory of Bulgaria is divided into municipalities and regions and 'other administrative territorial units and bodies of self-government shall be established by law' (Art. 135). Municipalities are free to associate in the solution of common matters; a municipality has its own budget, its permanent sources of revenue, established by law while the state is to ensure the normal work of the municipalities through budget appropriations and other means. Concerning the region, it is 'an administrative territorial unit entrusted with the conduct of a regional policy, the implementation of state government on a local level and the ensuring of harmony of national and local interests' (Art. 142). Each region is governed by a regional governor, appointed by the Council of Ministers and aided by a regional administration. The regional governor is to ensure the implementation of state policy, the safeguarding of the national interests, law and public order and exercise administrative control.

Specific regulations

Other regulations are designed to decentralize the administration and to bring the decision-making closer to the citizens. Important in this respect is the fact that both countries have ratified the European Charter of Local Self-Government, one of the corner-stone Conventions of the Council of Europe, which has had a high impact on shaping local self-government in Europe (understood as the right and the ability of local authorities to regulate and manage a substantial share of public affairs under their own responsibility and in the interests of the local population – Art. 2 of the Charter).[5]

The ratification of the European Charter by Bulgaria in 1995 and by Romania in 1998 and especially the pressure of the European Union on the two countries to implement the *acquis communautaire* and to create the mechanisms and institutions needed to manage EU funds allocated for economic and social development, led to an improvement of the legal framework related to decentralization and local and regional development in both countries.

The legal framework for decentralization in Romania

In Romania, Law no. 215/2001 on local public administration (amended and supplemented several times, especially by Law no. 286/2006), the Law on decentralization and the Law on local public finances (both adopted in 2006), supplemented by other regulations, are intended to create strong autonomous local communities, capable of possessing the necessary tools to promote local development. The aim of the Law on local public administration is to regulate 'the general regime of local autonomy, as well as the organization and functioning of the local public administration' (Art. 1). Local autonomy and decentralization are considered as the fundamental principles of this law, but their application 'shall not harm the character of national, unitary and indivisible state of Romania' (Art. 2). The law establishes that 'within the national economic policy, the communes, towns and counties have the right to their own resources, which the local public administration authorities shall manage according to the duties devolving upon them, under the terms of law. The financial resources of the local public authorities must be proportional with their competences and the responsibilities stipulated by law' (Art. 9).

The interesting provisions concerning financial decentralization are included in the Law on local public finances and the Framework law on decentralization. Specifically, the Law 273/2006 on local public finances[6] stipulates that the central government should transfer to the local public administrations sufficient funds to carry out their decentralized competences. The local authorities have the competence to establish the amount of local taxes and fees subject to approval by the local or county councils. In addition to their own income from taxes, fees, contributions and other payments, local budgets are supplemented by transfers, shared taxes and other subsides received from the state budget. Almost half (47%) of the income tax collected by the state at the level of each territorial administrative unit is allocated to the local budgets of the communes, towns and municipalities; another 13% to the budget of the county; and 22% to a distinct account opened on behalf of the county council for balancing the local budgets of the communes, towns, municipalities and county. The law also permits local authorities to collaborate in carrying out local public works and delivering services on the basis of conventions or contracts of association in which the financing sources representing the contribution of each local authority involved are stipulated.

The Framework law on decentralization,[7] adopted by the Romanian Parliament in 2006 (which replaced the law on decentralization of 2004) enhances the local autonomy and accountability of public institutions. Widely considered to be a real turning point, this law asserts the principle of subsidiarity as the basis for the decentralization process. The purpose of the law is to transfer new functions to local authorities, together with finance, thus strengthening their powers. It defines decentralization as the 'transfer of administrative and financial competences from the level of central public administration to the level of local public administration or to private sector' and makes a distinction between the exclusive competences of local public administration and those shared by local and central public authorities.[8] The elaboration of the strategy and general policies of decentralization, as well as the technical coordination and the effective implementation of this process are in the responsibility of the Ministry of Administration and Interior.

In order to fulfil its task in this field, this Ministry adopted in 2007 an Operational Programme titled *Administrative Capacity Development 2007–2013*, structured along two major axes: the first one refers to the horizontal management problems at all public administration levels (central and local), with a focus on key attributes that strengthen the reliability of the administration, decision-making, better regulation, accountability and organizational effectiveness; the second one focused on improving the responsiveness of the public administration towards the citizens' needs, and specifically oriented to improve the quality of service delivery in certain priority sectors (health, education, social assistance) and the absorption capacity of development funds (especially of structural funds from the European Union).[9] The document emphasizes Romania's experience in public administration reform, especially since 2001 when the Government adopted a strategy in this area supported by the EU-Phare Programme.[10] The legislative framework was improved and new institutions were set up at central level in order to accelerate the reform of public administration (among these, The National Agency of Civil Servants, the National Institute of Administration, the Central Unit for Public Administration Reform and the Public Policy Unit from the General Secretariat of Government). Nevertheless, the document recognizes that the progress has been uneven, the capacity to implement the new legislative framework is weak and the institutions mentioned previously not fully meeting expectations. As a remedy, it asserts the necessity of strengthening the coordination structures and procedures for implementation of the reform strategy. A strong management, coordination and cooperation between those organizations that share ownership of the reforms are seen as essential to achieve the desired long-term impacts. At the same time, special attention is given to consultation with civil society in the process of policy elaboration and to building up partnerships between interested stakeholders who share a common final objective.

Legal framework on decentralization in Bulgaria

In Bulgaria, the framework for decentralization is provided by various laws and strategies such as the Law on Local Self-Government and

Local Administration and the Local Taxes and Fees Act. The Local Self-Government and Local Administration Law of 2002 (replacing the law of 1991) regulates the relationships of local self-government and local administration.[11] It allows the municipalities to design and to implement development strategies, projects and programmes, to adopt the municipal budget and to control its implementation, to set the size of local taxes and charges within the statutory limits and to create districts and mayoralties (defined as administrative components and territorial units of municipalities) in order to perform their competences. Several provisions of law deal with the problem of the municipal finances. Thus, the Municipal Council compiles an autonomous municipal budget, separate from the Central Government Budget, on the basis of its own sources of revenue and subsides from the state.

These provisions are detailed by the Local Taxes and Fees Act,[12] which enumerates the taxes and fees collected by municipal administration and the principles determining their amount, including fairness in the determination of local fees and the creation of conditions for expanding services and improving their quality. The law does not stipulate the percentage of revenues destined to the local level but, according to a Freedom House Report on Bulgaria which used data collected from the National Association of Municipalities in the Republic of Bulgaria (NAMRB), between 7 and 10% of all tax revenues are shared with local governments (Freedom House, 2006). This makes the provision of high quality public services difficult and leaves local governments dependent on central government resources.

However, fiscal decentralization and a correspondence between the functions and responsibilities of municipalities are priorities of the *Operational Programme Administrative Capacity 2007–2013*, adopted by Bulgaria's Ministry of State Administration and Administrative Reform in March 2007.[13] According to this, in the process of implementing decentralization in Bulgaria, special attention will be paid to (i) linking the modernization of the state administration with the process of decentralization, (ii) uniting the process of decentralization of powers and functions with financial decentralization and (iii) ensuring a closer link between the process of decentralization and regional development policy, including actions strengthening the administrative and programming capacity for the absorption of EU funds at municipal and regional level.[14]

Regulation of the regional level

As concerns the regional level (the intermediate level) in both countries, regional development structures and policies have not been created as a bottom-up initiative, but as a direct result of negotiations with the EU and its politics in this field. Thus, in order to accomplish the EU requirements towards accession, Romania adopted legislation on regional development and created, in 1998, eight development regions, based on the association of neighbouring counties and named after their geographical position in the country.[15] According to the provisions of the *Law on regional development in Romania*,[16] the development region is not a territorial administrative unit and does not have a legal personality. The regions provide a framework for the conception, implementation and evaluation of regional development policies, and for collecting statistical data in accordance with EU regulations. The law enunciates the principles of subsidiarity, decentralization and partnership as being at the basis of regional development policy and the basic objectives of this policy, including the diminution of regional imbalances through the recovery of deprived areas, the avoidance of new imbalances, interregional cooperation and trans-frontier cooperation within the framework of the Euroregions. Also, it establishes other structures for regional development, including the Regional Development Council,[17] the Regional Development Agency[18] and the National Regional Development Council.[19] Romania has adopted an Operational Programme *Regional Development 2007–2013* which, together with the National Strategy of Regional Development of the National Development Plan and other sector-based programmes, aims to reduce the disparities between Romania's regions. This aim is to be achieved through providing the less developed regions with a higher financial allocation. This programme is financed from the State Budget and co-financed from the European Regional Development Fund.

Regional development in Bulgaria is regulated by the *Law on Regional Development*, which establishes six Planning Regions formed on the basis of districts depending on their geographical location, economic development, population size and prospects for development.[20] The purpose of this law is the balanced and sustainable development of Bulgaria guided by the principles of partnership, publicity and transparency at all levels of planning, financing, control and assessment. The Regional Council for Development is responsible for the implementation of policy for regional development at the level of the planning region.[21] Regional development policy is managed centrally through Regional Development Plans for each planning region (adopted by the Council of Ministers on a proposal of the Minister of Regional Development and Public Works and the Minister of Finance). These medium-term plans contain analyses of the social-economic state of the respective planning region, the main development objectives and priorities, the required actions and the indicative financial resources for achieving their objectives.

Bulgaria also adopted the *Operational Programme Regional Development 2007–2013*,[22] which incorporates the European Union priorities in the field of regional policy (especially sustainable development through strengthening growth, competitiveness and employment, social inclusion, and the protection and quality of the environment). Led by the principle of partnership and prepared in close cooperation with the European Commission, the programme proposes a set of integrated measures designed to contribute to the achievement of the long-term development goals of the country; its implementation will be financed by the structural funds from the European Union and national co-financing.

Beyond the legal framework

This brief description of the legal framework governing decentralization and regional policy shows that positive changes have been carried out in both Romania and Bulgaria, many under pressure and with the support of the EU. A legal framework regulating local autonomy, the decentralization of state power and regional development policy have been created in both countries. Also, strategic documents regarding the reform of public administration and its responsiveness to the needs of citizens have been adopted.

However, there are still steps that need to be taken to improve both legislation and implementation. As the laws and operational programmes presented previously emphasize, the concept of *administrative capacity*[23] is a central concept in the decentralization process. But the operational programmes and many other reports (including the regular reports of the European Commission) recognize the weak capacity of the institutions to implement the legislative framework. At the local level, the lack of administrative capacity is related to many factors, among them are the problem of human resources, corruption and, not least, political interference in the local public administration.

Corruption largely affects the public sector, both in Romania and Bulgaria, and the confidence of citizens in institutions.[24] Many irregularities and accusations of corruption in the management of the European Funds appeared over the last years and payments under several EU programmes were suspended in both countries. The corruption phenomenon could be, to a certain extent, related to the low level of salaries of public servants. Low pay and the weak correspondence between the level of income and the responsibilities of public servants are two of the main problems of the administrative reform. An important aspect of human resources concerns the issue of training and the necessity to enhance the qualifications and skills of civil servants with foreign language skills, computer literacy, and training for strategic planning and project development. The need for training is greatest in smaller municipalities.

Another factor related to the weak administrative capacity refers to the political interference in local public administration; this interference is high, particularly in Romania. The dependence of local communities on financial transfers from the state budget provokes a political migration of the elected mayors to the party that wins the elections at national level.[25] Also, the budgetary subordination reinforces, especially during electoral years, existing patterns of political favouritism and clientelism in the public administration.[26] Each political party tries to create an advantage for its local politicians in order to gain re-election. All these factors slow down the process of real decentralization.

As concerns the regional level, several conclusions, valid for both countries, could be derived from the brief analysis of regional policy. Firstly, regional policy is mainly managed by the central authorities and there is much reluctance to establish an additional government tier with strong regional institutions for regional development policies supported by the EU.[27] Secondly, the laws and strategies on regional development were adopted under the pressure of the EU, as a part of the *aquis communautaire* for EU accession (under Chapter 21 of the negotiations on 'Regional Policy and Coordination of the Structural Instruments'). Thirdly, the compatibility of norms in order to join the European Union (rather than the pressure from society) was the main motivation for adopting the legislation discussed here. The lack of societal expectations for such legislation could explain partially the difficulties of its implementation (see Monastiriotis, 2010).

The efficiency of the development regions and institutions remains to be demonstrated because until now these institutions have not worked very well in either Romania or Bulgaria.

Many reports, elaborated by Romanian NGOs and think tanks working on the issue of public administration, emphasized the failure of regional development policy due to weak regional institutions, their limited and unclearly defined competences and the delimitation of the eight regions without thorough research and analysis of relevant data (Institute for Public Policy, 2002). Such reports have suggested the necessity to rethink the status and the responsibilities of these institutions and even the administrative-territorial organization of Romania, as solutions for a more efficient decentralization and more effective local economic development.

Similarly, Bulgarian regional institutions have not demonstrated, until now, great efficiency in formulating and implementing regional development policy. The Councils for Regional Development are not very effective instruments for the coordination of regional policy. Being dominated by appointed representatives of the central government, these councils provide little room for representation of regional and local interests (Minkova, 2007).

In both countries, the magnitude of reforms needed at the regional level depends, beyond the adaptation of EU standards, on historical and other endogenous factors.[28] Romania and Bulgaria have to decide which the best solution is in order to improve their regional development policy performance. At least two options are possible in the future.[29] The first implies the maintenance of the established administrative system, in which the centre delegates specific planning, development, and implementation functions to the regional level and the rest remains the competence of the central authority. This strategy has not been very successful until now. The second option supposes a radical reform towards the creation of a second tier of government, with broad competence regarding regional development. It requires clear allocation of competences between the central and regional levels, clear prerogatives of each level and clear vision of the horizontal and vertical relationships among the units of power. From the perspective of political decentralization, the regional level makes sense only through the establishment of a Regional Parliament or Council, led by a president or regional governor (directly elected by citizens), and having substantial competences in programming and planning strategies and prerogatives in the field of economic and fiscal policies, including taxation.

Main challenges

Regardless of which of the two options will be chosen, there are several challenges in both countries concerning the sustainability of administrative reforms and the real transformation of the administrative system.

The main challenge for both countries seems to be the capacity to ensure an efficient implementation of the regulations and strategies. This goal could be achieved by strong management, coordination and cooperation between the institutions that share the ownership of the reforms and by building partnerships between interested stakeholders. It is important for the Government to realize the necessity of a broad partnership for good governance, including civil society organizations, the business sector and other stakeholders, as a prerequisite for creating and implementing better policies. Civil society organizations must become partners of the entire process of policy, from strategy and policy design, to policy evaluation and implementation.

The partnership principle also requires changes in the administrative culture and the modernization of the administrative apparatus. More training at all levels of administration is necessary in order to improve the competences of civil servants who are in charge of the implementation of reforms. Both Romania and Bulgaria have made progresses in recent years in improving the civil servants' qualifications, but more training is still needed to improve their skills, especially regarding foreign language skills, computer literacy and experience in working with EU funds. Given that low salary levels and lack of motivation are the main problems at both territorial and central levels of administration, it is necessary not just to increase the income levels in the state administration but also to develop methods for the evaluation of civil servants' performance and to bind their remuneration with their professional performance.

The reform of the state administration must be linked to the process of decentralization. Strengthening the administrative and financial decentralization process and monitoring the progresses of the decentralized public services should be priorities. Also, a closer link between the process of decentralization and regional development policy is necessary, including more and better-defined responsibilities for the regional institutions and other measures meant to increase the absorption of EU funds at the local and regional level.

At the same time, more efforts are needed to enhance the transparency and the accountability of public institutions and to fight against corruption. The high level of corruption in both countries affects the confidence of citizens in the institutions and the fight against it supposes, alongside with legal mechanisms and strategies, the concerted efforts of government, civil society and the business sector. Combating corruption has become a priority for the civil society organizations that monitor government policy in this field and provide anti-corruption information and educational campaigns; such efforts should be continued and improved.

Last but not least, a public and political consensus regarding the process of decentralization and regionalization is also needed, since all the aforementioned processes should be accompanied by public debates, efficient information and media campaigns in order to be effective and lead to an improved environment for the success of the decentralization process and to support local and regional development.

Notes

1. The approach of the World Bank Institute recognizes three types of administrative decentralization (op. cit.: 2–3): (1) *deconcentration* (the weakest form of decentralization, used frequently in unitary states) – the transfer of power to an administrative unit of central government (usually a regional office); (2) *delegation* – a more extensive form of administrative decentralization through which central government transfer responsibility for decision-making and management of public functions to semi-autonomous organizations not wholly controlled by the central government, but accountable to it; (3) *devolution* – a type of administrative decentralization that supposes an increased reliance on sub-national levels of government and underlines most political decentralization. It transfers responsibilities for services to local governments that have clear and legally recognized boundaries, within which they have independent authority to raise their own revenues and to make investment decisions.
2. For instance, one of dimensions by which the non-governmental organization Freedom House evaluates the progresses of democracy in transition countries refers to decentralization of powers and the measure in which local authorities exercise their powers freely and autonomously of the central government.
3. The Constitution of Romania is available at http://www.cdep.ro/pls/dic/site.page?id=371
4. The Constitution of Bulgaria is available at http://www.parliament.bg/?page=const&lng=en
5. Council of Europe, European Charter of Local Self-Government, Strasbourg, 1985, available at http://conventions.coe.int/Treaty/EN/Treaties/Html/122.htm. Considering that the right of citizens to participate in the conduct of public affairs can be most directly exercised at local level and that the existence of local authorities with real responsibilities can provide an administration which is both effective and close to the citizen, the Charter sets out the principles regarding the protection of local authorities' boundaries (Art. 5), the existence of adequate administrative structures and resources for carrying out their tasks (Art. 6), the conditions under which their responsibilities are exercised (Art. 7), the financial resources of local authorities (Art. 9) and the legal protection of local self-government (Art. 11). Briefly, all the ratifying member states have to guarantee the political, administrative and financial independence of local authorities and to recognize in domestic legislation the principle of local self-government.
6. Romania's Law 273/2006 on local public finances, published in the Official Gazette of Romania, no. 618/18 July 2006.
7. Romania's Framework law 195/2006 on decentralization, published in the Official Gazette of Romania, no. 453/25 May 2006.
8. According to Romania's Framework law on decentralization, the competences in the provision of local public services are divided into three main

categories: *exclusive competences* (mean that local public authorities have the right to decide in every aspect of the local affairs; they include public utilities, urban planning and land use, local cultural institutions, social services for elderly, management of hospitals and regional airports); *shared competences* (mean that local authorities share their responsibility towards the provision of certain services with the central level or with other levels of local public authorities; in this category are included public education through grade 12, public safety, public housing, management of crisis situations, etc.); *delegated competences* (including all services provided by the local administration, but financed by state, the local administration being, in this case, an agent of the state; in this category are included subventions for persons with disabilities and for their support personnel).

9. Romania's Ministry of Administration and Interior, Operational Programme Administrative Capacity Development 2007–2013, Official Proposal.
10. According to this document, the Phare allocations for the projects regarding Romanian public administration reform exceeded €72 million, between 2002 and 2004.
11. Bulgaria's Local Self-Government and Local Administration Law, available at http://www.urban.org/PDF/bulg_locgov.pdf
12. Bulgaria's Local Taxes and Fees Act (from 1997, as amended 2007) available at www.minfin.bg
13. Bulgaria's Ministry of State Administration and Administrative Reform, *Operational Programme Administrative Capacity, 2007–2013*, available at http://www.mdaar.government.bg/docs/en_OPAC_eng_09.03.2007.pdf.
14. Ministry of State Administration and Administrative Reform, Republic of Bulgaria, *Operational Programme Administrative Capacity, 2007–2013*.
15. These regions are North-East Region, South-East Region, South-Muntenia Region, South-West Region, West Region, North-West Region, Centre Region and Bucharest-Ilfov Region.
16. *Law 315/2004 on regional development in Romania*, published in the Official Gazette of Romania, no. 577/29 June 2004. This law replaced the former law on regional development, from 1998.
17. The Regional Development Council is a deliberative body, without legal status, established at the level of each development region, and made up of the presidents of the County Councils within the development region and a representative of the local municipal, city and communal councils from each county of the region. Among its responsibilities are to analyse and approve the regional development strategy, programmes and projects, to coordinate and support the development of regional partnerships, to approve the criteria, priorities and resources from the Regional Development Fund and to monitor the use of these funds.
18. The Regional Development Agency is a non-governmental body, non-profit, with legal personality, constituted in the framework of each development region and having as main responsibilities the following: drawing up and submission for approval to the Regional Development Council of the regional development strategy, plans and programmes and the planning for funds management; ensuring the implementation of the regional development plans; identifying and promoting, in partnerships, projects of local and regional interest and intraregional cooperation projects.

19. The National Regional Development Council is a national structure with a decisional role with regard to the elaboration and implementation the objectives of regional development policy. It has the attributions as proposing the mode of the utilization of the funds for regional development allocated to Romania by the European Union, analysing their utilization or advising the projects proposed by the Regional Development Agencies and approved by the Regional Development Councils for their financing from the regional development programmes.
20. The Planning Regions in Bulgaria are the following: North-Western Region, North-Central Region, North-Eastern Region, South-Eastern Region, South-Central Region, South-Western Region. For more details, see www.mrrb.government.bg (regional policy-menu option).
21. The Regional Councils for Development are set up in each planning region and include the representatives of certain ministries (seven members of line ministries), the district governors and one representative of a municipality from each district included in the respective planning region.
22. Bulgaria's Ministry of Regional Development and Public Works, *Operational Programme Regional Development 2007–2013*, available at www.mrrb.government.bg
23. The administrative capacity is understood as the institutional capacity of a public authority to formulate and to carry out plans, policies and other measures to fulfil public purposes; in terms of the Romanian law of decentralization, the administrative capacity means the totality of material, institutional and human resources in a administrative territorial unit, as well as the actions of this unit in exercising its competences established by law.
24. Both Romania and Bulgaria are situated on the 71st place in the *Corruption Perception Index* (2009), published by Transparency International, a report that ranks 180 countries in terms of the perceived level of public sector corruption.
25. For more details, see Dragos and Neamtu (2007). One of the most significant examples, cited in this article, is the political migration of mayors after the local elections in 2000, when the government party mayors increased from 35% in 2000 to 64.5% in 2003.
26. See Nations in Transit 2009, Romania-country report, by Alina Mungiu-Pippidi. According to this report, in 2008, just one month before the general elections, the government distributed approximately two billion lei (approximately US$ 800 million) from its reserve budgetary fund to local governments of counties and municipalities led by government party politicians. Thus, the mayors from the ruling party, 22% of the total number of mayors, received 42% of the total funds.
27. For more details in this respect, see *Progress Report on Local Democracy in Stability Pact Countries since the Zagreb Conference,* prepared by professor Gerard Marcou, after the Second South-Eastern Europe Regional Ministerial Conference on 'Effective Democratic Governance at Local and Regional Level', Skopje, 8–9 November 2006, pp. 4–7.
28. Poland is considered, in the former communist space, as a country which took radical steps towards decentralization and regionalization, based on its traditions of regional government. In Poland it's a clear correlation between development regions and the intermediate level of government (the 16

regional administration/voivods correspond to NUTS II region), territorial reform being reconciled with EU regional policy requirements and historical patterns and institutions.

29. See Minkova, op. cit., pp. 11–12.

References

Basta Fleiner, L. (1999) *Decentralisation: Key Issues, Major Trends and Future Developments*, Bern: SDC Publications on Development.

Byrne, S. (2005) 'Decentralisation and local governance in the Western Balkans: Literature review', *New Trends in Decentralisation Series*, International Research and Consulting Centre, Institute of Federalism, Fribourg.

Dragos, D. C. and Neamtu, B. (2007) 'Reforming the public administration in Romania: Trends and obstacles', *International Review of Administrative Science*.

Freedom House (2006) *Nations in Transit 2006: Democratization from Central Europe to Eurasia*, New York: Freedom House.

Institute for Public Policies (2002) *Aspects Regarding Decentralisation Process in Romania, The Administrative-Territorial Reform*, Bucharest.

Litvack, J. and Seddon, J. (eds) (1999) *Decentralisation: Briefing Notes*, Washington, DC: World Bank Institute.

Minkova, M. (2007) 'Regional policy effects of the preparation for EU accession in Bulgaria: Satisfying conditionalities or creating opportunities?' *Policy Paper*, Budapest: Local Government Initiative.

Monastiriotis, V. (2010) 'The emergence of regional policy in Bulgaria and the role of the EU', in S. Katsikas (ed.) *Bulgaria and Europe: Shifting Identities*, London: Anthem Press, pp. 173–92.

9

The Integration of Administrative and Fiscal Decentralization: The Case of Albania

Englantina Gjini

Introduction

The process of decentralization is an important element of local democracy and local development as it involves an overall effort to increase the powers and resources of the local government. The basis of this process is set out in the European Charter of Local Self-Government, which stipulates that public responsibilities ought to be carried out by authorities that are 'closest to the citizens' (CoE, 1985).[1] Decentralization relates to the fiscal, political and administrative framework in which different levels of government operate. It disperses power geographically and institutionally across different tiers of government, ideally creating more favourable circumstances for the exercise of local autonomy and greater responsiveness to local preferences.

Decentralization does not take place in vacuum; its effects depend to a great extent on its design in terms of legal and institutional arrangements and their implementation (Bardhan and Mookherjee, 2006). An effective administrative and fiscal decentralization should ensure a real devolution of power, responsibilities, financial resources and assets. It often requires capacity building within local government units (LGUs) since they need new expertise to fulfil their new responsibilities and carry out their new functions.

This chapter focuses on two main dimensions of the decentralization process in Albania – administrative decentralization and fiscal decentralization. It investigates this issue through an examination of the legal and institutional framework for decentralization in Albania, and an assessment of the challenges and trends of fiscal decentralization, and a critical review of the problems related to the implementation of decentralization. It questions whether decentralization has simply been a policy that has enjoyed the full support of the central government or whether it has been a cosmetic exercise to satisfy the requests of international donors. Finally, some policy recommendations are suggested.

The decentralization process in Albania

The first democratic changes in Albania occurred in 1992 with the transition from communist dictatorship to parliamentary democracy and in 1998, several competences and direct responsibilities were transferred to urban and rural municipalities. In 1999 the Strategy for Decentralisation and Local Autonomy set out a long-term vision for the development of LGUs in line with the European Charter, which was ratified by Albania in 1999.[2] The Strategy identified the general structure and tiers of government, the territorial divisions of local units as well as their main duties and responsibilities.[3] Further, it prescribed the steps involved in transferring duties from the central government to LGUs. The Parliament approved the Law on Territorial and Administrative Division as well as the Law on the Organization and Functioning of local government (the 'Basic Law') on 31 July 2000. The territorial reorganization led mostly to administrative fragmentation. Albania is divided into 65 municipalities and 309 communes, which represent the first tier of local government. The municipalities are grouped into 12 regions and 36+1 districts as the sub-division of the regions, which represent the second tier of local government.

Albania has an average of about 8200 inhabitants per unit of local government on the first tier. The size of communes varies considerably: all have fewer than 10,000 inhabitants, about half have fewer than 5000 inhabitants and 12 communes have less than 1000 inhabitants. The size of the municipalities also varies considerably: 55 municipalities have fewer than 25,000 inhabitants and only nine have between 25,000 and 100,000 inhabitants (INSTAT, 2004). Although the administrative division does not create a uniform size for LGUs, some duties and responsibilities linked to education, health, environmental protection, economic development, the mitigation of poverty and urban development are more effectively implemented in larger communities. Size has a substantial influence on the efficiency of local administration. In small municipalities there is a lack of human resources and few of the administrative staff have appropriate skills. The World Bank (2004) has suggested two different approaches to overcome this administrative fragmentation of LGUs. One approach would be to amalgamate the smallest communes and municipalities, while another approach would be to encourage voluntary reorganization of LGUs with financial incentives. The latter would likely be more effective as it would not require a change in the law.

The territorial reorganization was followed by the adoption of a new local government structure. The communes and municipalities were given their own decision-making power based upon elections to the commune and municipality councils and their own executive authorities in the form of the Mayor of commune or municipality. The elected mayors become automatically members of the Regional Council, which is the representative body of the region. In proportion with the number of inhabitants, there may be more than one representative from each LGU.

Communes and municipalities as legal entities have the competence to regulate and independently administer local issues within their jurisdiction, to exercise property rights, to administer their revenues independently, to implement economic activities, to collect and spend revenues which are essential for carrying out their duties and to impose local taxes and their level.

Communes and municipalities have their own functions according to the law on local government. They have full legal authority on issues of administration, services, investments and regulations respecting the national and regional policies in infrastructure and public services, in social services, in local economic development, in public order and civil defence. These competences cannot be shared with other local or central institutions.

The law clearly sets out the *shared functions* of LGUs with the central government being responsibility for the provision of pre-school and pre-university education, primary health care services, public health and environmental protection, social assistance and the mitigation of poverty. The LGUs implement delegated functions that are closely monitored and controlled by the central government.

The Regional Council, as a middle tier of local government, has the authority to draft regional policies in compliance with central government policies, to implement functions that LGUs delegate to them on the basis of mutual agreements, and to implement responsibilities delegated to them by the central government. However, these competences are not well elaborated and do not have any particular regulatory framework. The middle tier of local government has so far not found its role and has not been able to exercise its authority to any great extent. It does not have a clear electoral mandate or competences, nor any assets, funds or property of its own. It seems quite difficult to foresee how the regions will evolve in the future as the second tier of local government, or to identify the advantages they have to promote regional development. The regional councils reflect all the confusion and reservations that have arisen in the course of creating a middle tier of government. This handicap of the local self-government model makes it imperfect and not fully functional. As the World Bank has observed (2004: xi) 'establishing the regions as effective governing authorities will require a clearer assignment of their responsibilities and a commensurate degree of fiscal autonomy in order to ensure greater efficiency and accountability'. However, little has changed since these words were written almost ten years ago and it seems as if Regional Councils are becoming a redundant local government tier.

The LGUs are supervised by the institution of Prefect, which monitors the legality of their decisions and financial practices. According to the Albanian Constitution,[4] the Prefect is the representative of central government at the regional level and is appointed by the Council of Ministers. The Prefect is not accountable to the local self-government institutions, but is accountable to central government. The representatives of LGUs have expressed their criticism of the lack of influence they have over the actions taken by the Prefect. They consider that the prefect carries out too much monitoring of their budgets and the utilization of their funds, and prevents them from exercising their legal right to autonomous decision-making in relation to these funds. However, rather than being a legal or political issue, this would seem to be a question of how the Prefect exercises his or her authority.

The ministries and the other central government institutions continue to follow old regulations and behaviours that were practiced under the former centralized system of government. They continue to block initiatives that would transfer competences to LGUs. Thus central government has substantial political influence over LGUs, a feature of the system that will remain unchanged for as long as the latter have limited access to legal, administrative and monetary instruments to execute their autonomous competences.

While the LGUs should develop their own local capacities to carry out their new responsibilities effectively, it is debatable whether capacity building or the transfer of responsibilities should be the priority. The decentralization process has been adversely affected by inherited weaknesses in the skills and knowledge of staff, and from the migration of skilled professionals from rural to urban areas, or emigration abroad. However, the administrative employees of the municipalities have considerably improved their performance as the result of assistance and training offered by central government and donor organizations.

However, the employees of most communes have benefited far less as they have not been a target group of donor organizations. The administrative employees of both urban municipalities and central government are subject to the law on the civil service, while the administrative employees of the rural municipalities are excluded from this law. The rationale of this exclusion was that the implementation of the civil servant status in a small local unit would cost too much in comparison to the available local revenues. While the Inter-Ministerial Committee on Decentralisation has made some progress on this issue, it has not yet been completely resolved. The low salaries at the local level compared with those at the central level have also influenced the low quality of staff. With the aim of narrowing this gap, competitive compensation packages and salaries to attract local talent together with appropriate strategies on local human resources management should be introduced in all LGUs and not just in the larger municipalities. In order to reduce these discrepancies, unified budgetary procedures should be adopted at all levels of government, as well as in LGUs in order to managing financial resources based on clearly defined competences backed up by national training programmes on the management of local financial resources.

The adoption of the European Charter for Local Self-Government made fiscal decentralization a priority for Albania, while international donors encouraged the adoption of a legal framework for decentralization along with appropriate practices. The UNDP,[5] USAID[6] and the World Bank[7] were the lead donors in this process through different decentralization programmes and incentives, and assisted the Albanian government throughout the decentralization reform. Regardless of various shortcomings, and of the fragmented nature of the pilot programmes funded by the donors, decentralization became an indispensable part of the process of democratization and a requirement for EU integration. It is one of the main pillars of the National Strategy for Development and Integration 2007–2013 and taken into account in the Opinion of the EU Commission on Albania's application for membership of the EU (EC, 2010, 2011). Though it may have started as a 'cosmetic exercise' to meet the conditions for obtaining donors funds and investments, LGUs themselves are now forcefully requesting central government to fully transfer financial resources and responsibilities in order that LGUs may become self-sustainable and financially independent.

The process of designing and adopting laws on fiscal decentralization has taken more than ten years but the legal framework still requires further improvements. Its implementation was boosted during 2002–5 when the total local budget increased to 68 billion lek, or 10.2% of the state budget excluding welfare and healthcare funds.[8] Of this, almost half (49%) was raised from local resources. This was a major increase in comparison with 2001, when less than 27% of LGUs' resources were raised at the local level. Fiscal decentralization has significantly contributed to the improvement of quantity and quality of services provided by LGUs. During 2002–5, capital expenditure reached 42% of the total local budget, while salaries and other operational expenses were 23% and 35%. Before this, most of the budget of local government had been spent on maintenance and only 28% had been spent on investments. The increase in investment expenditure can be explained by the increased fiscal autonomy of local government. The year 2005 is considered to be the culmination of the fiscal decentralization process.

The decentralization reform process continued during 2006–9 without any change in the model. Its main developments included the decentralization of water supply, the practical application of the 'shared function' concept in education and social care, as well as improvements in other areas such as regional development, territorial planning and local government borrowing. In this four-year period, the reform of decentralization was supported by a substantial increase of local government financial capacity, mainly as the result of budgetary transfer.

In 2006–9, the total local budget reached about 129 billion lek, or 1.9 times more than that in 2002–5. The ratio of the local budget to the state budget reached 12.5%, revenues from local sources increased 1.6 times, while the state budget transfer increased 2.2 times. Although the level of the fiscal transfer to LGUs (60% of required resources) remained below that stipulated by law (88%), local expenditure on investment continued to increase. Capital expenditure increased to 47% of local budgets, while the structure of salaries and other operational expenses fell to 25% and 27% respectively of the total local budget. Additionally, local communities increased their participation in decision-making over issues of local interest.

Challenges and trends of fiscal decentralization in Albania

Fiscal decentralization is an essential and complex dimension of the decentralization reform. Every step forward has to be carefully considered. The Albanian government has adopted a policy of imposing a light fiscal burden, of providing public services at prices affordable to the citizens and of ensuring a modest share of public expenditure in GDP. Decentralization issues should be resolved in the context of this national fiscal policy stance. The key question is whether the LGUs have adequate financial resources to take over their legal functions, and how efficiently the funds are utilized. Not surprisingly, most LGUs consider their resources to be insufficient, while the central government argues otherwise.

According to the law on local budgets of 2001, a new equalization formula was applied for the transfer of grants from central government to LGUs that takes into consideration the size of population and territory, urban services and fiscal equalization based on the revenues generated from the previous budgetary year (Pigey and Hoxha, 2001). The equalization grant is unconditional, and LGUs therefore have full discretion on how the transferred resources may be used.

Unconditional transfers have increased from 2.8% to 5.5% of the total of central government revenues during the past decade, making it possible for LGUs to cover the costs of additional expenses associated with their newly delegated local administration functions. The LGUs' revenues from their own sources, including local taxes increased to half of their budget, with only half derived from central government transfers. However, the budget of medium- and small-sized LGUs is still based on conditional transfers which have, however, decreased to a rather small share of the total (around 7% by 2009) and continued to fall in 2010.

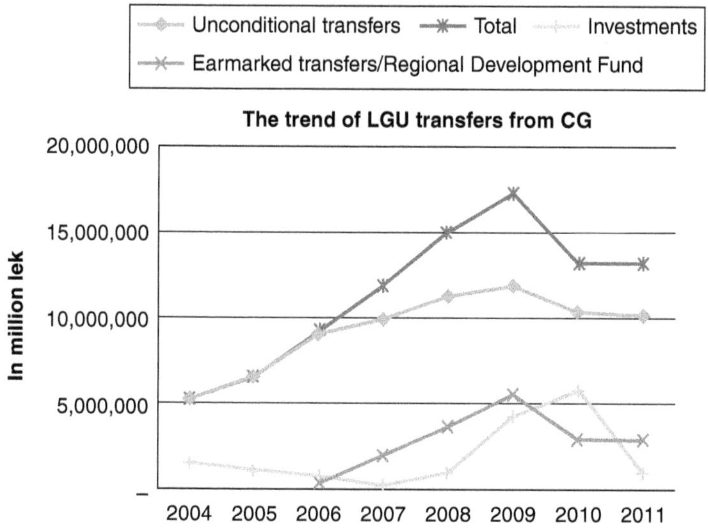

Figure 9.1 Transfers from the central government to LGUs (2004–11)
Source: Ministry of Finance Albania, 2012 (the data and the graph are elaborated by the author).

Due to the decentralization laws, LGUs now have greater fiscal and administrative autonomy, particularly related to investments. An integral part of the central government's financial support to LGUs during 2006–10 was the *competitive grant*. LGUs could apply for investment projects using the competitive grant mechanism through a central government technical committee. The total of the competitive grant fund allocated annually has increased significantly from 2.2 billion lek in 2006 to 5.5 billion lek in 2009. However, transfers for investments fell from 85% to zero in 2009 and a new scheme, the Regional Development Fund (RDF), was established in place of competitive grants in 2010. The RDF is a preparatory tool for regions and larger LGUs that was intended to build capacities for absorbing EU structural funds, as well as funds from internal and external financial markets. An inter-ministerial committee chaired by the Prime Minister has been established to monitor and supervise the funds of the RDF, while Technical Secretariats have been established in the respective line ministries in charge of examining technical and economic aspects of projects proposed by the LGUs. In addition, the process of transferring state assets from the central government to LGUs was completed in 2011. The municipal councils now have responsibility for asset management policies and priorities and for taking decisions concerning municipal assets. These competences are supervised by the Assets Management Unit of the central government.

Problems related to the implementation of decentralization

As has been pointed out before, the competitive grant has become the main means by which LGUs receive funds from the central government. This system has a number of drawbacks as the criteria and procedures for accessing funds are not transparent and are too complex for the smaller and more remote LGUs that lack capacities and skills to absorb funds. LGUs are apt to be financially fragile because of delays in the disbursement of funds from the central government. On the other hand, the scheme established by the RDF regarding the competitive grant allocation remains unclear and politically implicated since it is chaired by the Prime Minister and other senior politicians. The high political level representation on the evaluation committee – deputy ministers of the Ministry of Finance, Ministry of Integration and other line ministries – inevitably politicizes the evaluation process and introduces the possibility of discrimination against municipalities governed by opposition parties.

A further problem arises from the change to the tax law adopted in 2009, which restricts the amount of municipal taxes and tariffs that

LGUs can charge small businesses, which confirms the confusion in the central decision-making process that inhibits effective local decentralization and local democracy (Pigey et al., 2002). The Ministry of Finance has justified the change to the tax law as a step to protect small business from the economic crisis, to reduce fiscal evasion and to stimulate an increase in local revenues through more effective management of other municipal taxes and tariffs collection. Yet, other ways could be found to avoid the risk of an abusive increase of tariffs by LGUs. The revised local tax law was contested on the basis that it was approved without consulting interested parties or the international donors who provide support to the decentralization process. The revised law had a negative impact on the own revenues of LGUs which fell by 10–40% in 2009. In September 2009, an additional amendment to the law was adopted through which the tax for 'infrastructure impact' for all unauthorized buildings in the process of legalization was reduced to 0.5% of their investment value. Previously, the tax had amounted to 1–3% for all municipalities other than Tirana where the rate was set at 2–4%. This change considerably reduced the budgets of the LGUs and their borrowing capacities, and consequently it reduced the funds available for local investment, capital investment plans and LGUs' ability to implement strategic plans. It hampers the collection of local taxes making it difficult for LGUs to cover the costs of services through tariffs due to the elimination of the link between tariffs and the cost of service provision. It has undermined the fiscal autonomy of LGUs, which has reverted to the level before 2005 and has challenged the donors engaged in decentralization and local government financing issues.

Local tax offices face additional difficulties in collecting the tax on small business since small firms do not keep accounting records or cash registers. This additionally suggests that LGUs need more and better-qualified staff in order to successfully advance the decentralization process.

The lack of sufficient funds hinders the effective implementation of projects and policies, and leads to ineffective distribution of financial resources at the local level. As a consequence, the Ministry of Finance justifies the supervisory role of central government over LGUs finances, which goes against the law on local government as well as the aims of the decentralization strategy.

Several positive examples of decentralization reforms can be identified such as transfer of water supply and sewage functions to the LGUs, which took place from 2003 onwards. However, the management of these functions is inefficient and the revenues generated cannot cover the costs. In contrast, the decentralization process has been less

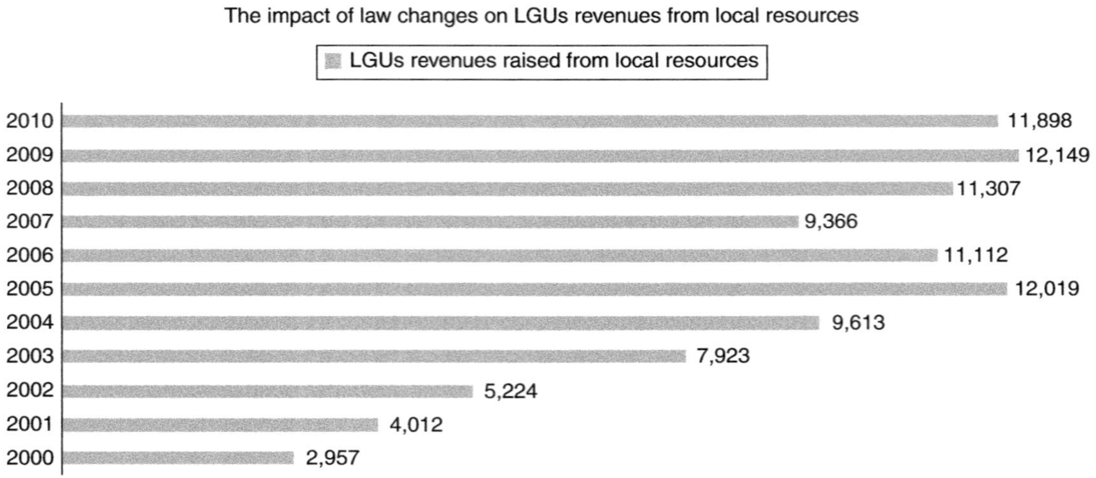

Figure 9.2 The revenues of LGUs from local sources (2000–10)
Source: Ministry of Finance Albania, 2012 (the data and the graph are elaborated by the author).

successful in education, social care and social assistance and in civil protection functions. A clear definition of these shared functions, as well as of the role of LGUs themselves, is still needed.

Furthermore, the transfer and registration of public assets has stagnated, hindering the transfer of responsibilities and functions. From one point of view, the restrictions set by the central government unify the use of public assets by LGUs; however, from another point of view they prevent LGUs on using these assets for local needs.

Finally, in order to proceed with further implementation of decentralization in a timely and responsive manner, political consensus through intergovernmental dialogue on decentralization will be of fundamental importance. Since the Democratic Party came to power in 2005, the opposition Socialist Party has almost abandoned the Parliament, blocking the adoption of several important acts, amendments and laws that would accelerate the fiscal decentralization process and break down bipartisan cooperation within the Albanian Association of Municipalities and Communes. The LGUs led by the opposition parties have established a separate municipality and commune association.

Conclusions

Decentralization has been a major policy aim of successive governments, and has been encouraged by international donor organizations and institutions often within the framework of conditionality related to financial and political support. Despite the progress that has been made in creating a legal framework for decentralization, in practice the implementation of the laws still faces many obstacles. The existing arrangements for fiscal decentralization are unlikely to increase local revenues since many restrictions are placed on the ability of LGUs to raise local taxes and user charges. Moreover, the vague procedure of applying for funds from the RDF suggests that the allocation of funds might be politicized, further limiting the fiscal autonomy of LGUs. In addition, LGUs have limited resources to carry out public investments for the development of their communities. Even the funds that had been originally allocated for public works and infrastructure investment are often used to cover budget deficits. Consequently, few LGUs can provide effective basic services such as waste management.

In its budgetary policies for 2010–11, the Ministry of Finance made a commitment to allow LGUs to borrow funds for local infrastructure development. However, in practice it is doing the opposite by placing limits on the ability of LGUs to raise their own funds and by requiring that LGUs have ministerial approval before raising funds in the form of loans for investment projects. The Ministry is understandably cautious because it is concerned about the possible adverse impact on macroeconomic stability if LGUs borrow in an uncontrolled manner and pile up debts. However, there are concerns that this caution is directed unfairly at large municipalities aligned with political opposition. Unfortunately, the political rivalry between the two main political parties at the national level has led to strained relations between the central government institutions and opposition-led LGUs.

In spite of the observed problems and difficulties, the decentralization reforms should continue. This is not only a local issue, but also an important aspect of the democratic transformation of the state as a whole. All interest groups, whether public or private, national or local, should be acknowledged through an approach based on solidarity. A constructive and professional dialogue among all interested actors would facilitate the completion of the decentralization process based on appropriate standards and transparency, rather than being simply a cosmetic exercise aimed to fulfil conditions imposed by international donors.

Notes

1. The Charter was ratified by Albania in 2000. Albanian Legislation is in full compliance with 22 important paragraphs of the European Charter of Local Autonomy. Of these, at least 12 are from the group of essential paragraphs.
2. Law no. 8548, dated 11 November 1999, 'On the ratification of the European Charter of Local Self-government'.
3. Several studies have outlined the process of decentralization in Albania: see Hoxha (2001, 2002), Hoxha, Dhimitri and Pigey (2002), Hoxha and Dhimitri (2006), Pigey and Hoxha (2001), Pigey, Hoxha and Ymeri (2008), Schroeder (2004).
4. The Constitution was approved by the Albanian Parliament on 21 October 1998.
5. UNDP has delivered US$41,964,301 for the period 2004–11. It allocated US$5 million for Local Governance Programme piloted in three regions and nine communes/municipalities in 2002–5 and US$4,795,222 for Art Gold Albania program in 2006–9.
6. USAID has delivered over US$500 million in foreign aid to support Albania's development, stability and integration into Europe in 1992–2012; and Only Local Governance Program in Albania piloted by USAID in ten municipalities is estimated at US$7.3 million for 2007–12.
7. The World Bank has financed 69 projects in different sectors totalling over US$1.4 billion during 1992–2011.
8. Personal communication with A. Hoxha, analyst for economic issues in Albania and Director of Institute for Contemporary Studies (ISB), 28 April 2010.

References

Bardhan, P. and Mookherjee, D. (eds) (2006) *Decentralisation and Local Governance in Developing Countries: A Comparative Perspective*, Cambridge: MIT Press.

CoE (1985) *European Charter of Local Self-Government*, Strasbourg: Council of Europe.

European Commission (2010) *Commission Opinion on Albania's application for membership of the Europen Union*, Brussels: EC.

European Commission (2011) *Commission Staff Working Paper, Albania 2011 Progress Report*, Brussels: EC.

Hoxha, A. (2001) 'Local government in Albania', in E. Kandeva (ed.) *Stabilization of Local Governments*, Budapest: Open Society Institute, pp. 41–88.

Hoxha, A. (2002) *Local Self-Government and Decentralisation – Case of Albania: History, Reforms and Challenges*, Tirana: Institute for Contemporary Studies.

Hoxha, A. and Dhimitri, J. (2006) 'Fiscal decentralisation in SEE countries, the case of Albania', *Stability Pact Conference*, Tirana, 30 September.

Hoxha, A., Dhimitri, J. and Pigey, J. (2002) *Albania, Local Tax and Fee System: Policy Options and Recommendations*, Urban Institute & Institute for Contemporary Studies, Washington, DC: USAID.

INSTAT (2004) *The Population of Albania: Gjirokastër 2001*, Tirana: Institute of Statistics.

Pigey, J. and Hoxha. A. (2001) *Albania Unconditional Transfers for Local Government and Objective Formula for Distribution*, Washington, DC: Urban Institute.

Pigey, J., Hoxha, A., Dervishi, P. and Dhimitri, J. (2002) *Albania: Analysis of Small Business Tax and Implications of Transfer to Local Governments – Policy Options and Recommendations*, Urban Institute & Institute for Contemporary Studies, Washington, DC: USAID.

Pigey, J. H., Hoxha, A. and Ymeri, S. (2008) 'Albania: Decentralization and local government finance – key successes and future challenges', in Z. Sevic (ed.) *Local Public Finance in Central and Eastern Europe*, Cheltenham: Edward Elgar, pp. 26–49.

Schroeder, L. (2004) *Albania: Fiscal Decentralisation Policy Study*, The Urban Institute & Institute for Public Administration, Washington, DC: USAID.

World Bank (2004) *Albania: Decentralisation in Transition*, Report No. 27885-ALB, Washington, DC: World Bank, Poverty Reduction and Economic Management Unit Europe and Central Asia Unit.

10
The Role of the Third Sector in Providing Social Services at the Local Level in Transitional Serbia

Marija Kolin

Introduction: Changes and challenges

The last 12 years of economic transition and social sector reforms in Serbia[1] have been focusing on modernization of the social welfare system and restructuring of the inherited 'paternalistic' concept of social welfare, where the welfare mix within which public, non-profit, non-governmental organizations (NGO) and private partners' operation is strongly encouraged. The main aims of reform in this area are in building an efficient social protection system and the further creation of new legislation in accordance with European Union (EU) standards. The new approach to policy planning is fostered by the Poverty Reduction Strategy Programme (PRSP), accepted by the Serbian government in 2003 as part of a joint effort of the national government, the UNDP, the World Bank, the International Monetary Fund and other international players active in Serbia (GoS, 2007). The PRSP started to promote a new concept for the alleviation of poverty and unemployment, but also underlined directions for systematic changes covering the spectrum of social policy reforms in which government, market and third sector have to act in an effective partnership.

Following the new European trend in social policy the third sector organizations are becoming integrated partners of governmental organizations as recognized by important national strategies that legitimize their role in the planning and implementation of policy as well as a significant actor in providing social services. At the beginning of this process, the Social Innovation Fund (SIF) has been established by the Ministry of Labour and Social Policy (MLSP) designed to promote the welfare mix concept, protect the most vulnerable groups of society, foster social dialogue and support reform projects in different areas of social welfare. The Ministry is a partner in EU/UNDP's funds-supported SIF which has been responsible for around 300 projects in local communities of Serbia dealing with different social problems such as those supporting children and youth welfare, organizing day care centres, home care for the elderly, clubs for pensioners, providing services for the disabled and other programmes fostering social cohesion at the local level. The most important documents initiated by the MLSP, such as the Strategy for the Development of Social Policy (2005) and the National Strategy for Aging (2006)[2] largely concentrate on the improvement of alternative social welfare programmes which would support day care centres, at-home social care, and programmes strengthening partnership and social cohesion at the local level.

Nevertheless, the described process of reform did not have a significant positive impact on people's well-being and the discrepancy between the proclaimed objectives and reality is one of the major characteristics in all important domains. It can be said that centralization of social policy is still a major problem that decreases the effectiveness of proposed actions for welfare services provision. The central government is still the key player and responsible body in defining the regulatory framework by passing strategy programmes, addressing legal issues and providing a budget for the core network of institutions (Bajec et al., 2008; Kolin, 2009). The main problem is that underdeveloped regions have no financial means for appropriate social protection and community care, considering day care service centres, field visits of the vulnerable, due to the deficiencies in financial resources and poor professional capacities for organization of community programmes. The analysis in this chapter seeks to identify and explain the variety of third sector entities focusing on organizations that are service providers and give a more detailed insight into the structure of the existing social services provision entities, their functions and activities, as well as the main populations served.

Disparities in regional and rural–urban development

The economic collapse of the 1990s, as a consequence of wars in the region, constant macroeconomic instability and distortions (hyperinflation in 1993–4), UN sanctions, and the NATO bombing of 1999 in the end have had a catastrophic impact on the regional economy and population in Serbia. This has resulted in low levels of economic activity and the emergence of regional disparities within Serbia. The gap between the more and less developed regions – that to a great extent is derived from the process of previous socialist industrialization and urbanization, often characterized by irrational regional arrangement of business activities on the ground of political decisions and sustained economic allocation of industrial enterprises – has continued to widen during the transition process. Disparity between the most developed region, the City of Belgrade, and the least developed one in South Serbia in 2005, measured by per capita income, was 6.8:1 (Bajec et al., 2008). Underdevelopment is evidenced by the demographic depletion of a number of regions, high unemployment rates and agricultural production of small scale, outdated technology and rural poverty. According to the Second Progress Report of the Implementation on the PRSP in Serbia, regional disparities are 1:7 at the district level and 1:17 at the municipal level. The same source argued that the population of rural areas is 2.5 times poorer that the city population and it is even worse as regards physical and social infrastructure (GoS, 2007). The region with the largest share of poor is Central Serbia or the Jablanicki region in South Serbia sub-region.[3] The poverty risk in this region is 21.6% higher than the average poverty risk of Serbia's population of 10.7%.[4] Regional differences in the unemployment rate are also high. According to the last data provided by the National Employment Service, the lowest unemployment rates are in Belgrade (13.5%) and Novi Sad (17%), while unemployment is the highest in Novi Pazar (51%) and Loznica (41.5%). The national unemployment rate (22% in 2010) is among the highest in the region and considerably higher than in the EU.

Poverty in Serbia has become a rural phenomenon, as in the majority of other transitional countries. Although the share of urban population in Serbia has been growing continuously, according to the number of inhabitants living in non-urban settlements, it seems that Serbia is still one of the most rural countries in Europe when approximately 55% of the total population in Serbia are living in smaller settlements. The rural population is significantly poorer than the urban population since the poverty index of the rural population is almost twice as high as the poverty index of the urban population. Various causes have contributed to the considerable differences among rural and urban areas. This can be partially explained by the fact that the growth of employees' earning and pensions, which represent a dominant source of income of the urban population, was relatively higher than the growth of other income sources (GoS, 2007).

The rising trend of regional and urban–non-urban differences has been affected by the financial crisis as it is concluded by the recent report of the Matkovic, Mijatovic and Petrovic (2010). According to these estimates the incidence of poverty increased quite rapidly in Central Serbia while non-urban areas of Serbia have experienced higher poverty risks during the crisis period, and the overall increase of poverty actually occurred in these areas. The rising trend in poverty has particularly affected population younger than 15 and the uneducated.

In recent years the reduction of regional disparities and improvement of rural quality of life has been one of the most important topics for policymakers and politicians. The absence of an institutional framework for a more balanced regional development resulted in the adoption of a new legal framework and strategies to improve and harmonize public administration legislation and practice. The most important event in the domain of local self-government was the adoption of the Law of the Local Self-Government on 2002 and the Law on Financing Local Self-Government,[5] which came into force at the beginning of 2007. In addition, the Government of Serbia established the Ministry of State Administration and Local Self-Government to address current decentralization issues. Since the beginning of 2007 municipalities have developed strategic documents (almost all of 167 municipalities in Serbia) and started to govern local institutions in education, health and social welfare. In the context of European integration, policy has considered specifically the decentralization experiences in EU countries and the wider European patterns of local government. The Ministry of Economy and Regional Development has started the preparation for developing a ten-year National Plan for Regional Development in accordance with the Law on Regional Development. Recently the Ministry of Economy and Regional Development established a National Agency for Regional Development supported by the Enterprise Europe Network to realize EU projects at the local level aiming at improving infrastructure, social capital and entrepreneurship. Besides, important strategies aiming at the removal of regional disparities and improvement of rural quality of life have been adopted, such as the National Strategy of Economic Development of Serbia for the period 2006–12, the Strategy of Regional Development of Serbia for 2007–12 and the Agriculture Development Strategy 2007. There is more emphasis on social inclusion and prevention of social exclusion in the recent period. The transition from the concept of poverty reduction to that of social inclusion is driven by the commitment of the government to finalize the European-integration process and harmonize with EU policies aiming at more effective targeting of social cohesion.

Beside recent efforts for more balanced regional policies, decentralization remains one of the most important issues for further improvement of the administrative capacity of local and regional development according to EU regional policy. In reality, uneven regional and rural–urban development is one of the most serious problems reflected at the community infrastructure, welfare policy and quality in provision of social services at the local level. One of the main difficulties is that underdeveloped regions have no financial means for appropriate social protection and community care, due to the deficiencies in financial resources and poor professional capacities for organization of community programmes. Decentralization of the social care and reforms for improving efficiency and active participation of the beneficiaries remain the key challenges for the near future.

Key features of the third sector

It is almost impossible to talk about the numbers and types of Serbian civil society organizations that have emerged as part of the third sector in Serbia. The problem is that the wide spectrum of civil society initiatives is not recorded by reliable statistics regarding their number, types and regional distribution. If we start with the official statistics, which are unreliable, about 20,000–25,000 civil associations are registered in Serbia as citizens' associations in accordance to the Law on Associations of 1989.[6] The third sector database provided by the Centre for Non-Profit Sector Development (CRNPS), a think tank organization established in 1996 by the Soros Foundation in order to support the building of autonomous civil organizations in Serbia, shows that only some of them – that is around 2000–3000 autonomous NGOs – were registered at the CRNPS Directory by 2005.

There is a wide diversity of what makes up the third sector and the relationship between the government and third sector reflects this diversity. Among various NGOs active in diverse fields, including education, culture, science, arts and ecological groups, local community development, and human rights organizations, there are 300–400 welfare organizations dealing with the provision of social services. In a situation of limited local funds, the role of the international community and civil organizations has been decisive for the provision of community care in Serbia through the network of NGOs which provide support to the elderly, sick persons, victims of violence, disabled and other marginalized social groups. This segment of NGOs has been providing various kinds of psychosocial assistance, legal aid, counselling, occupational therapy, job-creation activities, advocacy, and other supplemental and innovative programmes.

Due to the increasing number of elderly people and limited resources of governmental institutions to meet the corresponding needs, various third sector actors have started to provide *welfare services to the elderly* engaged in providing help at home and offering visiting services, transport, some kind of training for care workers, psychological support and recreation. A study by the Gerontology Association of Serbia (Dinic et al., 2008) documented that 68 third sector actors are active in providing some kind of help, advocacy, psychosocial assistance, education or services for the elderly. The most active is Humana's network established 2004 which now associates 15 non-profit and religious groups.[7] The study estimates that civil society actors provide home care for 27,720 elderly beneficiaries.

Women's NGOs have established a range of services and activities aimed at supporting survivors of gender-based violence within the last 15 years, and most of them are specialized in domestic violence, sexual violence, trafficking and sexual harassment. Their activities transcend service provision and range from basic awareness-raising programmes to creating a tangible policy and legislative changes through drafting legislation, monitoring state policy, organizing training and specialized services. According to a recent qualitative study that covered 37 NGOs dealing with gender-based violence (Brankovic, 2009), there are around 50 NGOs providing various types of support to all victimized and marginalized persons (domestic violence, violence at the workplace, trafficking, other violent crimes, robbery, etc.).[8] The study showed a high level of expertise and capacity of this network. Considering the geographical distribution of services, the findings of the survey pointed out that shelter services (primarily shelters for victims of domestic violence) are highly concentrated in Belgrade, while NGO-run hotlines and counselling centres are more or less evenly geographically distributed across Serbia.

Self-help groups for persons with disabilities are composed of well-organized traditional segments of civil associations focused on the handicapped population (blind, deaf, mentally retarded, paraplegics, disabled veterans). Some of these NGOs are newly established, like the Association of the Students with Disabilities in Novi Sad or the Centre for Independent Living in Belgrade, which are organized on a cross-disability principle. There are also a great number of pre-transition segments of the third sector which, like in other East-Central European countries, are composed of self-organized groups of handicapped people financially supported by the government. The vast majority of these organizations were established in the 1970s with the main task to implement supplementary services (recreation and sports). In the 1990s this segment of NGOs had a very important role in providing technical help and equipment (medicine, sanitarian help and wheelchairs) and their activities were important for many categories of disabled people. At the end of the decade some of them tried to reform themselves and build capacity by providing social services or more extensive services, such as the self-employment programmes and other activities in order to integrate people with mental or social handicap into active life.

Religious groups that provide social services to the elderly, sick or other disadvantaged groups registered according to the Law on Associations of 1989 or the Law on Churches and Religious Communities of 2006 could be considered as a specific type of third sector service-providing organization. The renaissance of religious groups in Serbia started during the 1990s when many renewed their programmes after several decades by providing direct relief and support to war victims. A key task of these organizations has been the distribution of humanitarian aid provided by numerous international organizations. After the democratic changes of 2000, religious groups started to provide social services, in particular to vulnerable and marginalized groups organized at the local level. Generally, religious networks consist of 30–50 medium-sized NGOs, operating in Belgrade or regional centres such as Niš, Uzice or Novi Sad. The elderly population forms the main beneficiary group of these religious organizations: they receive assistance ranging from nursing and medical treatment to nutrition, food provision and home assistance. Chronically sick individuals with weak family support are also supported by religious groups because many became extremely marginalized during the transition. Caritas is the biggest religious network in Serbia supported by international welfare organizations of the Catholic Church. Philanthropy, the humanitarian organization of the Serbian Orthodox Church, is one of the most influential religious groups involved in providing services for the elderly and sick. HEKS (Swiss Interchurch Aid) supports the ecumenical aid organization and EHO in Novi Sad with the development of social welfare services for the elderly and sick.

In recent years the *Serbian Red Cross* started offering programmes for the elderly, implementing home care, psychosocial support and other programmes. The Amity Report (2007) documented that the national Red Cross network covers around 10,000 elderly beneficiaries with service provision at the local level.

Social enterprises are the new third sector actors that could also be organized to provide services, improve quality of life and increase social integration at the community level. A range of social and economic criteria of social enterprises, known collectively as the EMES criteria,[9] have been identified to define social cooperatives and social enterprises that are predominantly involved in providing services to the community. A closer look at the Serbian social enterprise development shows that the following forms of organizations correspond to the concept of social cooperatives: associations of citizens, cooperatives and vocational enterprises for persons with disabilities (Kolin and Petrušić, 2008; Les and Kolin, 2009). Registered according to the 1989 and 2009 Law on Association of Citizens and 1996 Cooperative Law, these actors often deal with providing services to the disabled and other vulnerable groups. Beside the number of cooperatives which are mostly inherited from the past period, there are around 100–200 newly established cooperatives which represent innovative social enterprises created to integrate extremely marginalized groups of persons with disabilities or providing help to elderly and the sick persons.

Various forms of enterprises for the *vocational training and employment of persons with disabilities* registered under the Law on Enterprises for Vocational Training and Employment of Persons with Disabilities of 1996 and 2009 could also satisfy the social enterprise definition. Their activities promote social integration through job creation, micro-projects, self-employment and other types of activities fostering an enterprising atmosphere and supporting people with disabilities. According to evidence provided by the MLSP, 52 enterprises for the vocational training and employment of people with disabilities, primarily disabilities with work-related causes, were organized by 2006.

The regulatory framework for welfare provision

The currently applied concept of social protection in Serbia is not essentially different from the classic socialist welfare system developed before 1989. At the formal level, the social welfare system rests on the Law on Social Protection and Social Security of Citizens, adopted in 1991 (amended several times since then). It is characterized by a centralized approach in planning residential capacities, alongside insufficient resources at the local level that do not correspond to the real needs of the beneficiaries.[10] The main stakeholder in social protection at the central level is the MLSP, while local governments, Centres for Social Work (CSW) and public social welfare institutions that provide temporary or permanent accommodation to adults and children are the main stakeholders at the local level.

The majority of responsibilities for determining rights and decision-making on the way they will be realized and the necessary resources which are relevant for welfare users are concentrated at the level of the central government. Although much of the welfare programmes are centralized, some of them are decentralized and regulated by the Law on Local Self-Government, which referred on the significant role of local community in social protection provision and also welfare services and money transfers.[11] According to the appropriate document – Decision for Social Protection which determines the level of social welfare provided by the local communities – municipalities have to provide money transfers for urgent needs (for medical supplies, food, heating), home assistance, day care centres, shelters for homeless people, funeral reimbursements for the poor and 'soup kitchens'. The local government also has to support clubs for the elderly and other institutions that are organized at the local level with the objective to provide psychosocial support for the vulnerable groups of the local community.

The network of the CSW is the most important governmental institutions that regulates services and provision and also coordinates among providers. The whole country is covered by the CSW network that is well developed in each municipality (135 units: some municipalities have organized CSW or branch office) with multidisciplinary professionals in social work. On a practical level, the prime difficulties are connected with professional capacity and related skills, deficiencies in management capacities, the frequent changes in regulations and shortcomings of evidence-based policy to handle policy at different levels of implementation. With the exception of the top ministries, analytical skills are missing throughout all other levels of the social sector's administration. The core professionals have an official education but are often resistant of innovations, professionally unmotivated with poor salaries, providing more money transfers and accommodation than social services, field visit or other programmes which would be more appropriate to meet the needs of beneficiaries (Kolin, 2009).

The Law on Social Protection and Social Security of Citizens defines local self-government and municipalities as responsible bodies for the social protection programmes, and specifies two options in providing community care services: home care and day care centres. These schemes are regulated by MLSP and have to be provided in the domain of social protection of citizens in the local communities. This type of home care is provided on a means-tested procedure, while participation of the users and contribution of relatives is different in each community, depending on income and family status. The local government is also responsible to support clubs for the elderly that are organized at the local level to provide psychosocial support and recreation. It is estimated that 18,000 elderly persons are beneficiaries of the care at home or they are covered by the clubs for the elderly organized at local community level. These programmes are organized by the CSW and provided by the MLSP and local governments in Serbia.

Community Care (*kućna pomoć i nega*) could be provided as a health treatment by the network of health centres through Serbia and specialized health institutions – Institute for Gerontology, Home Treatment and Care – which cover only Belgrade, supported by the Ministry of Health. According to the recent study on the long-term protection of the elderly (Kolin, 2011) this institution provides health treatment and help at home without a means-tested procedure, and depends on the health status of the capital's beneficiaries. Respective authorities claimed that around 1500 beneficiaries per day in Belgrade are covered by the whole range of health services at home provided by multidisciplinary medical staff. A detailed analysis of the same study shows that the network of health centres throughout the country provides home treatment for needing beneficiaries according to their health status. Health care service provision is also inherited from the socialist system of social policy. New private arrangements and agencies have flourished in order to organize health services for the sick and elderly at home. One of the well known is ARWEN established in Belgrade, but the private services are expensive for most of the vulnerable with average income.

Various causes have contributed to the poor development of social services but shortages in financial means for social welfare provision and the low share of spending for different money transfers is the main reason for inefficient services. The PRSP Second Report (GoS, 2007) provides figures about public expenditure of GDP for social welfare from which it is clear that total spending is relatively high (14.5% share of total GDP) but the great share of this amount is spent on the provision of pensions and other money transfers, while the social welfare share is only 3.7%. The biggest share of GDP, which currently amounts around US$3300 per capita, concerns spending on Family Material Support (MOP or *materijalno obezbedjenje porodice*) as the most efficient social welfare programme in the country which is provided as a money transfer for poor families. According to the PRSP estimates this measure of social protection is at present untargeted (only 3% of poor families in 2005) and provided at the low level of compensation (around €50 per family).

Respective authorities and proclaimed strategies claimed that the whole range of services should be provided at the community level as the local government's responsibility, but still a significant number of municipalities does not have capacities for social policy implementation due to missing funds and lack of appropriate programmes and services at the same time and local self-governments not having enough autonomy, and neither is interested in fulfilling citizens' needs through the development of a wide range of community-based services. According to relevant research data only 2% of municipal budgets are on average spent on social protection at the local community level, while the level of spending is different across the country. The same source reported that only 39 municipalities (out of 167 municipalities in Serbia) provide home care services for the elderly (Amity Report, 2007). The majority of these programmes are implemented in big cities and regional centres with large variations in their service levels depending on the regional and rural–urban settings (the highest budget spending is in Belgrade with 2.8%).

Cash compensation for help – Payment for Care (*novčana naknada za pomoć i negu drugog lica*) is a benefit granted to a person who is incapable of fulfilling basic needs (cannot dress, feed, walk without help of the other person) while the level of the payment depends on the national average income (40% of the average income).

It should be mentioned that the Payment for Care is one of the benefit schemes inherited from socialism which continues to represent the most important welfare programme to the elderly and disabled, provided according to the Law on Social Protection and Social Security and the Law on Pension and Invalidity Insurance. This benefit is provided as a cash transfer to recipients, without a means-tested procedure, and the average level is €55 per person per month. This kind of help depends on health status and family structure, so that the elderly with the most difficult health problems are beneficiaries of the scheme, while the majority of them are immobile and 'older-old', sick persons.

The Payment for Care is provided by the MLSP and pension insurance programme and covers the whole country. If the beneficiary is out of the pension insurance scheme then he or she can be a recipient of this benefit if they are recommended by the CSW. In that case provision depends not only on health status but also on family status under a means-tested procedure. This money transfer is very important for the sustainability of family care – that is, for the provision of home care although there is no regulation about how this money should be used. The mentioned scheme is provided for the whole country through social welfare institutions and pension insurance network. Taken as a whole, €16.8 million per year is spent for this benefit which currently receives 63,000 users, the majority of whom are the elderly according to the MLSP.

A centralized approach in planning residential capacities and financing rights, alongside insufficient resources at the local level has created a bungling network of institutions that does not respond to the real needs of the beneficiaries and does not provide adequate services. Broadly defined and applied rights to residential accommodation, along with underdeveloped community-based services, have led to an institutional isolation of many beneficiaries whose needs would be better fulfilled through other types of services. Due to insufficiently developed foster care and unequal coverage, children without parental care and those with disabilities have often been placed in institutions. Beside significant improvement in fostering deinstitutionalization, 800 children without parental care are accommodated in these institutions, while 4700 are in foster family placement, according to MLSP. Children remain in institutions for long, whereas services provided in social welfare (residential) institutions are incomplete and do not empower them for independent living. Children with disabilities placed in five residential institutions are particularly vulnerable. They usually spend their entire life in an institution, so institutions that were originally meant for children with disabilities gradually became institutions for the accommodation of adults as well. These institutions are characterized by a large number of beneficiaries (from 300 to 650), children and adults ages from four to 50, even older, which exceeds the number prescribed by existing norms and standards. The facilities are in poor condition, the staff structure prescribed by norms is inadequate, and carers are insufficiently trained for the application of contemporary work methods.

Conclusion

Following the European integration process, the Serbian government has recognized and legitimized the role of civil society and NGOs, in particular those providing social services at the local level. It is estimated that such service-provider organizations fill the welfare gap that emerged from shrinking public welfare programmes. The evidence shows that NGOs are an additional or supplemental actor in the provision of services, while a classical welfare strategy with state responsibility remains the dominant welfare state regime. International organizations and donors are a key innovator and driving force in building the new welfare structure in different fields of social policy – health, education, social welfare, employment and environment. TACSO (2010) recently estimated that civil society in Serbia remains overly dependent on international donors and suggested that as much as 75% of all NGO funding in Serbia is from foreign sources. The various programmes and instruments through which EU supports NGOs and their activities represent the largest single source of civil sector funding (CARDS, IPA, Civil Society Facility and other EU funding forms).

The analysis showed that a regional disparity within Serbia and centralization of social policy still decreases the effectiveness of proposed actions for welfare services' provision. The gap between the more developed and less developed regions has continued to widen during the transition process and Southern Serbia is one of the most economically disadvantaged areas. As the population in Belgrade, Vojvodina and urban centres has greater accessibility to social services than the population living in Southern Serbia and non-urban areas, the following issues emerge as key problems: low level of contracting-out of services, underpaid or poorly paid public contracts, emerging shortage of skilful leaders for social enterprises/work-integration social enterprises, chronic financial instabilities on the part of social enterprises, including a lack of funds for running services, incomplete and unstable legal and fiscal frameworks, and other reasons.

Decentralization of social care and reforms for improving efficiency and active participation of civil society is increasingly high on the policy agenda in Serbia. The main intentions of the new decentralization trend of social welfare focuses on the development of a greater variety of more feasible local services for the beneficiaries at the local community level which would depend on local needs assessments and on the sustainability of programmes. Strengthening the local potential in the service-oriented welfare system, promoting new, alternative and community-financing services through community foundations, partnership and third sector funds and the development of innovative local financial institutions supporting the third sector, among other measures will require greater attention from policymakers and service providers.

Notes

1. Following the dissolution of Yugoslavia, the Republic of Serbia consists of about 7.3 million people with around two million living in the capital Belgrade.
2. Available at http://www.minrzs.gov.rs/cir/index/php.option.com
3. The PRSP project considers Serbia divided into Vojvodina, Central Serbia and Belgrade. The problem is that Serbia is not administratively regionally divided. Serbia is officially divided into 24 districts and the city of Belgrade.
4. The persons considered to be under the absolute poverty line live below the minimum required for food and other expenses according to the Living Standard Measurement Survey conducted by the Republic Statistics Office.

5. Official Gazette of the Republic of Serbia No. 9/2002, No. 33/2004 and No. 62/06. These laws introduced a number of changes in extended municipal competences and limited central government control. The Law of Financing Local Self-Government prescribes stabilization of the scope of transfers and more equal income disbursement; authorizes local self-government to establish the tax rate and collect the property tax; and introduces other innovations important for local social and economic development.
6. The legislation under which 'modern' NGOs operated in the last two decades basically comes from the communist period. The new Law on Associations has been accepted on 2009 in accordance with European standards and best international practices, creating a supporting environment for NGOs and other civil organizations. In other areas of law, particularly those concerning tax and fiscal measures, the law is treating NGOs as if they were profit-making enterprises.
7. The study argued that, among others, the Red Cross provided social services for 10,000 elderly, the Caritas network for 2700 beneficiaries, the NGO Amity for 2500 beneficiaries and the Association for Judah Community for 600 beneficiaries.
8. Among the NGOs providing gender-based activities are Autonomous Women's Centre, Belgrade; Legal Clinic, Niš; Women's Network, Smederevo; Women's Alternative Workshop, Kikinda; SOS Helpline for Women and Children Victims of Violence, Grocka; Centre for Girls, Belgrade; and many others across the country.
9. EMES is a research network of established university research centres sponsored by the EU to study the third sector and social economy, solidarity-based economy and social enterprises. Social enterprises consist of organizations that have developed between the market and the state to pursue social and economic goals. A range of social and economic criteria of social enterprises – which include both the production of goods or provision of services on a continuous basis as well as a trend towards paid work and autonomy – have been identified according to EMES criteria. For more, see http://www.emes.net
10. A new draft Law on Social Protection has been prepared and is in public debate. According to estimates, the new law will enable a wider coverage of poor households and eliminate the largest weakness of the current programme.
11. Law on Local Self-Government, 2008/03-L040, Republic of Kosovo.

References

Amity Report (2007) *Vaninstitucionalna zastita starih ljudi u Srbiji* [Community Care of the Elderly in Serbia], Belgrade: UNDP (unpublished report).

Bajec, J., Krstić, G., Pejin-Stokić, L. and Penev, G. (2008) *Social Protection and Social Inclusion in the Republic of Serbia*, European Commission and Economics Institute in Belgrade.

Brankovic, B. (2009) *Responding to Silent Screams: Mapping of Provision of Non-Governmental Organizations in Serbia in the Area of Gender-Based Violence*, Belgrade: UNDP.

Matkovic, G., Mijatovic, B. and Petrovic, M. (2010) *Impact of the Financial Crisis on the Labour Market and Living Conditions Outcomes*, Belgrade: Centre for Liberal-Democratic Studies.

Dinic, D. (ed.) (2008) *Detekcija i hraniteljstvo starijih ljudi* [Detection and Foster Family Placement for the Elderly], Belgrade: Gerontological Association of Serbia.

GoS (2007) *Second Progress Report on the Implementation of the Poverty Reduction Strategy in Serbia*, Belgrade: Government of Serbia.

Kolin, M. (2009) 'The role of the Third Sector in changing the welfare system', *Teorija in Praksa* (Ljubljana), XLVI(3): 255–70.

Kolin, M. (2011) 'Ageing and the welfare mix policy in Serbia', in A. Osterle (ed.) *Long-term Care in Central and South Eastern Europe*, Frankfurt am Main: Peter Lang, pp. 151–75.

Kolin, M. and Petrusic, N. (2008) *Socijalna preduzeca i uloga alternativne ekonomije u procesima evropskih integracija* [Social Enterprises in Serbia and the Role of Alternative Economy in the European Integration Process], Belgrade: European Movement in Serbia.

Les, E. and Kolin, M. (2009) 'East Central Europe', in J. A. Kerlin (ed.) *Social Enterprise: A Global Comparison*, Lebanon, NH: University Press of New England, pp. 35–64.

TACSO (2010) *Serbia: Needs Assessment Report, Technical Assistance to Civil Society Organisations in the IPA Countries*, EuropeAid/127427/C/SER/Multi/5, Belgrade: TACSO Serbia Office.

11
Strategic Planning of Local Economic Development in Vojvodina

Dragiša Mijačić[1]

Introduction

Decentralization is among the foremost governance-transforming policies in developed, developing and transitional economies. National governments decide to shift powers and resources to sub-national units of government for a variety of reasons, but the results are undeniably that – now more than ever before – local governments and other lower level actors are becoming engaged in the planning and implementation of economic development policies in their own territories. Nevertheless, local development remains more of a movement rather than a strict economic model defined by a prescriptive approach.

Local development initiatives tend to adopt a territorial approach as a means of achieving economic growth (Pike, Rodriguez-Pose and Tomaney, 2006). The focus falls on building the wealth of a territory, central to which improvements in the economic, institutional and social foundations are regarded as prerequisites for entrepreneurial success (Amin, 1999). However, traditional top-down development policies – usually designed by national planning and development offices and often supported by academics – have not generally given way to a more bottom-up, tailor-made approach to territorial development, in part because the latter is not based on any clearly-defined theoretical underpinning (Vázquez-Barquero, 2003; Pike, Rodriguez-Pose and Tomaney, 2006).

The problems created by an imprecise definition of local economic development are compounded by the fact that it can be seen as both a product and a process. Defined as a product, local economic development is usually measured in terms of outcomes such as increases in economic growth and the volume of enterprises, jobs, investment or wealth created. On the other hand, defined as a process, local economic development can be seen as a means to encouraging the development of commercial and physical infrastructure, support for industry, labour force development, the attraction of inward investment and all those issues with which economic development planners are typically concerned. Unfortunately, it is often difficult to demonstrate the congruence between the desired outcomes of economic development and the processes used to achieve them, due to the unstable and changing nature of the economic environment beyond the local area, which tends to involve a high level of 'externalities' (including exchange rates, new technologies and foreign competition). This chapter is focused on local economic development defined as a process rather than a product, and therefore the economic outcomes of the development planning process are not examined in detail.

There are several working definitions of local economic development as a process that are widely used by both academics and practitioners. Blakely and Bradshaw (2002) define local economic development as 'a process in which local government or community-based (neighbourhood) organisations engage to stimulate or maintain business activity and/or employment'. Beer, Haughton and Maude (2003) view it as 'a set of activities, usually organised by local governments yet also by the community ... aimed at improving [the] economic well-being of an area'. Among the most popular, however, is that employed by the World Bank (2006), which defines local economic development as 'the process by which public, business and non-governmental sector partners work collectively to create better conditions for economic growth and employment generation'.

The aforementioned definitions all emphasize local economic development as being a collaborative process that mobilizes public and private actors to work collectively in the creation of economic prosperity and well-being in a given territory. It is a process that involves the vertical and horizontal coordination of different levels of government as well as local public and private actors, thus demanding a shift to an increasingly complex system of governance – one which supplements the government hierarchy and market exchange through institutionalized negotiations, with the aim of reaching consensus and building mutual understanding between all actors involved. Such an approach to governance requires new institutional forms of networking, cooperation and coordination, which in turn provide a basis for economic and social progress (Jessop, 1998; Amin, 1999).

The key to successful governance is the ongoing commitment to dialogue of all the actors concerned in order to generate and exchange information, reduce opportunism by locking governance partners into a range of interdependent decisions over a range of short-, medium- and long-term objectives, and build on these interdependencies by encouraging solidarity between the participants. Public actors may choose to give up part of their capacity for political decision-making in exchange for greater influence over economic agents and more effective overall economic performance. Private actors, meanwhile, may renounce part of their autonomy in economic decision-making in exchange for political influence and better overall functioning of the socio-economic system (Jessop, 1998). Nonetheless, local authorities retain the leading role, acting to promote processes that will lead to a mutual consensus on the vision and developmental objectives among all the actors involved.

The interaction and dialogue between public and private actors is organized within a process of strategic planning for local economic development. This strategic planning is defined as 'a disciplined effort to produce fundamental decisions and actions shaping the nature and direction of an organisation's (or entity's) activities within legal bounds' (Olsen and Eadie, 1982). In essence, therefore, strategic planning is a process that facilitates face-to-face communication with the participation of different actors. It accommodates divergent interests and values, fosters intelligent decision-making and promotes successful implementation and accountability (Bryson, 2004). A high degree of mutual trust and understanding among all those involved is crucial for the success of the process.

Due to its tailor-made character, strategic planning has quickly been accepted by international development organizations, technical assistance agencies and the public sector as one of the main instruments for local economic development. In that regard, numerous international organizations have invested efforts in developing methodological guidelines for the design and delivery of local economic development strategy plans, the essence of which is the mobilization of all community actors from the public, private and non-profit sectors to work together with the aim of creating better conditions for economic growth and employment generation.

The process of strategic planning of local economic development in Serbia's municipalities was first introduced and facilitated by international and bilateral organizations. As a result, close to 700 strategic and action plans have been developed at the local level in the field of economic development, environmental protection, tourism, social welfare, empowerment of youth, women, Roma people and other disadvantaged groups, as well as other related issues (SKGO, 2011). The majority of these plans have been developed in a participatory manner, mainly using the World Bank five-step approach (World Bank, 2006) or comparable methodologies designed by various development organizations and technical assistance agencies.

The focus of this chapter, therefore, is to explore whether the early experiments in strategic planning of local economic development were successful in fostering dialogue between the public and private sectors at a local level in Serbia. To that end, the chapter presents the results of field research conducted between 2009 and 2010 in the Autonomous Province of Vojvodina with local self-government institutions that were or had been involved in the strategic planning process, as well as with representatives of private sector enterprises in two cities and three municipalities.

The chapter first provides an overview of the strategic planning process in the Republic of Serbia, before going on to explore the scale and scope of the planning process in Vojvodina and the results of empirical research on the subject of the extent to which strategic planning contributed to the dialogue between Vojvodina's public and private sectors. The chapter ends with concluding remarks on the first cycle of the strategic planning process in the Autonomous Province of Vojvodina.

Strategic planning of local economic development in Serbia

The Republic of Serbia was a latecomer to the transition process, making its conversion to a market-driven economy more than ten years after other former communist countries in Europe. Consequently, the model of strategic planning in which public and private actors work together in order to determine and achieve local economic development objectives is an approach that does not have a long history in the country.

The strategic planning of local economic development in Serbian municipalities is a concept that was initially introduced through projects and programmes implemented by international development organizations such as the UNDP, USAID, the World Bank and UN-Habitat, as well as by the Standing Conference of Towns and Municipalities.[2] The European Agency for Reconstruction, later replaced by the Delegation of the European Union to the Republic of Serbia, also had a significant role in this process, primarily in providing financial support for technical assistance in the design of strategic plans for local economic development in Serbian cities and municipalities.

The first local economic development strategic plans in Serbia were formulated in 2005 in the municipalities of Ada, Lazarevac, Kraljevo, Nis, Pancevo, Prijepolje and Zrenjanin. However, in a short period of time, the number of such strategies grew exponentially due to the fact that, among the main donor agencies targeting local levels, strategic planning of local economic development had become the most dominant form of technical assistance. In a mapping research conducted in 2011 by the Standing Conference of Towns and Municipalities, 696 local development strategies and action plans were identified, out of which 536 had been finalized and adopted by local assemblies, while 160 were either still in the development phase or pending assembly approval. The average number of strategic or action plans per local self-government unit in Serbia was 4.16 and represented a 67% increase on the figure recorded in 2008 (SKGO, 2011).

Influenced by the growing importance of bottom-up initiatives for strategic planning at the local level, the new Law on Local Self-Government of the Republic of Serbia, introduced in 2007, cited planning of local economic development as one of the key responsibilities of Serbian municipalities.[3] However, there were no other legislative acts, by-laws or policy documents that further elaborated or explained in a practical manner how to plan local economic development in a pragmatic way.[4]

Consequently, although both international and local technical assistance agencies have continued in their efforts to facilitate the process of designing local economic development strategic plans in Serbian municipalities, these agencies have shown a tendency to replicate standardized strategic planning methodologies rather than focusing on the economic, political or social fabric of the respective territories as they should. Moreover, the whole process has remained supply-driven and donor-oriented, since the vast majority of strategies have been both initiated and paid for by international donors.

As discussed previously, the strategic planning of local economic development requires a system of governance characterized by partnership, face-to-face communication and interdependency of the involved actors, as well as a high degree of mutual trust and understanding. In order to explore to what extent early experiences in strategic planning of local economic development were successful in fostering dialogue and mutual trust between public and private sectors at the local level, the author conducted field research in the Autonomous Province of Vojvodina, the findings of which are presented in the following two subchapters.

Empirical evidence on the strategic planning of local development

The first part of the research aimed to identify the municipalities involved in the strategic planning of local development in Vojvodina, as well as the methodologies used. Based on the findings from this first phase of research, the second phase focused on establishing how far the strategic planning process had contributed to increased cooperation between the public and private sectors in the five municipalities, with a particular emphasis on the methodological differences in their approaches.

The Autonomous Province of Vojvodina is divided into 39 municipalities and six cities, altogether comprising 45 local self-government units (see Figure 11.1). By 2010, when the field research was carried out, the first cycle of strategic planning of local economic development in Vojvodina's local self-government units was almost complete. In total, 40 cities and municipalities had already developed strategic plans and the respective local assemblies had adopted all of these. One municipality (Vrbas) was still in the process of developing a strategic plan and four municipalities (Bela Crkva, Coka, Mali Idjos and Senta) had not yet initiated the process.

Strategic planning in Vojvodina began in 2005 when three local self-government units (Ada, Pancevo and Zrenjanjin) designed local development strategies. Thereafter, the number of cities and municipalities that became involved in strategic planning gradually increased with each passing year, reaching a maximum of 19 local strategies developed in 2009. Two further strategies were designed in 2010 and, as discussed earlier, one municipality was still in the process of developing a strategic plan at the time the research was conducted. It should also be noted that, by 2010, the city of Subotica had already begun the process of developing its second strategic plan for local economic development.

The Standing Conference of Towns and Municipalities pioneered the introduction of strategic planning at local level, not only in Vojvodina but also in Serbia as a whole. During the period 2005–7, under the project *Local Agenda 21*, financed by support from the Norwegian Government and with technical support from the Norwegian Association of Local and Regional Authorities, the Standing Conference of Towns and Municipalities assisted seven Serbian municipalities to develop local strategic plans; two of these (Becej and Sombor) were in Vojvodina. On the basis of good results of this project, the Standing Conference then initiated a follow-up project that was funded by the European Agency

Figure 11.1 Map of local self-government units (cities and municipalities) in Vojvodina
Source: InTER, www.lokalnirazvoj.org

for Reconstruction, as part of the Hungary–Serbia Neighbourhood Programme. The new project saw the development of strategic plans in a further six municipalities: Irig, Kovin, Kula, Novi Becej, Odzaci and Sremski Karlovci. Thereafter, the Standing Conference continued to use this methodology in providing technical support, either through the EU-funded 'Exchange 2' programme or with the backing of other donor agencies such as the Spanish Agency for International Cooperation.

Technical assistance in the development of local strategies was also provided by other donor agencies. In 2005, for example, the World Bank supported strategic planning in the city of Pancevo, one of the first strategies to be developed in Vojvodina. The USAID-funded *Municipal Economic Growth Activity* (MEGA) supported the development of strategic plans in four units of local self-government in Vojvodina (Indjija, Novi Sad, Subotica and Vrsac) while the Hungarian foundation, Szülőföld, funded the strategic planning process in Kanjza municipality, which was completed in early 2006.

However, strategic planning of local development in Vojvodina really took off in 2009 when its importance was recognized by the Secretariat for Inter-Regional Cooperation and Local Self-Government of the Government of Vojvodina, which decided to provide financial support for technical assistance in designing 15 local development strategic plans in the province. In that regard, several service providers were selected, among the most involved of which were the Alpha Resource Centre for Development, engaged in the development of five strategies, and the Vojvodina Centre for Strategic Economic Studies (Vojvodina CESS), on a further four. The remaining providers (including Alma Mons d.o.o., Micro Project d.o.o and the Initiative for Democratic Transition, among others) were each engaged in the development of a single strategy.

Strategic planning has not been a uniform process across Vojvodina's local self-government units and has differed according to the service providers involved. However, these differences are most notable in terms of the plans' titles and time periods, while being less evident in the choice of methodology for developing the plans.

Although these strategic documents bear a number of different titles,[5] they can all be regarded as local economic development strategies, as defined earlier. Most of the local self-government units in Vojvodina have also been engaged in the development of strategic plans concerning other issues such as social protection, youth, employment and child rights. The experiences of local self-government units in strategic planning for these issues were not included in the herewith-presented research, however.

The duration of the strategic plans varies across municipalities and corresponds to the methodology of the selected technical assistance provider. Most strategies were planned for either five or 11 years (13 strategic plans each), with a further nine strategies programmed over a six-year period. Two strategies (in Ada and Zrenjanin) were programmed for eight years and one (in Sombor) for nine years. It is worth noting that two strategic plans (in Backa Topola and Novi Knezevac) did not stipulate the time period for their implementation.

The structure of the strategic plans is quite similar across local self-government units. It usually includes a welcome note from the Mayor, a methodological explanation of the planning process and a socio-economic assessment of the territory, along with an (often romanticized) history of the territory concerned. This is followed by a SWOT[6] analysis, vision, mission statement and strategic priorities. In some cases the strategy also includes an operationalization of the objectives through certain identified priority projects, an action plan and occasionally, though rarely, a financial plan. In the majority of cases, the length of the strategic plan is extended by the inclusion of definitions and theoretical explanations of local economic development and each of the strategy's aspects.

The most common strategic objectives for development are in the fields of infrastructure (26 strategies), agriculture (25 strategies), tourism (23 strategies), environmental protection (21 strategies), small- and medium-sized enterprises and entrepreneurship (20 strategies) and education and human resources (20 strategies). The objectives of competitiveness and an enabling business environment are presented as an objective in 19 strategies. Less commonly mentioned is industrial development, which appears in only nine strategies, covering development of industrial zones (two strategies) and the development of the processing industry (three municipalities). Out of 41 strategies, the attraction of foreign direct investment is presented as an objective by only eight local self-government units. Innovation is recognized an objective in three strategies (Novi Sad, Subotica and Zitiste), but renewable energy is only a strategic objective for the City of Pancevo, and the sole municipality which lists energy efficiency as an objective is Zabalj. The municipalities of Beocin, Kula and Kikinda include forestry and water management as their strategic objectives, although competences in these sectors are allocated to the provincial and national levels.

Increasing the efficiency of local self-government administration is recognized as a strategic priority in seven municipalities, while local marketing is an objective in two strategies (Ruma and Subotica). Three local self-government units (Kikinda, Pancevo and Zabalj) cite the strengthening of public-private networks as a strategic objective, while the municipality of Zabalj goes further in aiming to promote the accession of the Republic of Serbia to the European Union.

A significant number of strategies (28 in total) have objectives in non-economic fields such as social cohesion, social welfare, culture, sports, health protection and similar. Civil society development is recognized as a priority in three local strategies (Backi Petrovac, Irig and Vrbas).

The vast majority of local strategic plans were developed using a participatory approach in which representatives from the public and private sector, along with civil society organizations, worked together in determining a joint vision and mission statement and identifying strategic objectives and priority projects. Only the municipality of Beocin, which contracted the Institute for Agricultural Economics in Belgrade to design and deliver a full local strategic plan, failed to take this approach.

It is important to mention that there is a dearth of institutional records on the process of strategic planning in Vojvodina's local self-government units. Consequently, it is very difficult to determine how many people were involved in the process, whom they represented, how they were selected to join the planning group, and how engaged they were in discussions. Some answers on these questions were received through a questionnaire that was sent to all cities and municipalities in Vojvodina as part of this research and, in a few cases, information on the planning process was given in the strategic plans themselves.

In all cases, the participatory process of strategic planning was led by the local authorities and facilitated by technical assistance agencies. The methodology usually included the creation of a core group to organize the whole process and coordinate all the necessary steps in developing a strategy. In many instances, a thematic or sector-based group was also created, engaging additional representatives from the public and private sectors. There are also cases where large community groups were consulted in the strategic planning process (such as Stara Pazova, where over 600 people were involved, as well as 400 in Vrsac).

In the majority of cases, the public sector was the most strongly represented within the working groups. Representatives from the private sector and civil society organizations usually became involved in one of two different ways: either through receiving a direct invitation or by responding to a public call for participation. Regardless, the question over adequate representation by all stakeholder groups remains unanswered.

Notwithstanding, representation by civil society organizations seems to have been more substantial than that of the business sector. There are several possible reasons for this, including having a better networking capacity, being more acquainted with the community's needs or possessing better technical knowledge of the planning process itself. Furthermore, from the local authority's point of view, civil society organizations are preferable as partners due to their familiarity with donor initiatives and available funds. The last is especially important, bearing in mind that many of the priority projects identified in the local strategic plans were foreseen to be funded with the support of external actors.

There are many possible reasons for the weak – and sometimes inadequate – representation of the business sector in the planning process. To cite but a few, they include: a lack of interest among local authorities to involve a wider representation from the business sector; the animosity of business executives to cooperating with local authorities; a lack of information about the planning process and on the criteria for participation in it; a lack of capacity among business associations to represent all their members; and the absence of business associations at the local level. Furthermore, none of the municipalities included representatives of foreign investors when discussing their strategies.

However, these strategic planning efforts represented the first organized attempt at cooperation between the public and private sector at the local level in Vojvodina. Earlier examples of cooperation between private and public agents had mostly been one-sided, supply-driven and/or problem-oriented. It was therefore important to examine whether the early experiments in strategic planning in Vojvodina had made a positive contribution to ongoing public–private dialogue at the local level.

Has strategic planning of local economic development improved cooperation between the public and private sectors?

In order to establish to what degree dialogue between the public and private sectors at local level has been improved through the experience of strategic planning, five local self-government units were selected for analysis: two cities (Subotica and Zrenjanin) and three municipalities (Beocin, Indjija and Kula).

The selection was made on a number of grounds. Both Zrenjanin and Subotica were among the first cities in Vojvodina (and indeed, Serbia) to have developed strategic plans, but each did so in a different way.

Zrenjanin developed its strategy using its own resources, while Subotica developed its strategy with technical assistance from an external consultant. The three municipalities had also adopted different methods of strategic plan development. Indjija developed a strategy with technical support from the USAID MEGA programme, Kula with the support of the Standing Conference of Towns and Municipalities and Beocin by contracting the Institute for Agricultural Economics in Belgrade. In terms of focus, two strategies bear the title *Local Development Strategy* (Indjija and Beocin), two of *Sustainable Development Strategy* (Kula and Zrenjanin), while the one in Subotica was named *Local Economic Development Strategy*. All the strategies, with the exception of Beocin's, were developed using a participatory approach. The chosen sample of two cities and three municipalities is therefore a fair representation of the range of differences in approach to the process of strategic planning at the local level in Vojvodina.

In order to obtain a similarly representative response to the strategic planning process from the private sector, a total of 46 executives from private enterprises operating in the five selected units of local self-government were interviewed. These representatives, a number of whom had been directly involved in the strategic planning process, were chosen from a range of large, medium and small enterprises, entrepreneurs, business associations and clusters.

In those cities and municipalities that had employed a participatory approach to planning (Indjija, Kula, Subotica and Zrenjanin), the vast majority of executives interviewed had some knowledge – or were at least aware – of the existence of the local development strategies. Some had actively participated in the strategic planning process, whereas others had been informed by the local media. However, this was not the case with executives in the municipality of Beocin, where the strategy was the product of a consultancy contract and none of the interviewees from the private sector claimed any acquaintance with it.

Moreover, even in the cities and municipalities that had taken a participatory approach to planning, many of the business executives were not familiar with the procedures that had been used to select participants in the strategic planning process. Those who were interviewed but had not participated in the planning process blamed local authorities for not sending out proper invitations and for keeping the whole process opaque. The involvement of large enterprises in the participatory planning process was particularly weak, which, among other factors, can be attributed to the low degree of privatization of the majority of these entities at the time the consultation process was implemented.

However, dissatisfaction with local authorities was also evident among the majority of those executives that had been directly involved in the planning process, many of whom claimed that their role had been rather nominal since they had felt powerless to influence strategic orientation and policy interventions, and complained that their feedback on draft versions of the strategies had not been properly taken into consideration. The interviewees also expressed their dissatisfaction with the local authorities for not having sent them the final versions of the strategies.

Similar claims were made by executives in all four cities and municipalities that had conducted participatory planning, regardless of the technical assistance agency involved and minor differences in the applied methodology. The implications of this finding are twofold: firstly, there were significant gaps in the facilitation of the participatory planning process, which can be attributed to a lack of knowledge and skills among those who were organizing and implementing the process, including professionals from the technical assistance agencies. As discussed before, participatory planning is a new phenomenon in Serbia and there is therefore a lack of methodological guidelines, clear procedures and qualified specialists who could successfully moderate the whole process. Secondly, the participatory planning process did not succeed in creating a sense of ownership over the strategic plan by those representatives of the private sector involved. Consequently, the strategies are perceived as policy documents that are only relevant to the city/municipality and their institutions, and extraneous to the private sector. This also means that the strategic planning process failed to create synergy between public and private sector organizations for the promotion of economic development or the fulfilment of other planned objectives.

Although awareness of the existence of the strategic plans was quite significant among the executives interviewed, at least in the four local self-government units where a participatory planning process had been applied, their knowledge about the strategy's implementation and priority projects was inadequate. Specifically, those interviewed could not identify a single mechanism for implementing the strategies, claiming that the local authorities had never invited them to discuss modalities for implementation of the priority projects nor progress towards achieving the strategic objectives. Moreover, press releases and media coverage of these issues locally were lacking.

Statements from interviewed executives to the effect that strategic planning of local economic development had not directly contributed to the advancement of cooperation between the public and private sectors were common, regardless of the methodology applied. However, interviewees from cities and municipalities that had taken a participatory approach did say that the work of their local self-government units had become more transparent. They also stated that cooperation with local authorities had improved since the creation of Local Economic Development Offices,[7] which serve as a good channel of communication between different actors at the local level. In addition, some voiced the opinion that local authorities had become much more trustworthy than before. However, interviewees from Beocin – the municipality that did not employ participatory planning mechanisms – did not share the point of view of their peers from the other four local self-government units. Rather, they were persistent in their complaints about the performance of their local authority.

From the executives' interviews it is reasonable to conclude that the business sector was not adequately included in the first efforts at strategic planning of local economic development in Vojvodina. This is especially true when the strategy was developed solely as a consultancy output. In cases of participatory planning, where business executives were included in the process, their participation was not adequately facilitated and their opinions were not effectively utilized. In neither case did follow-up activities around strategy implementation include the participation of private sector actors. There was also no evidence of a systemic increase in public–private dialogue on any important issues, whether related to the implementation of the strategy or to any other question. Nevertheless, opinions were expressed which suggested that participatory planning had contributed to the transparency of the work of the local administration, and did to some extent increase trust in local authorities.

Conclusion

There is little evidence to show that the first attempts at strategic planning of local development in Vojvodina's units of local self-government have created conditions favourable to the emergence of a public–private dialogue at the local level. The reasons may be found in the traditional lack of trust between the actors on both sides, as well as in the procedural issues and lack of facilitation skills of individuals providing technical assistance for strategy development.

Due to its late transition to a market economy, the private sector in Vojvodina, as in the rest of Serbia, is weak in terms of employment generation and investment capacity, particularly since the global financial crisis, which has hit businesses in the province severely. Micro- and small enterprises dominate the private sector, primarily in the provision of basic services, while the few remaining large companies mostly work with limited capacity or are in administration for insolvency. The capacity of the Serbian Chamber of Commerce and other business associations that represent the private sector is also weak, especially in terms of expressing a collective voice and articulating the need for business development. Moreover, the volume of net foreign direct investment is somewhat symbolic and mainly concentrated in Belgrade, Novi Sad and a handful of other large towns located either in the vicinity of these two cities or on the main highway corridors (Sestovic, 2010). Therefore, the reason for the rather negligible participation of the private sector in the process of strategic planning may partly be attributed to the weak capacity of the local business community to contribute to job creation, wealth generation and economic development.

The empirical research conducted by the author has revealed differences in attitude between businesses from cities and municipalities that apply a participatory approach to the planning process and those that do not. Private sector representatives are much more aware of the existence of a strategic plan and its objectives in local self-government units where a participatory approach has been taken. In addition, business executives' perceptions of the transparency of local authorities are higher in those cities and municipalities that have adopted a participatory approach. The recent initiatives for creation of Local Economic Development Offices within the local self-government units have also been warmly welcomed by the private sector.

The implementation of strategic plans is expected to be financed either from the local budget or through external funding, whether national or donor. Financing by the private sector is not yet seen as an option. Therefore, it behoves local authorities to create formal mechanisms for involving private sector representatives in the implementation of the local development initiatives identified in the strategic plans, and particularly to seek synergy between developmental interventions and priorities for private investment. To that end, the establishment of a permanent forum for public–private dialogue at the local level could prove invaluable in increasing trust between the actors, as well as their sense of ownership, both of which are fundamental preconditions for any successful and sustainable strategic planning for local economic development in the future.

Notes

1. The author acknowledges financial support from the Austrian Development Agency which covered part of the research that is presented in this chapter. The author is grateful for feedback received from a number of reviewers, most notably Dr William Bartlett, Sanja Malekovic and Tomislav Novovic. Many thanks also to Olivia Lalonde for proofreading and English language editing.
2. The Standing Conference is Serbia's national association of municipalities.
3. 'Službeni glasnik RS', No. 129/2007, Article 20, paragraph 9.
4. In 2011, the Government of the Republic of Serbia adopted a by-law that regulates development of the methodology and structure of planning documents at national and regional levels ('Službeni glasnik RS', no. 15/2011). Although this by-law does not directly refer to local levels of administration, it is the first official document that provides guidelines regarding the planning process in Serbia.
5. Among 41 strategies in Vojvodina's local self-government units, most have the title Local Development Strategy or Sustainable Development Strategy (each of these two titles covers 16 projects). Only six strategies are referred to as a Local Economic Development Strategy and one (in Bac) is named Local Socio-Economic Development Strategy. The remaining two strategies are called Rural Development Strategy (Alibunar) and Strategy of Communal Services (Titel).
6. S – Strengths, W – Weaknesses, O – Opportunities, T – Threats.
7. A Local Economic Development Office is a unit of the local administration, usually established with the objective of promoting an enabling business environment in the local area and coordinating activities on the implementation of strategies.

References

Amin, A. (1999) 'An institutionalist perspective on regional economic development', *International Journal of Urban and Regional Research*, 23(2): 365–78.

Beer, A., Haughton, G. and Maude, A. (2003) *Developing Locally: An International Comparison of Local and Regional Economic Development*, Bristol: Policy Press.

Blakely, J. E. and Bradshaw, K. T. (2002) *Planning of Local Economic Development: Theory and Practice*, London: Sage Publications.

Bryson, J. M. (2004) *Strategic Planning for Public and Nonprofit Organizations: A Guide to Strengthening and Sustaining Organizational Achievement* (Third Edition), San Francisco: Jossey-Bass.

Jessop, B. (1998) 'The rise of governance and the risks of failure: The case of economic development', *International Social Science Journal*, 50(155): 29–45.

Olsen, J. B. and Eadie, D. C. (1982) *The Game Plan: Governance with Foresight*, Washington, DC: Council of State Planning Agencies.

Pike, A., Rodriguez-Pose, A. and Tomaney, J. (2006) *Local and Regional Development*, London: Routledge.

Sestovic L. (2010) 'Mapping Serbia's growth', *FREN Quarterly Monitor No. 20*, January–March, pp. 69–87.

Službeni glasnik RS (2007) 'Zakon o lokalnoj samoupravi', *Official Gazette of the Republic of Serbia*, no. 129/2007.
Službeni glasnik RS (2011) 'Uredba o strukturi, metodologiji izrade, načinu usklađivanja razvojnih dokumenata, načinu sprovođenja javne rasprave, kao i načinu i rokovima izlaganja na javni uvid razvojnih dokumenata regionalnog razvoja', *Official Gazette of the Republic of Serbia*, no. 15/2011.
SKGO (2011) *Mapiranje postojećih lokalnih strategija i tela za njihovu primenu u opštinama i gradovima Srbije*, Beograd: Stalna konferencija gradova i opština.
Vázquez-Barquero, A. (2003) *Endogenous Development: Networking, Innovation, Institutions and Cities*, London: Routledge.
World Bank (2006) *Local Economic Development: A Primer, Developing and Implementing Local Economic Development Strategies and Action Plans*, Washington, DC: World Bank.

12

Towards Policy Entrepreneurship at Community Level: The Impact of Decentralization on Local Public Services in Macedonia

Marija Risteska

Introduction

Sub-national governments are often thought to be closer to the people than the central government as they have better information about the preferences of local population (Hayek, 1945). Hence, it may be argued that they are better informed and thus more responsive to the variations in demand for goods and services. By tailoring the outputs of goods and services to the particular preferences and circumstances of their constituencies, decentralized provision may increase economic welfare above the levels of such services under uniform national provision (Wallace, 1999). Decentralization is also argued to improve governance in public service provision in at least three ways: by improving the efficiency of resource allocation, by promoting accountability and reducing corruption within government, and by improving cost recovery (Azfar et al., 1999).

Tiebout (1956) proposed that competition among sub-national governments allows for a variety of local public goods to be produced, which in turn enables individuals to reveal their preferences for those goods by moving to the jurisdictions that satisfy their tastes (thus 'voting with their feet'). Such 'voting by foot' is thought to provide strong incentives to local officials to engage in 'policy entrepreneurship' in order to satisfy the changing distributions of voter preferences. The policy entrepreneurship approach is rather novel as traditionally, literature on entrepreneurship focuses on the capabilities and resources of private entrepreneurial agents and their networks. The policy entrepreneurship approach, unlike traditional entrepreneurship studies, shifts its attention to the broader institutional environment, and scholars such as Ostrom (2005) began to perceive policymakers as policy entrepreneurs. This chapter assesses how the decentralization process affects policy entrepreneurship in Macedonian municipalities since the decentralization reform of 2005. It begins with the hypothesis that in a decentralized environment, local policymakers, including the Mayor, the Councillors in the municipal council, and the public service managers become policy entrepreneurs who strive to match the design of the public services offered by municipalities to the preferences and needs of their constituents. The chapter assesses the local policymakers' potential to engage in such policy entrepreneurship in the social sector, especially in childcare services, as well as on the necessary institutional environment for the development of such policy entrepreneurship at the community level in Macedonia.

Unpacking the decentralization reform in Macedonia

With 34 local government units established since 1976, Macedonia had a reasonably well-developed system of local self-government within former Yugoslavia. Municipalities were responsible for a wide variety of public services, enjoying a substantial budgetary autonomy, and significant revenue raising powers (Levitas, 2004). In independent Macedonia, a new legal basis for local self-government was established in 1991 through the new Constitution that defined the municipalities as the basic units of local government and established the general principles for the organization, functions and financing of the local governments. The 1995 Law on Local Self-Government established an impressive range of competences of the local government, but did not include fiscal decentralization. Furthermore, the central government's unwillingness to effectively transfer competences was visible. The Law on Territorial Organization (adopted in 1996) announced the government's aim to ensure the development of smaller settlements and a more balanced development of the country by expanding the number of municipalities to 124. However, many of the newly created municipalities were too small and had insufficient administrative capacity to effectively provide the services they had been assigned (Daskalovski, 2006).

The most recent decentralization reform in Macedonia came into effect in 2005. Several prior events influenced the decision to decentralize competences to the local governments. In 1997 Macedonia ratified the European Charter of Local Self-Government, which deems it to be appropriate for public services to be provided by the lowest level of government (Rafuse, 2000). Subsequently, the Ministry of

Local Self-Government was established, with the aim of monitoring the development and recommending measures for improving local self-government as well as developing policies and instruments that would enable a more balanced regional development. The institutional preconditions were set for launching the decentralization reform once the Ministry of Local Self-Government was established. However, the decentralization actually only gained momentum following the reforms agreed within the Ohrid Framework Agreement in 2001.[1] The Ohrid Framework Agreement literally put an end to the inter-ethnic conflict between ethnic Albanian rebels and the government security forces, and introduced formal mechanisms for conflict resolution at national and local levels. The Ohrid Framework Agreement (hereafter OFA) set out a strategic agenda concerning equal representation of different ethnic groups in public life and local self-government and the devolution of powers from the central government to the municipalities (henceforth decentralization). In the process, the government has committed itself to devolve the responsibilities of the central government to the local government units. The OFA called for the establishment of a decentralized government as well as legal changes of the 1991 Constitution,[2] and of numerous laws and by-laws, in three main areas: (i) *Devolution of competences* in the area of public services, urban and rural planning, environmental protection, local economic development, culture, local finances, education, social welfare, and health care;[3] (ii) *Territorial division* to 84 municipalities, including the capital Skopje and its ten municipalities; and (iii) *Municipal funding* that should ensure an adequate system of financing, thus enabling local governments to fulfil all their responsibilities.

The decentralization also implied transferring responsibilities to local self-government in terms of collecting taxes and reallocation of funds for financing public services on a local level. With the fiscal decentralization that commenced with the passing of the Law on Financing of the Local Self-Government, the government aimed at correcting the deficiencies in the functioning of municipalities and enhancing their capacity to create sustainable local economic development by using their own revenues. With the reform the municipalities are now financed from own-revenue sources, government grants and other sources of revenue and by borrowing. The own-revenue sources comprise property, inheritance, gift taxes, sales taxes on real estate and rights, and municipal fees. Moreover, the municipalities are responsible for setting the rates on these taxes, as well as for communal fees and charges like the hotel charge and the sign fee, with maximum and minimum limits specified by the Laws on Property Taxes. Other revenues of the municipalities include a 3% share of the personal income tax paid by people living in the given municipalities.[4] In addition to own revenues, the Law on Financing the Local Self-Government Units specifies a number of grants provided from the central Budget as additional revenues for the municipalities: revenues from value added tax (general grants), block grants, earmarked grants, capital grants, grants for delegated competences. The law also allows municipalities to borrow additional funds in the capital markets, if approved by the Ministry of Finance.

The implementation of the decentralization reform was conducted in phases. In the first phase, ownership of primary and secondary schools, cultural institutions, homes for the elderly, sports facilities and fire protection units were transferred to local governments. They were also given earmarked grants to cover the maintenance costs for these facilities. These grants were to be used for financing of specific costs such as electricity, heating and other maintenance-related costs. They were generally distributed to the municipalities based on the historical costs of the designated local institutions (schools, culture institutions, homes for the elderly) though objective criteria also applied (kindergartens and schools were financed on per capita basis).

Local governments who had met specific conditions[5] progressed to the second phase of decentralization. In this second phase the municipalities were given responsibility for hiring and firing employees as well as covering the wages of those employed in the respective facilities. At this point, earmarked grants are transformed into sectoral block grants. The Law on financing local self-government units (OG 61/2004) foresees block grants for financing municipal activities in four sectors: education, social policy and child protection, culture and health. The formula for allocating the sectoral block grants is made by the responsible ministry (Art. 46). Using these grants increases the spending discretion of the local government within, but not between sectors. Currently all municipalities, except one, Plasnica, have progressed to the second phase of decentralization.

Improving democracy, equality and development

The main objectives of the decentralization process in Macedonia were to improve democratic governance and enhance economic and social development, with an aim to decrease regional disparities and enhance equality. The reform process introduced a policy design for improving the delivery of education, cultural and social protection services (childcare and care for the elderly). In these sectors, as mentioned before, the central government first transferred the ownership of the buildings and then provided earmarked grants to finance their maintenance, and later sectoral block grants to pay for the salaries of the staff. The municipality has complete autonomy to decide on the management model, the place where the services will be delivered and on the type of services to be offered. The decision-making related to these issues is the responsibility of the municipal council whose members are elected through direct local elections. The municipal public services are managed by Directors who are appointed by the Mayor on a proposal from the management boards in which all relevant community stakeholders are represented (i.e. in the board of the kindergarten the municipality, the caregivers and the parents are represented; in the school board the municipality, the teachers and the parents are represented). Although the management of these services was fully transferred to the individual municipalities in the second phase of decentralization, the policymaking in these sectors remained under the competence of the central government. For example, in the education policy area the Ministry of Education and Science adopts laws and bylaws on education, and together with the central bodies, such as the Bureau for Development of Education and the State Education Inspectorate, ensures quality of education. The education service is delivered to citizens by schools that are managed by the municipality. The municipality itself has limited competences in policymaking: it can adapt 20% of the education curriculum to local needs while quality assurance is strengthened through municipal education inspectors. This option allows for the municipal policymakers – the Mayor, council members and public sector managers – to tailor public services to the specific needs of their communities.

For the tailoring of services to be satisfactory to the local population, it is necessary that municipalities gather information of their needs and preferences. Therefore, under the decentralization reform, various mechanisms were introduced to enhance voters' participation so that their needs and preferences can be identified. This in turn has an impact on the democratic processes in Macedonian municipalities. The CRPM Decentralization Survey, carried out in 2010, revealed that a quarter of citizens are consulted on the decisions of the municipal council by organizing public debates (25%). The municipalities also keep the citizens informed on their decisions and services that are on offer through information published in the local media (23%), through postings on the municipal website (21%), and by publishing local newsletters that are delivered to people's homes (17%). Furthermore, democratization at the municipal level is strengthened through the system of double majority voting[6] in the municipal council which enables ethnic groups representing more than 20% of the population to influence municipal decisions related to their identity (cultural preferences). This system is designed to provide a voice to the minority communities and is intended to ease inter-ethnic tensions.

Prior to the reforms, it had been thought that inter-ethnic tensions were provoked by the unequal distribution of public funds, and so decentralization aimed at decreasing economic disparities between the municipalities. The main tool used for achieving this was a redistribution of some of the revenues from the personal income tax and the value added tax to municipalities. Under this system, 3% of the VAT revenue is allocated to the municipalities in accordance with a formula. Of the distributed VAT, 2% is assigned to a reserve to be available to municipalities unable to meet their expenditure obligations. Of the remainder, 10% is allocated to metropolitan area Skopje (out of which a proportion is assigned to the city of Skopje, whereas the rest is shared among the other ten municipalities that make the city), while the residual 90% is allocated to the municipalities outside of Skopje taking in consideration the size of the population, land area and number of settlements. The distribution model prioritizes the rural areas and is designed to gradually promote convergence in revenues between the metropolitan and non-metropolitan areas. Levitas (2009) argued that 3% of the VAT revenue is insufficient to promote such convergence and concluded that 'too little of Macedonia's too small fiscal pie is going to local governments,[7] and too much of that too small piece of the fiscal pie is going to Skopje'[8] (ibid.).

The attempt to achieve more balanced development is especially visible in the way that the formula for financing education is designed. This includes three elements: a lump sum for each municipality, an amount based on the number of pupils attending schools in the municipality (including weights for students with specials needs) and an element inversely related to population density designed to ensure that education is delivered in rural areas (Ordinance No. 1700 OG 129/2007). By adopting this redistribution formula, the government has made a commitment to moving towards a system of financing that will ensure that municipalities are rewarded for providing schooling in less populated areas (Art. 12, point 2 OG 61/04). How has this system worked in practice? Levitas (2006) analysed data from the municipalities that had participated in the second phase of decentralization and found that 'money is flowing to local governments not on the basis of the number of pupils attending schools in their jurisdictions but primarily on the basis of the number of teachers teaching in them' (Levitas, 2006). Considering that each class is taught by one teacher and especially since in urban areas over-crowded classes are very common, the current system of redistribution of resources seems to be rewarding the schools with more teachers rather than those with more children. On the one hand this suggests that the system of redistribution moved to more equitable allocation of resources and is decreasing urban–rural disparities taking into consideration that in rural areas there are less children in class than the legally binding 22–4 students. However, on the other hand, in Macedonia, there are rural areas that have high birth dates (i.e. the Polog region) and therefore schools in these areas provide education service to more than 24 students in one class. Under the current redistribution of resources, these schools receive less money than other schools with a smaller number of students. By not putting in effect the decision for per capita financing of education, the Government is running the risk of increasing inequalities and putting in danger the achievement of the objective of the decentralization reform to enable a more coherent and equitable development.

Moreover, the scope of the redistribution policy was limited to the field of education; similar equalization formulas were not adopted in other policy areas such as childcare, sports and recreation, culture and care for the elderly. For example, in the childcare sector, in the municipalities that had kindergartens on their territory prior to decentralization, the ownership of the buildings was transferred and funds were provided to cover maintenance costs in the first phase of the decentralization reform. In the second phase, the whole management responsibilities were transferred to the municipalities to provide childcare. As per capita formula for financing was not adopted in the childcare sector, the municipalities without kindergartens gained childcare competences, but did not have the institutional network to provide the services nor the finances to deliver them. Gaining the function to organize and provide childcare, without gaining the necessary financial resources to carry out the responsibility is contrary to the European Charter of Local Self-Government. What is more, the experience of the childcare sector shows that, despite the intention to redistribute resources to the poorer municipalities, the decentralization process in practice has perpetuated the historical concentration of childcare services in urban areas. As noted previously, kindergartens are still available mainly in the capital city, Skopje, and in the Eastern region, which due to the small towns located there is also rather urbanized and has a better network of service provision than the rest of the country. On the other hand, the most rural areas – Polog and the South-western region – have between nine and

Table 12.1 Childcare facilities in Macedonia by region

Region	**Total number of childcare services**	**Total number of children (0–5 years)**	**Number of children per childcare service**
TOTAL 2010	54	114,801	2126
Vardar	5	8153	1631
East	9	8417	935
South-west	6	10,880	1813
South-east	5	9591	1918
Pelagonia	6	12,279	2046
Polog	2	17,470	8735
North-east	3	10,035	3345
Skopje	18	37,976	2110

Source: State Statistical Office, 2010.

eight times less childcare infrastructure and services delivered to their citizens compared to Skopje. The disadvantages are most emphasized in the Polog region, which has the highest number of children in the kindergarten age group and the lowest provision of childcare services (with only one kindergarten being located in Tetovo and another in the town of Gostivar). The Table 12.1. above also demonstrates the huge disparity in provision of childcare services per number of children between Polog and the rest of the country (four times lesser than Skopje and eight times lesser than the Eastern region).

Hence, it may be concluded that through the decentralization process while a devolution of competences took place, the financial resources allocated for these competences have been allocated according to pre-existing distribution of assets, which are still financing the existing network of service delivery rather than being tied in any meaningful way to an effective process of redistribution. The decentralization process therefore has only a limited effect on the achievement of a more balanced development. This policy has therefore failed to encourage local economic convergence and it is likely that it may further widen the differences and inequalities between rural and urban areas.

Policy entrepreneurship – a mission impossible in decentralized Macedonia

In this section I would like to address the question of whether managers in municipalities without childcare institutions can act as policy entrepreneurs, and establish new childcare institutions on their territory. Under the new Law on Social Care (OG 79/2009) that regulates the system of social care, the central government has the right to determine the number of public institutions for social care that can be established by private and public entities. Municipal governments are empowered to follow the preferences of their voters and establish public institutions for institutional and non-institutional care of children, people with disabilities and the elderly. Consequently, municipal policymakers – the Mayor, the municipal council and public sector managers – may act as policy entrepreneurs and establish childcare services if these are desired by voters. However, such policy measures must be approved by the central government with the consent of the Ministry of Labour and Social Policy. They must be financed from their own financial resources. As demonstrated in the previous chapters, while already established institutions that provide social services – such as childcare services – receive central budget financing through block grants, the municipalities themselves must raise the revenues for any new institutions. This puts the municipal governments without childcare services in an unequal position in relation to the municipalities with established childcare services prior to the decentralization. Since the municipalities' lack of financial resources, presents the main problem in the implementation of the decentralized competences of municipalities,[9] this unequal approach in financing has a direct influence on the capacity of the municipality to successfully implement decentralized competences. Therefore it is not surprising that in the CRPM Decentralization Survey almost all (94.6%) of surveyed municipalities responded that the provision of elderly care is the least successful of their services considering that there are only four homes for the elderly in the whole country, while 83% replied that childcare services were not being provided successfully (see Figure 12.1). On the other hand a majority of municipalities considered that their provision of education services and urban planning was successful.

Furthermore, the municipalities in the Polog region and those in the South-east and South-west have the greatest difficulties in implementing the decentralized competences related to childcare provision (see Figure 12.2). Such results are to be expected since the Polog region has largest number of children in the kindergarten age group (17,470) and smallest number of kindergartens on their territory (2).

As policy entrepreneurship relates to policy innovation, it is important to know what would happen if municipal managers wanted to innovate and establish a public service that has not been provided before decentralization commenced. In the case of childcare services,

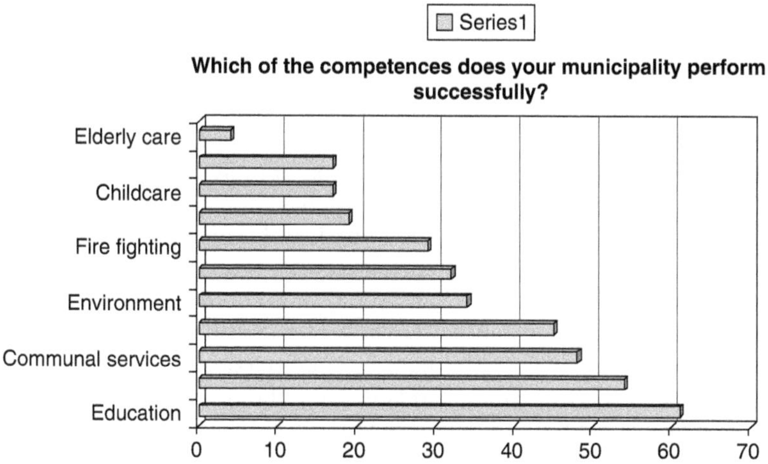

Figure 12.1 Municipal perceptions on execution of decentralized competences
Source: CRPM Decentralization Survey 2010.

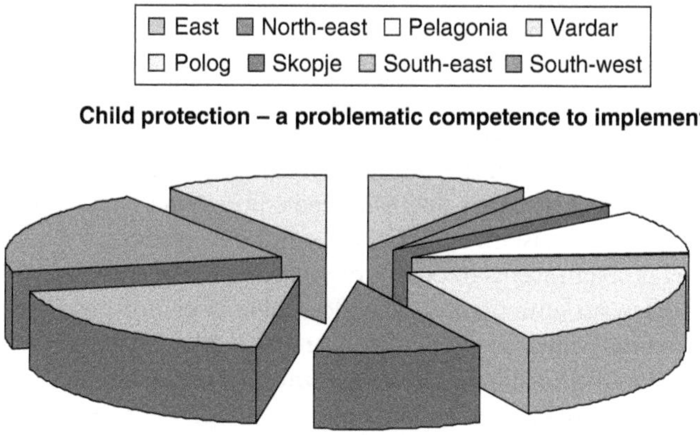

Figure 12.2 Implementation of child protection competence per region
Source: CRPM Decentralization Survey 2010.

this might involve the establishment of a new kindergarten that will provide childcare or the provision of a new home-based childcare service.[10] It is important to note that none of the municipalities have established an innovative childcare service at the community level (such as a home-based service organized on an efficiency basis) although there is an increasing trend of hiring private providers of day care at home (especially in Skopje). In more rural regions, many families arrange childcare for their children at home on the basis of inter-generational solidarity. Needless to say, these arrangements are not standardized and do not provide education or monitoring of early child development. What they demonstrate, however, is that there is a pressing need for an institutional response and for the provision of more childcare services.

Another question relates to the institutional framework and structures that encourage local policymakers to wish to become policy entrepreneurs. The Law on social care encourages the municipalities to establish public institutions for institutional and community-based care. Moreover, as regards guidance on to how to establish extra institutional childcare services, no decisions have been taken concerning who would approve such services, what standards they should reach, who would be responsible for training and providing licences to the caregivers or who would be responsible for monitoring and evaluating the performance of such services. All these issues need to be regulated so that the policy entrepreneur can make effective decisions. Without an effective framework of regulation and support, it is difficult to see how such a policy entrepreneur would be able to change established practice and design new policies or introduce new services. The absence of guidance from the central government has been identified as the main problem for municipalities (CRPM Decentralization Survey 2010). According to the findings of this survey, 19.6% of the municipal governments consider that the lack of clear legislative provisions is an obstacle for the implementation of the new decentralized competences, and almost half (44.6%) lack any assistance from the central government.

The key problem seems to be one of entrepreneurial capacity. As North (2005) argues, an entrepreneurial policymaker does not need particular entrepreneurial skills or particular entrepreneurial characteristics, but needs to be well embedded in the organizational and socio-political environment. What makes him or her a policy entrepreneur, and not a local government administrator, is the need to 'act sensitively towards developments in the policy environment, and to ensure cooperation from other policymakers' (Nooteboom, 2000). Policy entrepreneurs, Mayors and councillors, in order to secure their votes, should aim to match their voters' preferences with the public services delivered to them. In order to bring government closer to the people and 'act sensitively', policy entrepreneurs need to develop mechanisms through which they will be able to identify the interests of their electorate. Opening the local administration to the citizens, increasing transparency in the work of the municipality and increasing citizens' participation in decision-making are some of the avenues through which voters' preferences maybe gathered. Since transparency, accountability and participation are core principles of good governance, we might conclude that policy entrepreneurship is empowered by good governance practices at the local level.

Embedding the voters' preferences into policy solutions and public service design is pertinent to the political willingness, the power of persuasion and building political support among the councillors for the decisions to be made. But the decision only sets the environment for entrepreneurial behaviour. What is also essential for policy entrepreneurship is the capacity of the local administration to pursue the decision. Many municipalities do not have the necessary administrative or financial capacity to enforce decisions or deliver services that match voters' preferences and bring government closer to the people. The CRPM Decentralization Survey 2010 showed that the administrative capacity of Macedonian municipalities is insufficient due to poor qualifications and that local administrators lack essential skills and competences to carry out their functions effectively. Since the enabling conditions for policy entrepreneurship are set by the central government, cooperation between central and local government is important. While the CRPM Decentralization Survey revealed that over three quarters (76%) of municipalities have established cooperation with other municipalities, it also showed that cooperation with institutions at the central level is less evident. Cooperation between central and local government should ensure the adoption of clear and widely accepted rules and prevent disagreement on important policy issues and effective instruments (van der Steen and Groenewegen, 2008). Without such cooperation the central government cannot gather information on the needs of local governments and will most likely not set up the institutional and legal environment for municipalities to develop new social services. This makes cooperation between the central and local level of government important for potential policy entrepreneurs, since it is the finance, institutional framework and structures, and guidance from central government that encourages and enables local policymakers to become policy entrepreneurs. Finally, if these conditions are not met, it is highly unlikely that policy entrepreneurship could be achieved at the community level in Macedonia.

Conclusions

The recent decentralization of competences in relation to social services has transferred new responsibilities to local self-governments in Macedonia, but has provided insufficient corresponding financial resources. Municipalities have only received sufficient additional resources for the maintenance of the existing infrastructure and for payment of staff salaries to deliver these services. New services, which did not exist prior to decentralization, are not financed through the central budget but are expected to be financed by the municipalities' own financial resources. Such an approach serves to reinforce existing inequalities, hinders economic and social development at the local level and prevents the diminution of existing rural–urban disparities. Despite this, the legislative framework that has been put in place by the central government allows municipalities to become policy entrepreneurs and establish new social services if there is need for them. However, many elements of a supportive environment for policy entrepreneurship are still missing: (i) finances, (ii) institutional and legal framework, and (iii) cooperation with central government.

In order to enable municipalities to make more effective use of their transferred competences, and to encourage them to establish new local public services where voters' preferences call for such policies, the following steps should be implemented:

- Firstly, it is necessary to provide a more effective redistribution of finances that will enable a more balanced development, since the current financing model only covers maintenance costs of the existing network of public services, and provides limited incentives to establish new social care services.
- Secondly, an appropriate institutional framework should be established along with guidance from central government on various issues such as who should approve applications to establish new social services, what standards such services should reach, who would be responsible for training and providing licences to the caregivers, as well as who would be responsible for monitoring and evaluating the performance of such services.
- Thirdly, it would be necessary to strengthen the cooperation between local and central government in order to create channels for the flow of information concerning the needs of the local governments for the creation of an appropriate institutional framework and legal environment, for finances and for guidance to support their efforts to develop new social services and to act as effective policy entrepreneurs.

Notes

1. The main goal of the Ohrid Agreement was to accommodate the grievances of the Albanian community, while at the same time preserving the unitary

character of the state, thus addressing the concerns of the Macedonian majority who feared 'federalization' of the country and its eventual disintegration.

2. See the Ammendments of the Constitution of Republic of Macedonia at http://eudo-citizenship.eu/NationalDB/docs/MAC%20Const%20Amendments%20IV-XVIII%20(English).pdf
3. A full list of competences are specified in Art. 22 of the law: (i) urban and rural planning; (ii) environmental protection; (iii) local economic development; (iv) communal activities (including water supply, waste water treatment, solid waste collection and treatment, heating supply, and road construction); (v) culture; (vi) sports and recreation; (vii) social welfare and child protection; (viii) education; (ix) health care; (x) civil protection; (xii) fire fighting; (xii) supervision of municipal responsibilities; and (xiii) any other activities defined by law.
4. More precisely, 3% of the personal income tax on the salaries of employed people, collected in the municipality in which they are registered as having a permanent place of residence, and 100% of the personal income tax from individuals dealing with craftsmanship (Law on Craftsmanship, Official Gazette No. 62/2004), registered on the territory of the municipality in which they are registered to perform activity.
5. At least two financial officers responsible for financial management, budget preparation and execution and accounting; a chief accountant appointed by the mayor; and procedures and system for internal audit endorsed.
6. When voting on issues related to minority rights, the proposal can be accepted not only if the majority of all members in the municipal council votes for it but also the majority of the representatives of the minorities in the municipal council is required to vote for the proposal in order to be accepted.
7. Local government revenues in Macedonia in 2008 were 4.60% of the GDP compared with Albania and Croatia (in 2006) where they amount to 5.80% of the GDP or Serbia where local government revenues are 6.60% of the GDP in the same year.
8. The total per capita revenues of Skopje are almost three times more than the average elsewhere. Indeed, Skopje accounts for almost 50% of all the revenues in the system despite that fact that only 25% of the population resides in the capital.
9. According to the findings of the CRPM Decentralization Survey carried out in 2010.
10. Home-based care is care and education provided by adults in either their own home or the child's. It is usually organized for one to five children and is an appropriate form of family day care in rural areas where the density of children is not high enough for organizing regular kindergarten.

References

Azfar, O., Kähkönen, S., Lanyi, A., Meagher, P. and Rutherford, D. (1999) *Decentralisation, Governance and Public Services: The Impact of Institutional Arrangements: A Review of the Literature*, College Park: University of Maryland, IRIS Center.

Daskalovski, Z. (2006) 'Subnational budget monitoring in Macedonia: Case studies of municipalities of Shtip and Gostivar', in K. Ott (ed.) *Making Public Finance Public: Subnational Budget Watch in Croatia, Macedonia, and Ukraine*, LGI: Budapest, p. 3.

Hayek, F. (1945) 'The use of knowledge in society', *American Economic Review*, 35(4): 519–30.

Levitas, T. (2004) 'Background paper on Macedonian intergovernmental finance', paper presented at the *South-east European Regional Ministerial Conference on Effective Democratic Governance at Local and Regional Level*, August.

Levitas, T. (2009) *Local Government Finances in Macedonia Today: Possible Reforms for Tomorrow*, Skopje: Macedonian Local Government Activity, USAID.

Levitas T. (2009) 'Local Government Finances in Macedonia today: Possible Reforms for Tomorrow'. Urban Institute on international development and governance available online (last visited 17/10/2012) http://www.urban.org/uploadedpdf/412030_local_government_finances.pdf

Van der Steen, M. and Groenewegen, J. (2008) 'Exploring policy entrepreneurship', *Discussion Paper Series on the Coherence between Institutions and Technologies in Infrastructures, WP0801*, Ecole Polytechnique Fédérale de Lausanne and Delft University of Technology.

Nooteboom, B. N. (2000) 'Institutions and the forms of co-ordination in innovation systems,' *Organisation Studies*, 21(5): 915–39.

North, D. C. (2005) *Understanding the Process of Economic Change*, Princeton: Princeton University Press.

Wallace, O. (1999) 'An Essay on Fiscal Federalism', *Journal of Economic Literature*, XXXVII, 3.

Ostrom, E. (2005) 'Unlocking public entrepreneurship and public economies', *Discussion Paper no. 2005/01*, UNU World Institute for development Economics Research (UNU-WIDER), Helsinki.

Rafuse, R. W. Jr (2000) *Why Fiscal Decentralisation in Macedonia?, mimeo*, Skopje: USAID Local Government Reform Project.

Tiebout, C. (1956) 'A pure theory of local expenditures', *Journal of Political Economy*, 64(5): 416–24.

Part V
Spatial Inequalities

13
The Nature of Spatial Inequalities in South East Europe and the Scope for Decentralized Regional Policy: An Analysis of Bulgaria and Serbia

Vassilis Monastiriotis

Introduction

Throughout the former communist European space, the process of transition and, later, EU association has brought out important questions about the extent and evolution of regional disparities in these countries. The processes of industrial restructuring, economic openness and privatization, while generally supporting economic development nationally, have naturally favoured some regions at the expense of others – at least in relative terms. At the same time, as is discussed elsewhere in this volume, two key spatial-administrative processes, of decentralization and regionalization, developed in these countries under perceived or direct pressures for democratization and Europeanization. In turn, these developments too have a potentially important bearing on local capacities to stimulate economic development and, by implication, on regional disparities in incomes and rates of growth.

The literature examining the evolution of spatial disparities among the front-runners of post-communist transition, in Central and Eastern Europe (CEE), has helped identify a number of stylized facts that, broadly speaking, describe the pattern of local economic development in all European transition countries (see, inter alia, Petrakos, Maier and Gorzelak, 2000; Herz and Vogel, 2003; Iara and Traistaru, 2003; Petrakos, Psycharis and Kallioras, 2005; Resmini, 2007; Niebuhr and Schlitte, 2009; Kallioras and Petrakos, 2010; Monastiriotis, 2012a). These include:

- An emerging trend of polarization, with central places (typically, capital cities and their hinterlands) growing faster, benefiting from the concentration of financial and political capital and the attraction of disproportionate shares of FDI, international aid and skilled labour supply.

- An underlying trend of East–West dichotomy, underpinned by differences in proximity to the 'Western core' (the so-called blue banana) and the sharing of physical borders with the old EU15 (itself signifying existing, although possibly inert, cultural, historical and structural linkages with EU15 regions bordering the former Eastern Bloc).
- And a tendency for overall regional convergence, despite polarization, which is essentially driven by a process of club formation with the most well-off regions following a high-growth trajectory and the vast majority of the remaining regions converging towards a less dynamic second steady-state.

Of course, the actual trajectories that have been followed by specific regions vary. Beyond the central trends there are important variations that are related to a multitude of context-specific factors, such as the extent of past dependence on CMEA trade, the natural resource base, the position of specific regions in relation to past conflicts or active ethnic tensions, and others (Resmini and Traistaru, 2003; Longhi, Nijkamp and Traistaru, 2004; Monastiriotis and Petrakos, 2009). But the central trends seem to apply throughout the European transition space irrespective – or even despite – these case-specific particularities.

As the CEE countries offer a wealth of experience and, generally speaking, more 'normal' paths to transition and EU accession, in the sense of being much less subjected to inter-ethnic conflicts and much less interwoven with problems of underdevelopment, naturally much of the focus in the relevant literature has been on these countries. Thus attention to the extent, spatial manifestation and temporal evolution of regional disparities in the countries of South-east Europe (SEE) has been much more limited (for exceptions see, inter alia, Petrakos, 1997; Petrakos and Economou, 2002; Getimis and Kafkalas, 2007; Monastiriotis and Petrakos, 2009; Horvat and Hajdu, 2011).

In this chapter we seek to add to this literature by providing an exploratory spatial analysis for the cases of Serbia and Bulgaria, two countries of relatively similar size and levels of development, but with different positions in relation to EU accession and at different points in the transition process. Bulgaria represents the least successful of the CEE transitions, having only joined the EU in 2007 and having experienced in the early phase of transition (until 1997) many policy reversals and unsuccessful transition policies. Serbia, on the other hand, entangled in nationalist wars following the dissolution of Yugoslavia, only really started its democratic and economic transition after 2001 while it only managed to obtain an EU Candidate status in the last few months. Despite this, both countries have experimented with decentralization from rather early on (Monastiriotis, 2010, 2012b) – although in both cases no substantive form of decentralization had taken place until at least the late 2000s. Given the slow progression of both countries with regard to fiscal decentralization and administrative regionalization, as well as with regard to privatization and FDI attraction, it is interesting to examine to what extent developments commonly observed in the CEE space are also found in these two countries – which we take to typify developments across the SEE region more generally. It is moreover important to examine this in relation to the processes of decentralization and regionalization, as these processes affect the scale at which regional policy is designed and delivered. Thus, our exploration in this chapter is motivated by an underlying question about the spatial scale at which regional disparities in the two countries are located – with a possible mismatch between the revealed economic geographies and the administrative divisions at which policy is delivered representing an area of potential policy failure.

Our approach in this chapter is as follows. In the next section we analyse the extent and evolution of regional disparities in the two countries, corresponding to what is known in the literature as an analysis of sigma-convergence. We also look closer at the scale at which disparities are located, comparing the extent of disparity within and between regions and analysing the regional evolutions separately at the municipal, district (NUTS3) and regional (NUTS2) levels. In the later section we turn our attention to the geography of regional disparities and examine through the application of an Exploratory Spatial Data Analysis (ESDA) and the use of Local Indicators of Spatial Association (LISA) the extent of spatial clustering and spatial association in the two countries. As it will be shown, despite some notable differences between the two countries, our analysis reveals largely a set of problems for regional economic performance and regional policy that follow a common thread, relating broadly to issues of polarization and (lack of) spatial connectivity – albeit at very different scales in the two countries. We discuss the implications of this, and the future outlook of regional performances in the two countries, in the concluding section.

Regional disparities in Bulgaria and Serbia

Our starting point is the examination of the extent, as well as the scale, of regional disparities that have emerged in the two SEE countries of our focus throughout the process of transition. For this, we look at the level of regional disparities and how this has evolved since the mid- to late 1990s at various spatial scales, from the macro-regional (equivalent to the NUTS2 level) to, where available, the local (municipalities). We measure regional disparity by the coefficient of variation of various indicators that proxy for the level of regional development – using wages, per capita GDP and productivity depending on data availability.

Figure 13.1 presents the evolution of the coefficient of variation of regional incomes and productivity (measured in terms of Gross Domestic Product per capita and Gross Value Added per worker, respectively) for the NUTS2 regions of Bulgaria. As can be seen, following a period of relative stability in the mid- to late 1990s, regional disparities in the country increased rapidly with the turn of the century, reaching very high levels at the advent of the global financial crisis. In terms of GDP per capita regional disparities in 2008 were over twice their level in 2000 (and almost three times higher than in 1995), while in terms of labour productivity (GVA per worker) the increase was also significant – albeit much lower – at about 60%. Data on wages further corroborate this, showing an increase between 2000 and 2008 of 228%.[1]

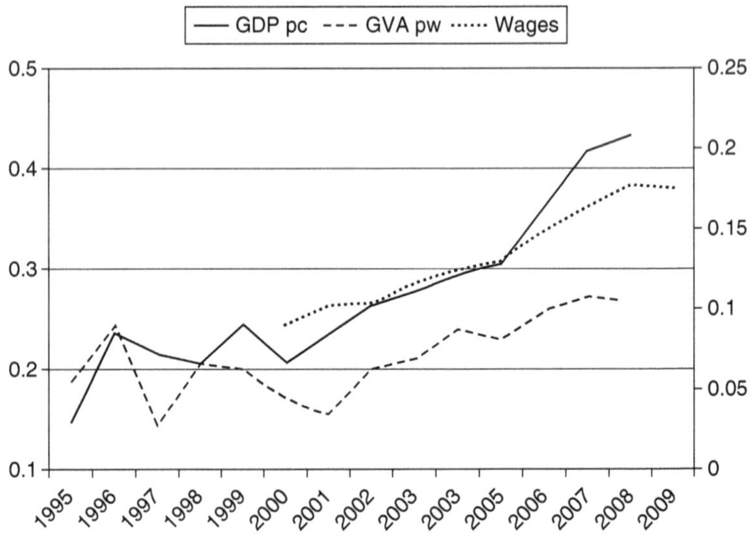

Figure 13.1 Regional disparities across the NUTS2 regions of Bulgaria (coefficient of variation)

Source: Data from Eurostat and the National Statistical Institute of Bulgaria; author's own elaborations.

The picture obtained for Serbia is only partly similar. Unfortunately, data on regional GDP and GVA are not yet available for Serbia. However, we can get a picture of the extent of regional disparity using data from the now discontinued series of national incomes that was published annually by the Statistical Office of the Republic of Serbia between 1996 and 2006.[2] Figure 13.2 presents the coefficient of variation of this series using District level data that have been aggregated at the macro-regional level using the NUTS2 regional classification established in Serbia in 2009. As is depicted there, and consistent with the picture observed for Bulgaria, regional income disparities in Serbia have been on the rise more or less throughout the period and their widening has been accelerated particularly post-2000. For the period 2000–4 this pattern is also revealed in the official data on average wages[3] published by the Statistical Office of Serbia. According to this series, however, post-2005 and at least until the eruption of the global financial crisis, regional disparities in Serbia (in terms of wages) were declining at an accelerated pace. Although it is not possible to know whether this decline is also to be found in regional incomes and GDP per capita levels, on the basis of the evidence derived from the wage data it is reasonable to assume that this has been the case.

This finding, of declining regional disparities in Serbia in the second half of the 2000s, is in many respects rather counter-intuitive.

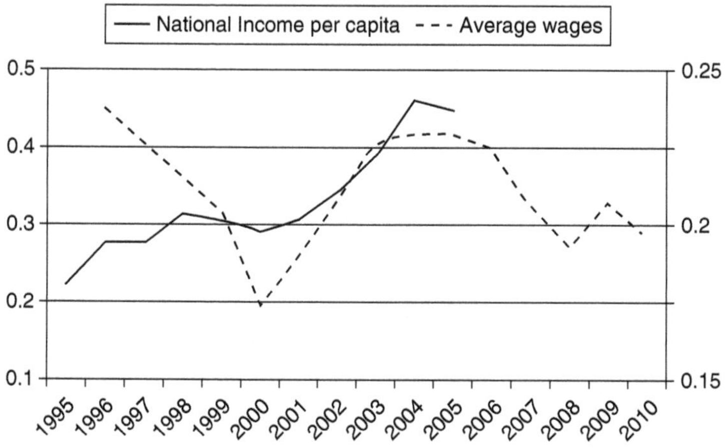

Figure 13.2 Regional disparities across the NUTS2 regions of Serbia (coefficient of variation)
Source: Data from the Statistical Office of Serbia; author's own elaborations.

Although for Bulgaria, as is found elsewhere in the literature for other CEE countries, the process of transition and EU integration has been associated with a widening of regional disparities, for Serbia the period associated with the take-off of transition and the intensification of the EU approximation process seems to be one of regional convergence. The question follows: is this finding due to some unique process of equilibration in Serbia, or is it rather an artefact of the regional aggregation – in which case we could expect to find regional disparities in the country to widen when measured at different scales? To examine this we take a closer look at the size and evolution of spatial disparities at the (sub-)regional and local levels.

The evidence from Figure 13.3 (left panel) seems to suggest that indeed Serbia has seen a process of spatial equalization at all scales in recent years. Despite the increase in regional disparities that was registered in the first years of the new millennium – as is evidenced mainly in the incomes data – the regional (districts) and sub-regional (municipalities) distribution of wages has clearly been narrowing since around 2003–4 and disparities appear to be lower today than those found in the country in the 1990s. In contrast, the district-level data for Bulgaria (Figure 13.3, right panel) remain consistent with the patterns found for the macro-regional level, with disparities rising continuously both in terms of incomes as well as in terms of productivities and wages.[4] In both countries, disparities at the local level (across municipalities) are notably higher than disparities found at the regional level (across districts), although the latter are either comparable (in Bulgaria) or in fact lower than the extent of regional disparity found at the macro-regional level (NUTS2). However, important differences exist in the location and scale of regional disparities in the two countries. Table 13.1 presents a decomposition of regional disparities into a within and between component to illustrate this fact.

As can be seen, in Bulgaria, consistently across all measures and over time, the main bulk of disparity is located within its NUTS2 macro-regions. Specifically, between 75% (for productivity) and 89% (for wages) of the spatial inequalities observed at the district level is located within each macro-region, leaving only a small fraction of disparity (between 11 and 25%) to be accounted for by differences across macro-regions. In other words, for Bulgaria, differences in incomes and productivities across macro-regions are not particularly significant and, in contrast, each macro-region contains within it a significant degree of disparity. The implication of this is that the high- and low-productivity districts in the country are not separated along macro-geographical

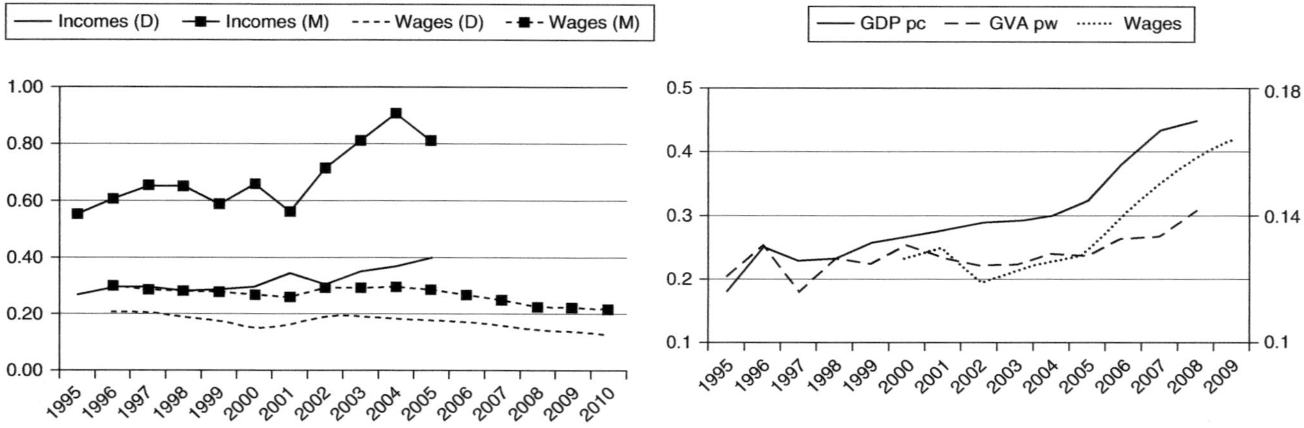

Figure 13.3 Regional disparities at the district and municipal level in Serbia and Bulgaria (coefficient of variation)
Source: See Figures 13.1 and 13.2.

Table 13.1 Relative importance of intra-regional disparities in Serbia and Bulgaria

	Bulgaria			Serbia	
	Within NUTS2, across districts			Within NUTS2, across districts	Within districts, across municipalities
Year	GDP pc	GVA pw	Wages	Wages	Wages
1995	0.86	0.62			
1996	0.82	0.77		0.51	0.53
1997	0.65	0.82		0.49	0.55
1998	0.72	0.68		0.49	0.63
1999	0.76	0.70		0.41	0.63
2000	0.85	0.76	0.87	0.41	0.70
2001	0.87	0.84	0.89	0.28	0.63
2002	0.86	0.74	0.86	0.27	0.64
2003	0.84	0.77	0.84	0.34	0.62
2004	0.82	0.74	0.83	0.42	0.61
2005	0.85	0.76	0.86	0.44	0.58
2006	0.85	0.77	0.85	0.45	0.59
2007	0.84	0.73	0.86	0.53	0.58
2008	0.82	0.75	0.89	0.46	0.59
2009			0.89	0.40	0.60
2010				0.46	0.63

Source: Author's elaboration of data from Eurostat, the Statistical Office of Serbia and the National Statistical Institute of Bulgaria. Figures show the part of the overall variance, across spatial units, of each variable that is due to differences observed within the region to which each spatial unit belongs. This corresponds to the 'within' component of a simple Oaxaca decomposition (for details see Monastiriotis, 2002).

lines (e.g. north–south or East–West dichotomies) but, instead, a core-periphery pattern characterizes each of the country's macro-regions. This is a finding that separates Bulgaria's experience from the experience of most CEE countries, where polarization around single poles (typically located in the capital cities) has been the norm for most of the transition period.

For Serbia, however, the picture is markedly different. For this country, less than half of overall cross-district disparity is to be found within each NUTS2 region, with the bulk of disparity being accounted for by differences across these macro-regions. The same, although to a slightly lower extent, seems to be true for disparities within districts (across municipalities), which account on average for some 60% of total cross-municipality disparities. This suggests that, relative to Bulgaria, spatial inequalities within the districts of Serbia are low while municipal outcomes seem to differ much more notably across districts. As a result, for Serbia, inequalities seem to be much more of a macro-geographical phenomenon than a localized core-periphery pattern.

In the next section we turn to the geographical manifestation of these patterns of regional disparity in order to analyse more closely how they differ between the two countries.

Distribution and spatial association of productivities and incomes

A first step for the geographical analysis of regional development differentials (as captured by measures of incomes, productivity and wages) is the visual examination of the geography of economic outcomes in the two countries. Figure 13.4 allows us to do this, by depicting the distribution of such outcomes (GDP pc and average wages) across the districts (for Bulgaria and Serbia) and municipalities (for Serbia) of the two countries along four quartiles and over three periods: the period before the take-off of transition (1995 for Bulgaria, 1996 for Serbia), the period of early transition (2002) and the period just before the financial crisis (2008).

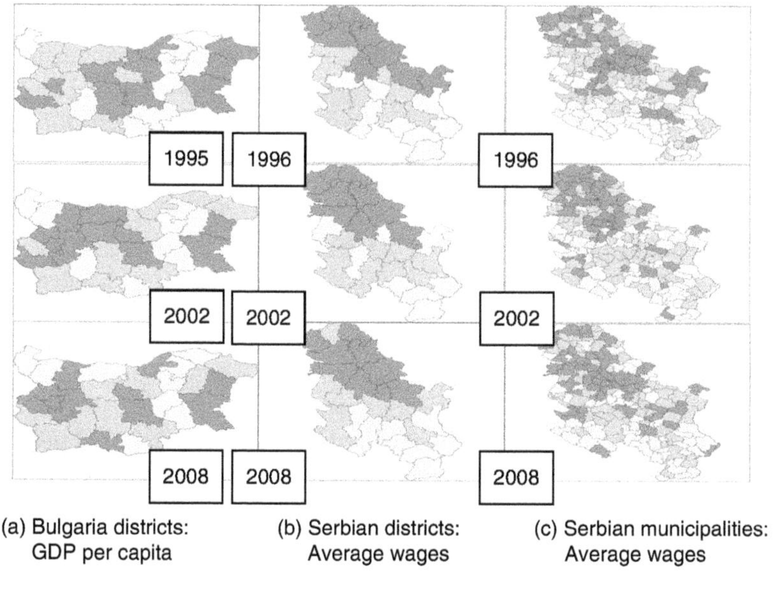

Figure 13.4 Geographical distribution of GDP pc and wages across districts and municipalities in Bulgaria and Serbia

The maps show clearly the validity of the conclusion reached earlier. In Bulgaria, neither the north–south nor the East–West dichotomy is sufficient to describe the pattern of disparities in the country. High-income regions are located both in the West (especially the region of the capital city, Sofia) and in the East (the regions of the two main coastal cities, Burgas and Varna) as well as both in the North and in the South. With regard to the latter, it is important to note that none of the three high-wage clusters found in the east, centre and west of the country (covering the regions of Burgas and Varna, Strata Zagora and Gabrovo, and Sofia, Pernik and Vratsa, respectively) is located within a single NUTS2 region: each and every one of the three clusters cross NUTS2 (and sometimes NUTS1) borders. Concerning the temporal evolution of this geographical distribution, it is worth noticing the narrowing of the eastern and central clusters and the strengthening of the cluster around the capital city of Sofia, which has been gaining in relative economic importance at least since the late 1990s.

In contrast, deciphering a macro-geography in the regional distribution of wages in Serbia is much more straightforward. At the district level, there is a clear north–south pattern, with high-wage regions concentrated invariably in the Autonomous Province of Vojvodina and the North-east part of Central Serbia (covering the capital city of Belgrade and the districts of Branicevo and Podunavlje to the east). The pattern is not much different when inequalities are examined at the municipal level. A large cluster of high-wage municipalities is located in the north and the incidence of high wages is limited to a few locations in the rest of the country, such as the municipalities of Despotovac (in the Pomoravjle district), Kusevac (in the Rasina district) and Sokobanja (in the eastern district of Zajecar).

Interestingly, however, whereas the geography of incomes and wages at the district level seems to be very stable in both Serbia and Bulgaria, at the level of municipalities important geographical shifts can be observed – at least in the case of Serbia where reliable data are available at this level. In the 1990s the incidence of high wages was more strongly concentrated along an axis running from Belgrade to the east (South Banat district of Vojvodina), an axis further north closer to the borders with Hungary (e.g. around Subotica) and a few other clusters in the north (around Novi Sad), the east (district of Bor) and the south (in the districts of Nis and Rasina). In the early 2000s the northern axes seem to have shifted westwards while the clusters in the rest of the country seem to have become weaker – with the incidence of high wages being more sporadic. More recently this geography seems to have shifted again (especially so for 2010 data), with the northern cluster becoming somewhat dissolved, the eastern cluster in Bor being strengthened, the Belgrade–South Banat axis re-emerging and the incidence of high-wage becoming much more dispersed towards the south. Relating to the findings from the aggregate analysis of the previous section, it is clear that these developments – mainly the dissolution of the northern high-wage cluster in Vojvodina and the emergence of high-wage 'hotspots' in the south – account for much of the overall decline in the coefficient of variation of municipal wages, as was discussed in the previous section (in relation to Figure 13.3).

Although these patterns of clustering are obviously very interesting and informative, it is important to test how strong they are statistically – as the visual identification of patterns can often be deceptive. To do so, we rely on the Moran's I statistic, which examines the degree of spatial association both globally (on aggregate, across the country) and at the local level (for each municipality individually and for emerging groups of municipalities).[5] Figure 13.5 presents a set of measures of global spatial association for the two countries of our analysis.

A first observation that can be made is the absence of any evidence of spatial association in the case of Bulgaria – at least at the district level. Although using different datasets at the municipal level (see Monastiriotis,

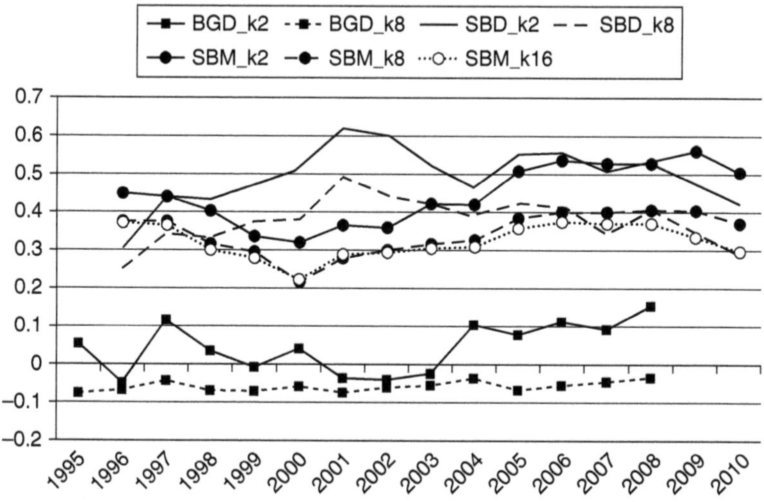

Figure 13.5 Spatial association of regional outcomes: Global Moran's I
Source: See Figures 13.1 and 13.2. All Moran's I statistics have been calculated in GeoDa.

2010), some evidence of very localized clustering (positive spatial association) can be found – together with negative spatial association at longer distances – at the district level there is in fact very little to show. Spatial association is marginally positive (but increasing post-2004) at the very localized level (in terms of Figure 13.5, when only two neighbours are considered for each district) while it is negative but very close to zero for spatial association using wider definitions of neighbourliness (here the eight nearest neighbours). This finding verifies the earlier conclusion, that in Bulgaria the distribution of advantageous economic outcomes is rather dispersed.

In contrast, for Serbia, evidence of spatial association (clustering) is much stronger. At the district level localized spatial association (two neighbours) reached very high values in the early 2000s and, although it has followed a subsiding trend more recently, remains very high today. Spatial clustering is also present at wider scales (eight neighbours), following largely the same trends as with localized clustering. Interestingly, spatial association for municipalities has followed a different trend, reaching its lowest value in 2000 but rising quite fast ever since. Here too, however, clustering remains rather localized, with the narrow-geography Moran's I coefficient (for two neighbours) having a value around one and a half times higher than the coefficient obtained for much wider geographies (eight or 16 neighbours).

How do these patterns of clustering translate into the actual geography of the two countries? To answer this we map in Figure 13.6 the location of statistically significant clusters of high and low outcomes, based on the local version of the Moran's I statistic.[6] In contrast to the picture of relative stability seen before, the location and incidence of statistically significant local clusters in Bulgaria seems to shift notably over time. In the 1990s the most notable feature is not the presence of high-outcome clusters (there is only one, whose centre, as depicted in Figure 13.6, was located in the north-east) but of a large low-outcomes cluster running across from the northern to the southern borders in the central-east part of the country. These clusters had effectively dissolved by the turn of the century while more recently a new cluster, encompassing a large number of districts and signifying the increasing clustering of high-value outcomes, was formed around the capital city – with Strata Zagora forming a separate statistically significant 'hotspot' of high-value outcomes (i.e. surrounded mainly by low-value regions).

These shifts are much more comparable now to those observed for Serbia. Here too, as was also discussed earlier, we observe notable shifts of patterns of clustering over time. The north-east cluster of high-value

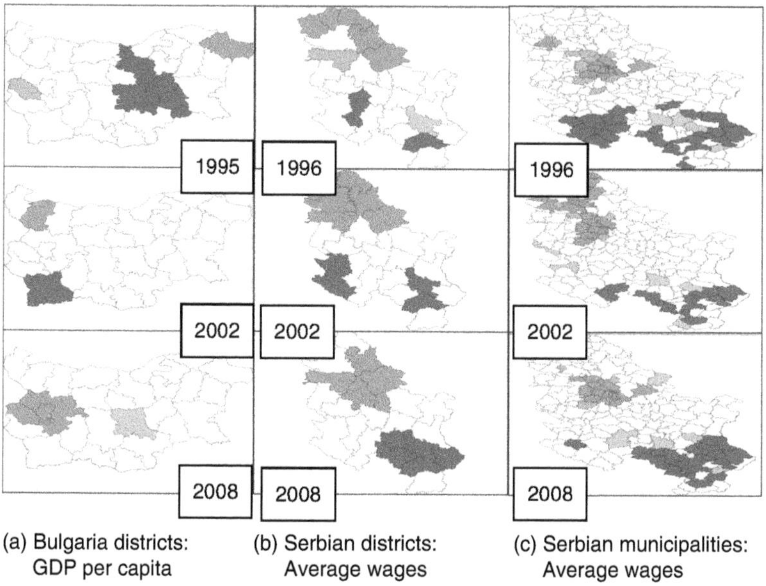

Figure 13.6 Local spatial association in Bulgaria and Serbia

outcomes of the mid-1990s shifted westwards and became much larger in the early 2000s before dissolving somewhat and shifting much closer to Belgrade, which seems to have consolidated its centrality in terms of economic performance more recently. In turn, the small clusters of low performance found in the mid-1990s in the south have become over time larger and have consolidated more recently into a single mega-cluster of relative underperformance in the southern parts of the country. Importantly, as is the case with Bulgaria, both of these clusters cross the NUTS2 boundaries of the country.

When examining these patterns using municipal-level data, the picture is broadly consistent but evidently there are also important differences. The northern high-high cluster found in the 1990s at the district level did not translate into a similar cluster across municipalities (with the implication that within-district outcomes in the region were at the time rather diverse). Instead, Belgrade formed the only inter-municipal cluster of high-value outcomes. Although this cluster expanded clearly northwards in the early 2000s, it appears that more recently this movement has been retracted and today the area around Belgrade constitutes the only statistically significant cluster of above-average outcomes. In the south, the low-low western cluster seems to have narrowed substantially, but the eastern low-low cluster has, if anything, become larger. Some hotspots of above-average economic performance have, however, remained present inside the otherwise underperforming south.

Discussion

The evidence presented in the previous two sections sketches an interesting picture about the extent, location and evolution of spatial disparities in the two countries under study. In Bulgaria, regional disparities seem to have increased substantially since the mainstreaming of the transition effort (after 1997) and the trend may have even accelerated more recently (in the advent of EU accession), resulting in high levels of disparity especially at the regional (NUTS3) and local levels. Geographically, however, the incidence of high-performance is rather spread and thus a dichotomous macro-geography is not discernible. An implication of this is that the extent of spatial association across the country is particularly small. Especially at the local level, this suggests that within wider regions (e.g. districts or NUTS2 areas) there is co-location of over- and under-performing localities. At a wider scale, this further suggests that positive economic outcomes, like those found in the coastal districts in the east and increasingly in the large high-high cluster around the capital city of Sofia, do not diffuse either at the micro- or at the macro-scale (i.e. across underperforming municipalities within the better-off districts or from the better-off districts to the ones in their periphery). Thus, whereas regional disparities at the level where policy is designed (NUTS2 regions) are not worryingly high, disparities at lower scales are much more heightened and – given the evidence of extremely weak spatial association – much more problematic from a spatial equalization perspective.

In Serbia the patterns are markedly different. The intensification of the process of transition and EU association after the early 2000s, has seen a relative decline in spatial disparities overall[7] – although good data on regional incomes and productivities are not available and could present a rather different picture from that obtained from data on wages that have been used here. In any case, spatial disparities in Serbia have a much more macro-geographical character, with no less than half of overall disparity being located across, rather than within, districts and the recently established NUTS2 regions. The geographical distribution of economic outcomes follows a clear north–south divide, with a remarkable concentration of above-average performances in the north and strong concentration of underperformance in the south.

Moreover, despite the evidence of declining overall regional disparities, the north–south dichotomy has, if anything, been strengthened, as is the dichotomy between the high-performance cluster around the capital city Belgrade and the rest of the country. It thus seems that here too, the process of transition and EU association has been accompanied by increasing polarization – even if this has not resulted so far to a widening of overall spatial disparities, as disparities between the two clusters have instead narrowed.

Are there any common lessons to be drawn from the experiences of the two countries regarding the evolution and pattern of their spatial disparities? On a casual inspection, it seems that the patterns are too dissimilar. Disparities in Bulgaria have increased while in Serbia they have subsided. Spatial association is much stronger in Serbia (and practically non-existent in Bulgaria) and while Bulgaria appears to have a number of high-performing clusters outside the capital (although of declining significance statistically), in Serbia the pattern is much more evidently one of polarization and north–south dichotomy. On closer inspection, however, our analysis suggests that some similar patterns are also identifiable. In both countries the importance and centrality of the capital cities seems to be on the rise. Similarly, in both countries the importance of clusters outside these central city-regions (e.g. Novi Sad in Serbia and Burgas-Varna in Bulgaria) appears to be declining. This seems to be consistent with the broader experience of the transition countries in Central and Eastern Europe, where economic openness coincided with a rising dominance of the capital city-regions (polarization) and relative gains for the regions bordering the old member states of the EU (Petrakos, 2000; Niebuhr and Schlitte, 2009; Monastiriotis, 2012a). In the two countries examined here, the pattern of polarization and capital-region dominance is also replicated, although the developmental gains for border regions are much less accentuated (perhaps owing to the fact that both countries lack physical borders with the industrial clusters of the old EU: Vojvodina and south Bulgaria border the least developed parts of Hungary and Greece, respectively).

Beyond these commonalities, however, it appears that the regional problems and needs for the two countries are qualitatively different. In Bulgaria the main problem seems to be the lack of spatial connectedness, as manifested in the very low spatial association of economic outcomes across space. An implication of this is that, whereas areas of above-average performance are to be found in many parts of the country, they largely fail to build wider and sufficiently strong agglomerations that could mobilize economic development more robustly and more equitably across the different localities within the regions of the country. In contrast, in Serbia the main problem seems to be with the macro-geography of the country and the persistent and widespread relative underdevelopment of large parts of the south (essentially, the whole of the country south of Belgrade). As spatial association appears much stronger in the case of Serbia, the policy implication is not one of seeking to improve spatio-economic connectivity but rather of aiming at strengthening the areas that can act as potential growth poles in the underperforming regions of the south.

A final note can be made about the ability of policy to identify and address these problems. As was shown in both the descriptive and the statistical analysis of the section 'Distribution and spatial association of productivities and incomes', in both countries the economic geography does not seem to coincide with the administrative geography and especially with the geography of the NUTS2 regions – where EU policymaking takes place. Effectively in all cases, spatial clusters cross the NUTS2 borders while at least in the case of Bulgaria regional disparities are at a much more localized scale than that of the NUTS2 region. Still, as is discussed in other parts of this book, for most countries in the SEE region, including Bulgaria and Serbia, policy has shifted towards a model of decentralization (to the municipal level) and regionalization (to the macro-regional level of NUTS2) that is largely driven by wider political–economic considerations (e.g. for compliance with perceived or binding EU rules) and pays little attention to the scale at which on-the-ground economic problems and needs are located. This appears to be a common challenge for regional policy in the two countries examined here and in South East Europe more generally.

Notes

1. Importantly, the level of regional disparity appears to be much lower on the basis of the wages measure (being at around 40% of the level of disparity suggested by the GDP pc measure). This is of course intuitively consistent, as cross-regional equilibration is more likely in the case of factor prices (e.g. due to capital mobility) than in the case of total incomes (which include rents from immobile factors). That said, the evidence for wages, as is the case with the evidence on incomes and productivity, is clearly of a fast-increasing trend for regional divergence.
2. The Statistical Office of Serbia recommends against the use of this series, as the definition and measurement of the national incomes series is not consistent with the Eurostat definition. Thus the use of the series here is for indication only, although we note that as long as the measurement bias (e.g. not accurately taking into account tax receipts) is constant across macro-regions

over time the measure of regional disparity produced by this data should be directly analogous to the true extent of regional disparity.
3. The series depicted in Figure 13.2 is average per capita labour income of dependent employees (salaries and wages). Alternative measures produce essentially identical pictures.
4. A similar picture is obtained from unofficial data that is available to the author for wages at the municipal level – although the quality of the data here is not sufficient to allow a confident analysis.
5. This is similar to a correlation coefficient showing correlation between local and neighbouring values. Values closer to 1 show a high positive association (so that similar regions tend to cluster together in space) while negative values (negative association) reflect a tendency for high-outcome regions to cluster together with low-outcome ones – with values close to zero showing that the spatial distribution of economic outcomes is (close to) random. For further details and exposition, see Anselin (1985).
6. The local Moran statistic gives a measure of coincidence of high or low values around a neighbourhood for each location individually. Following, a so-called LISA analysis can be performed (Anselin, 1995), whereby statistically significant clusters are divided along four groups: high-high (high local values surrounded by high neighbouring values), high-low (high local values with low neighbouring values), low-high (low local values with high neighbouring values) and low-low (low local with low neighbouring values). These four groups are depicted in different colours in the resulting LISA maps (red, pink, light blue and dark blue, respectively).
7. It should be emphasized that the evidence discussed and analysed in the chapter does not allow us to make any claims about causal links between the observed patterns and the wider political–economic processes underway in the two countries.

References

Anselin, L. (1985) *Spatial Econometrics: Methods and Models*, Dordrecht: Kluwer Academic Publishers.

Anselin, L. (1995) 'Local Indicators of Spatial Association – LISA', *Geographical Analysis*, 27(2): 93–115.

Getimis, P. and Kafkalas, G. (eds) (2007) *Overcoming Fragmentation in Southeast Europe: Spatial Development Trends and Integration Potential*, Aldershot: Ashgate.

Herz, B. and Vogel, L. (2003) 'Regional convergence in central and Eastern Europe: Evidence from a decade of transition', in C. Hausen, M. Resinek, N. Schürmann and M. Stierle (eds) *Determinants of Growth and Business Cycles: Theory, Empirical Evidence and Policy Implications*, Berlin: Springer, pp. 155–79.

Horvat, G. and Hajdu, Z. (eds) (2011) *Regional Transformation Processes in the Western Balkan Countries*, Pecs: Centre for Regional Studies, Hungarian Academy of Sciences.

Iara, A. and Traistaru, I. (2003) 'Integration, regional specialization and growth differentials in EU accession countries: Evidence from Hungary', in C. Hausen (ed.) *Determinants of Growth and Business Cycles: Theory, Empirical Evidence and Policy Implications*, Berlin: Verlag für Wissenschaft und Forschung, pp.181–202.

Kallioras, D. and Petrakos, G. (2010) 'Industrial growth, economic integration and structural change: Evidence from the EU new member-states regions', *Annals of Regional Science*, 45(3): 667–80.

Longhi, S., Nijkamp, P. and Traistaru, I. (2004) 'Economic integration and regional structural change in a wider Europe: Evidence from new EU and accession countries', *Journal for Institutional Innovation, Development, and Transition*, 8: 48–55.

Monastiriotis, V. (2002) 'Inter- and intra-regional wage inequalities in the UK: Sources and evolution', *LSE Research Papers in Environmental and Spatial Analysis No. 70*, London: London School of Economics and Political Science.

Monastiriotis, V. (2010) 'The emergence of regional policy in Bulgaria and the role of the EU', in S. Katsikas (ed.) *Bulgaria and Europe: Challenging Identities*, London: Anthem Press, pp. 173–91.

Monastiriotis, V. (2012a) 'Regional growth in Central and Eastern Europe: convergence, divergence and non-linear dynamics', in R. Crescenzi and M. Percoco (eds) *Geography, Institutions and Regional Economic Performance*, Berlin: Springer, pp. 77–94.

Monastiriotis, V. (2012b) 'Decentralisation and inter-municipal competition in SEE: Evidence from Serbia', *LSEE Paper on Decentralisation No. 1*, London: London School of Economics and Political Science.

Monastiriotis, V. and Petrakos, G. (2009) 'Local sustainable development and spatial cohesion in the post-transition Balkans: Policy issues and some theory', in M. Vujosevic and J. Petric (eds) *Regional Development, Spatial Planning and Strategic Governance*, Thematic Conference Proceedings Vol. I, Belgrade: Institute of Architecture and Urban and Spatial Planning of Serbia, pp. 1–20.

Niebuhr, A. and Schlitte, F. (2009) 'EU enlargement and convergence: Does market access matter?' *Eastern European Economics*, 47(3): 28–56.

Petrakos, G. (1997) 'The regional structure of Albania, Bulgaria and Greece: Implications for cross-border cooperation and development', *European Urban and Regional Studies*, 4(3): 195–210.

Petrakos, G. (2000) 'The spatial impact of East-West interaction in Europe', in G. Petrakos, G. Maier and G. Gorzelak (eds) *Integration and Transition in Europe: The Economic Geography of Interaction*, London: Routledge, pp. 38–68.

Petrakos, G. and Economou, D. (2002) 'The spatial aspects of development in Southeastern Europe', *Spatium*, 8: 1–13.

Petrakos, G., Maier, G. and Gorzelak, G. (2000) 'The new economic geography of Europe' in G. Petrakos, G. Maier and G. Gorzelak (eds) *Integration and Transition in Europe: The Economic Geography of Interaction*, London: Routledge, pp. 1–37.

Petrakos, G., Psycharis, Y. and Kallioras, D. (2005) 'Regional inequalities in the EU new member-states: Evolution and challenges', in J. Bradley, G. Petrakos and I. Traistaru (eds) *The Economics and Policy of Cohesion in an Enlarged European Union*, New York: Springer, pp. 45–64.

Resmini, L. (2007) 'Regional patterns of industry location in transition countries: Does economic integration with the EU matter?' *Regional Studies*, 41(6): 747–64.

Resmini, L. and Traistaru, I. (2003) 'Spatial implications of economic integration in EU accession countries', in I. Traistaru, P. Nijkamp and L. Resmini (eds) *The Emerging Economic Geography in EU Accession Countries*, Aldershot: Ashgate, pp. 3–24.

14
A NUTS2 View of Regional Inequality in Croatia, 1968–2008

Ivo Bićanić and Vedrana Pribičević

Introduction

Croatia is a small economy. This is true both with respect to its GDP (pre-recession, 2008 GDP was €47.4 billion, only 25% of almost equally populated Finland), population (with 4.4 million inhabitants according to the 2011 population census, it is approximately the size of metropolitan Milan or St Petersburg) and area (with an area of 56,542 square kilometres, it is slightly below the size of Lake Michigan). Furthermore, it is sparsely populated (with 81 persons per square kilometre, it is at 72% of the EU average) and ranked as an upper middle-income economy (with US$17,336 per capita in PPP in 2008, it is 65% higher than the World Bank average for this income group and ranks 64th on the World Bank GDP per capita PPP ranking). With regard to its population the whole country could easily be one NUTS2 region (out of 271 NUTS2 regions in the EU27, 13 have a larger population and 79 a larger GDP).

However, in spite of its small size, it harbours many differences making it a spatially very diverse economy and society (both in relative and absolute terms). Two climates (Mediterranean and continental), three geographical regions (Mediterranean coast, Dinaric mountains and Pannonian plain) and longitudinal mountains acting as barriers favoured the maintenance of diversity. As such natural circumstance have been combined with lasting and very diverse external influences (more recently: Italian, Austrian, Hungarian, Turkish and Serb) and the borders these created (administrative, internal and state), Croatia's relatively high levels of regional differences and the maintenance of isolated less developed pockets should not come as a surprise.

Given such a setting, it is interesting to see how spatial inequality developed over a long period of time. Obviously it would be nice to have historical regional data going back to the nineteenth century. However, historical regional data do not exist. The only pre-1945 regional data come from Good (1992) who offers partial estimates of pre-World War I Austro-Hungarian administrative regions for selected years. Comparable and reliable post-1945 regional data exists only after the pro-market reforms of 1965 improved the quality and quantity of data gathering. But even then, due to social accounting and regional changes during the 40-year period, regional differences after 1969 can only be measured indirectly. Admittedly, such a short time series prevents the extremely interesting analysis of the effect of the many external influences, but even in the short 40-year period for which data exists there were major changes, as shown in the next section, which should have had regionally asymmetric effects.

In an earlier paper (Bićanić and Pribičević, 2009), we discussed the changes in the development gradient of Croatia's present counties. In this chapter we further develop this analysis. Here we use an updated version of the same database but instead of concentrating on the county level we take the NUTS2 level as the basic unit of our analysis. For this level we calculate indicators of inter-regional inequality and rankings as well as intra-regional inequality during the 39-year period from 1969 to 2008. The first year of the period, 1969, is the first year useful data was collected. The last year, 2008, was chosen as the last pre-recession year and is the most recent year with data at the desired level of aggregation.

The chapter has four sections. In the first we discuss the trend and shocks to which the Croatian economy was subjected during the period. We deduce their spatially asymmetric effects and offer some a priori conclusions about their influence on regional inequality. In the second section we define the spatial unit of the analysis – that is, the NUTS2 level – in Croatia and then briefly describe the data and inequality measures used in the calculations. The third section presents the results of our measurement. The fourth and final section is the concluding section in which some policy implications are discussed.

Croatia's shocks and trends from a spatial viewpoint[1]

During the almost 40-year period from 1969 to 2008 analysed in this chapter, the Croatian economy was under three kinds of influences each of which should have had an impact on spatial inequality. The first were the long-run changes resulting from long-term development (primarily urbanization and industrialization). The second were a result of attempted social engineering and the path dependency it created (socialism and self-management together with the specifics of socialist industrialization policies). The third kind of influence resulted from shocks (the 1948 break with the Soviet Union that heightened the importance of strategic considerations in location decisions, the market-oriented reforms of the 1960s and the world debt crises of the 1980s).

It is quite understandable that with a long-term growth rate of per capita income of 3% over the almost 40-year period Croatia would have undergone major social and economic changes. Indeed, during this period it was transformed from a less developed economy to an upper middle-income one. The structural changes involved are well known and do not require special explanation. The obvious examples of the extent of these changes can be seen in urbanization (the share of non-farming population according to the 1971 and 2001 population censuses was 71% and 95% respectively), industrialization (employment in industry increased from 19% in 1971 to 24% in 2001, while the share of agriculture in GDP fell to 4.5% in 2005) and human capital formation (the share of population with a secondary education according to the 1971 and 2001 population censuses was 20% and 47% respectively). Such changes involve major population shifts and changes in patterns of economic activity and one would expect that they have had pronounced regional and spatial effects linked to urbanization and agglomeration. Consequently, an increase in spatial inequality could be expected. While there is no analysis of the regional impact of these statewide changes over the whole period, an analysis of their impact from 1945 to 1990 is given in Bogunović (1991) while the best general overview of national economic development is in Bartlett (2002).

The second influence on the spatial allocation of economic activity is a result of social engineering. During the 40-year period under consideration, Croatia experienced two fundamentally different socio-economic systems. Each of them covers a half of the period under consideration (about 20 years each) and each of them involved a significant degree of social engineering. The first, which started after World War II, lasted up to 1990. During this period Croatian policymakers were constructing what they perceived to be a socialist economy. After 1990 the economy embarked on a still ongoing transformation towards modern regulated capitalism and EU membership. In both periods the institutional framework was unstable with policymakers consciously searching for, building and redesigning an institutional framework, thereby creating a specific political economy in both cases. The 'grand project' of socialism was based on workers' self-management, while capitalism opted for a social-market economy. In both cases the intentions of these social engineering policies and their consequences were frequently in mismatch, and pathological results abounded. The socialist project generated a substantial economic slowdown in the 1980s that led to its demise, while the transition project led to the emergence of crony capitalism.

The spatial aspect of these engineering efforts should also have been important. Socialist social engineering included three important policies with regional asymmetric effects. The first had to do with the bias towards industry and the design of one-employer cities, often referred to as 'enterprise space'. In the case of Croatia, heavy industry in Sisak, manufacturing in Slavonski Brod and aluminium processing in Šibenik provide obvious examples – but there are many others. The second policy was a tolerance of mixed-income 'worker-peasant' households (almost a third of households were 'mixed' in this way). This tended to reduce pressures of urbanization. The third policy was one of managed exports through which planners, working with an administratively regulated trade and exchange rate, preferred exporting single valuable objects (which in the Croatian case were basically ships, leading to the building of numerous shipyards on the coast). Later, tourism also developed on the coast but not as part of any 'grand project'. Spatial equality was an important policy priority during socialism as is seen in the organization of administrative units and their changes, the inter-regional income redistributions and the support for less developed regions (for more details see Bogunović, 1985, 1991; Bićanić and Pribičević, 2009). The success of these policies should be reflected in relatively low and stable spatial inequality.

The transformation project of replacing socialism with capitalism did not have such a spatial policy focus. Of course, all the correct generalized political statements and policy declarations about spatial equality were made but there were no actual policies of regional redistribution. There were, however, policies targeted at other goals that had important spatial side effects. These policies concern post-war reconstruction and the return of refugees and displaced persons to the less developed areas of the country from which they originated. However, such transition policies should have profound spatial effects. Redressing socialist over-industrialization (employment in manufacturing fell from 33% in 1991 to 24% in 2001), the privatization path chosen and rapid internal liberalization (the loss of subsidies) all led to the implosion of overgrown, vertically integrated, regional, mono-employer firms and with it the economic lag of 'their cities'. The new openness to FDI was also asymmetric (with most of it going into tourism and large banks). The consequence of the aforementioned policies and their effects should be an increase in spatial inequality.

The third influence on spatial equality came from a series of shocks, most of them coming from policy, but with one important exception. Policy shocks are largely related to 'stabilization policies' (i.e. anti-inflation policies) and attempts for ironing out business cycles. While these did not have lasting effects, they certainly temporarily put regional issues on the backburner. During the period from 1968 to 2008, there were numerous stabilization policies (in 1971 and 1978, then in 1982, two in 1989 and the last one in 1993) and three cycle-related recessions (in 1971, 1981 and 1999 – the period ends before the 2009 recession). With regard to spatial inequality all the stabilization policies involved fiscal contractions, which reduced inter-regional redistribution, and wage and price controls, which also had spatially asymmetric effects.

However, arguably, the greatest shock during the period was in 1990. With the dissolution of Yugoslavia each of the successor states, Croatia included, faced two changes. Both of them should be of fundamental consequences for spatial inequality. The first was the emergence of new outside borders and, with them, new points of spatial discontinuity. The second was the emergence of new capitals and metropolitan areas. In the case of Croatia the third effect was the Homeland War of 1990–5. With the exception of the agriculturally rich Baranya and parts of Western Sirnium, all the other regions involved in the conflict were the least developed areas of Croatia.

NUTS2 in Croatia, data and inequality measures

With EU membership pending in 2013 (the negotiations were completed in 2011) Croatia had to divide its territory into NUTS2 regions. In order to close the EU accession chapter on statistics in 2005, Croatia had to accept some proposed statistical division. EU regulations stipulate that a NUTS2 region must have at least 800,000 inhabitants and the capital city cannot be a separate region which means Croatia could divide into a maximum of five NUTS2 regions (see Regulation (EC) No. 1059/2003). Following these guidelines the Croatian Parliament divided the country into three NUTS2 level regions: Eastern (Pannonian) Croatia, North-west Croatia and Adriatic Croatia (see Narodne Novine No. 35/07). These three regions have been constructed from the current administrative division of 22 counties and the capital city (Zagreb). Thus, from a statistical point of view, Croatia is complying with EU territorial divisions. The NUTS1 level is the largest statistical unit and includes the whole of the country. The NUTS2 level is made up of three regions – Eastern (Pannonian), North-west and Adriatic Croatia. The NUTS3 level units are all the existing 22 counties and Zagreb. The units in the lowest statistical division LAU2 are the 427 municipalities and 127 cities. The NUTS3 units make up the NUTS2 units in the following way:

- East (Pannonia) Croatia consists of eight counties: Sisak-Moslavina, Karlovac, Bjelovar-Bilogora, Virovitica-Podravina, Pozega-Slavonia, Brod-Posavina, Osijek-Baranja and Vukovar-Sirmium.
- Northwest Croatia consists of six counties: City of Zagreb, Zagreb county, Krapina-Zagorje, Varazdin, Koprivnica-Krizevci and Medjimurje.
- Adriatic Croatia is made up of seven counties: Istria, Primorje-Gorski Kotar, Lika-Senj, Zadar, Sibenik-Knin, Split-Dalmatia, and Dubrovnik-Neretva (see Figure 14.1). The current state of disparities between assembled regions is illustrated in Table 14.1.

Regarding the current statistical and institutional division, there is a widespread opinion that the NUTS3 and LAU2 division with their respective fragmentation are neither functional nor cost-effective and cannot provide a coherent and meaningful framework for a regional policy.[2] There is also dissatisfaction with the number of NUTS2 regions. However, any change was always politically contested at both the local and national levels, became controversial and was thus regularly postponed. Other boundaries for NUTS2 were discussed. Lovrinčević, Marić and Rajh (2005) in their article experiment with a number of different regional groupings using two, three or even four statistical regions. Using various regional boundaries they generate varying homogeneity within regions. The authors argue for the establishment of four NUT2 regions and that with its level of development the capital (Zagreb) is a statistical outlier and should hence be a separate NUTS2 region (which is not in line with EU guidelines). With Zagreb excluded they form three relatively homogenous regions: the North-west (different from the current NUTS2), East (Pannonian) Croatia and the Adriatic region. They also point out that by isolating Zagreb into a separate region the averages of the remaining ones would fall making them more eligible for EU funds. The World Bank in its papers routinely divides the country into seven regions (World Bank, 2006). Another more recent proposal argues in favour of five NUTS2 regions.[3] Its major novelty is that it splits the proposed Adriatic region into two: the Northern Littoral and Dalmatia (and makes small changes in boundaries to satisfy the population requirements) leaving the rest similar to the Lovrinčević,

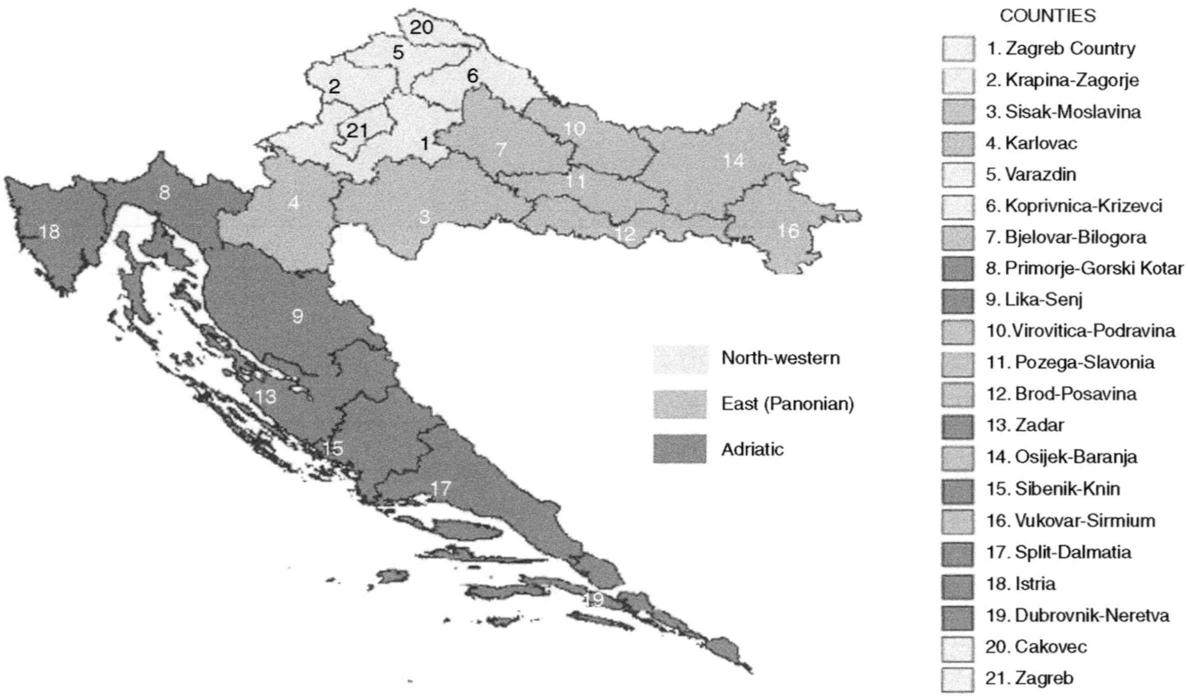

Figure 14.1 Croatian NUTS2 regions
Source: Statistical Yearbook, Croatian Office of Statistics.

Table 14.1 Disparities and inequality of Croatian counties

	Population			GDP (€ million)			GDP per capita		
	Size	Share	% of NUTS2 average	Size	Share	% of NUTS2 average	Size	% of NUTS2 average	% of EU average
East (Pannonia) Croatia	1,351,517	29%	76%	10,088	21%	11%	6851	34%	28
Adriatic Croatia	1,427,008	33%	81%	15,096	32%	17%	9471	45%	38
North-west Croatia	1,658,935	38%	94%	22,185	47%	25%	12,010	58%	48
CROATIA	4,437,460	100%		47,369			9656		100

Sources: EUROSTAT, CBS, 2008.

Marić and Rajh (2005) proposal. All these proposals (and other less formalized ones) are inward looking and reflect current local politics. They certainly do not consider the 'big picture' either in relation to the growth potential of defined regions or of their lobbying power in Brussels relative to other regions with which they are competing for funds. Prior to 1990, when Croatia, in contrast to the present, did have a regional policy it experimented with various regional boundaries.[4] From a historical point of view the division into three NUTS2 regions has no precedent; the closest to it were the four macro-regions in the late 1960s and early 1970s. Despite this and other papers originating from both the scientific community and politicians, in 2005 Croatia was divided into three regions with Zagreb City included within one of them (North-west Croatia).

The object of this chapter is not to dispute the current division into three NUTS2 regions. This division is a 'fact of life' that will probably not change, so it should be used as a basis for Croatia's future regional decentralization. In the remainder of this chapter we discuss the long-term relationship of these regions with regard to inter-regional and intra-regional inequality.

Data problems

When analysing Croatia's NUTS2 regions over a long period, two data problems stand out. The first problem is that there is no historical data on the three NUTS2 regions (they did not exist before 2005) so that this data has to be reconstructed. The second is that the data had to be recalculated to try to achieve acceptable comparability of data from the pre-1990 socialist period, based on material balances in national accounts and gross material product and data from the post-1990 capitalist period, based on UN national accounts and gross national product. Broadly, with regard to data comparability, three periods can be recognized.

The first period is from 1968 to 1991. This was the period during which Croatia was a socialist republic and part of Yugoslavia. At that time Croatia had a well-developed regional policy, so a wealth of data was collected: for example, income and income per capita, employment, industrial structure at the one-digit level, assets, and social and demographic statistics, all covering local territorial units and regions. These data were made publicly available. However, the difficulty with these data is that during socialism, data were collected according to different social accounting principles and the Gross Material Product (called 'social product') data it generated does not translate into Gross

Domestic Product (or Net Domestic Product). A detailed description of translating Yugoslav (and hence Croatian) GMP into GDP is given in Dubey (1975; especially appendix A) who concludes, 'Historically, GDP is higher by about 14 percent than GMP' (Dubey, 1975: 311). Fink and Havlik (1989: 60) come to a similar conclusion: 'Experience shows that the GDP may by as much as 10 to 15 percent higher than the corresponding NMP.' But for Croatia there are no reliable recalculations of the national level GMP data into national level GDP data for the entire period. The way around this is, as we have done in our calculations, is to use relative measures that do not require recalculation but implicitly use the assumption of a linear relationship between the two systems of national accounts.

The next period is from 1990 to 2005. For the second part from 1996 to 2006, GDP data was collected and national accounts were based on UNSNA principles. However, data was not collected for the county (NUTS3) level and NUTS2 level did not exist. There has been no attempt to estimate regional values for the main economic indicators at counties or NUTS2 level. At the disaggregated level only labour statistics (employment and unemployment) exist since employment offices are organized along county lines. As a result of this lack of data little can be said about territorial economic activities for that period. For the first part of the period – that is, from 1990 to 1995 – data are even less reliable. This was the period of the Homeland war, from 1991 to 1995, and high inflation, from 1990 to 1993. As a result this period is in many respects a data lacuna, when not even national GDP statistics are reliable.

The third period is the one after 2005. This was the first year regional NUTS2 data was published and during which Croatia implemented EUROSTAT data collecting principles. The data was published according to the National Classification of Territorial Units for Statistics harmonized with the Regulation (EC) No. 1059/2003 of the European Parliament and the Council on the establishment of a common classification of territorial units for statistics (NUTS). After 2005 the National Bureau of Statistics published statistics for GDP and GDP per capita and gross value added at the county level and, with necessary methodological corrections, the informal economy was included. Population data can be gathered from semi-annual demographic estimates, also at the county level. The counties can easily be aggregated into NUTS2 regions.

The second problem concerns regional boundaries. This can easily be solved for the whole period. Even though there were three different divisions of Croatia into regions, the boundaries of counties did not change significantly. In 1990 Croatia was divided into 106 communes and, luckily, they neatly fit into county borders and so into NUTS2 borders (for a more detailed discussion about recalculating pre-1990 counties into NUTS2, see Bićanić and Pribičević, 2009).

Inequality measures

In this chapter we use descriptive statistics for inter-regional differences and two inequality measures for intra-regional differences. Descriptive statistics for inter-regional differences are unavoidable since we are discussing only three regions, an insufficient number of data points for a more complex analysis. As a result all inter-regional analysis is conducted in very simple terms.

For the case of intra-regional inequality we chose what seemed to be the most adequate measures. Cowell (1995) identifies four distributional axioms an acceptable inequality measure should satisfy. The first is anonymity (no other specific characteristics but the one measured, in our case income, can influence the ordering principle), the second is scale independence (multiplying all incomes with the same positive scalar should not change inequality), the third is population independence (replicating each income an arbitrary number of times should not change inequality) and the fourth is the Pigou-Dalton condition (transfers from a richer to a poorer person reduces inequality).

With the aforesaid in mind, we selected two inequality measures to analyse both overall and intra-regional spatial inequality. The first is the Gini coefficient, arguably the best known and most often used inequality measure. The second is the Theil index whose popularity is increasing because of some of its very useful characteristics.

Since we deal with ungrouped data, the Gini coefficient is calculated according to the following formula:

$$G = \frac{1}{2n^2\bar{y}} \sum_{i=1}^{n} \sum_{j=1}^{n} | y_i - y_j | \tag{1}$$

where n represents the number of units, $\bar{y}$ is the average income per capita for all the regions and y_i is the income per capita of region i. The Gini coefficient satisfies all the inequality measurement axioms as well as yielding values in the interval [0,1] with higher values reflecting higher levels of inequality. Its two best-known disadvantages are that it is not naturally decomposable and it is oversensitive to changes in the middle of the distribution (thus the extremes are underrepresented).

The second inequality measure we chose is the Theil index. To account for both inter- and intra-regional disparities, a number of empirical studies (Terassi, 1999; Gezici and Hewings, 2007) use the Theil index and its attractive property of decomposability. The Theil index belongs to the class of generalized entropy inequality measures. To calculate the index of inter-regional inequalities, the chapter uses the following formula:

$$T = T(y:x) = \sum_{i=1}^{n} y_i \log\left(\frac{y_i}{x_i}\right) \tag{2}$$

where x_i is the population of county i relative to the national population, while y_i is the share of national income/gross value added of county i relative to the overall national income/gross value added and n represents the number of regions. Hence, the sum of inter-regional and intra-regional inequalities can be written as:

$$T = \sum_{i=1}^{n} y_i \log\left(\frac{y_i}{x_i}\right) + \sum_{g=1}^{n} Y_g T_g(y:x) = B + W \tag{3}$$

The first sum in the equation measures inequality between regions (inter-regional inequality) where Y_g is the region's share in total national income/gross value added, the second sum with $T_g(y:x)$ is the Theil index measuring inequality within regions (intra-regional disparities). In this way global inequality is decomposed into the contribution of inter-regional disparities and intra-regional disparities.

Regional inequality in Croatia at the NUTS2 level

The NUTS2 view of spatial inequality in Croatia is discussed in the following three subsections. The first discusses the influence of size on the reliability of inequality measurements. The second subsection presents results of intra-regional analysis in the form of descriptive statistics, while the third addresses regional disparities through relevant inequality measures.

Size and NUTS2 inequality

When choosing the appropriate measure of spatial inequality, size is important. As was illustrated in the introduction to the chapter, Croatia can be classified as a small country on all accounts. The economic implications of size have been extensively discussed in the literature and here we survey only those relevant for spatial inequality. There is a consensus among economists that size per se does not influence economic outcomes. Thus it does not influence the level of development, growth rates, policy reactions and their formulation, or national inequality levels. It is, however, argued that size does have an influence on spatial inequality. Portnov and Felsenstein (2005) specifically address the issues of country size in spatial inequality metrics. Testing a set of inequality indicators for a small country, the authors establish that most measures do not pass all tests required for robust inequality indicators. While a good deal of measures remain stable when the number of regions is varied, the Theil index and Gini coefficient show sensitivity to uneven population distribution but remain invariant to the order in which regions are introduced into the calculation. In that sense, using regional division with uneven population may result in erroneous inequality estimates. Novotny (2007) remarks on adjacency and comparability of analysed regions, especially with regard to area size. Furthermore, metropolitan regions should not be separated from their peripheries as this could increase measured inequality. Small countries often have one dominant metropolitan centre casting a shadow over other regions and dominating the country and economy. This dominance, it is further argued, decreases possible spillover effects. The rise of such a metropolitan centre is further strengthened by the distance between the centre and the hinterland. Even in a small country context, this distance is too large for daily commuting (Portnov and Erell, 2001). Croatia certainly does have a dominant metropolitan area. The City of Zagreb as the administrative, socio-economic and cultural capital of Croatia has over a quarter of the population and over half the registered firms. As a result it is expected to contribute greatly to overall spatial inequalities as a gravitational centre with its own growth and development path. On the other hand, small countries generally have smaller numbers and sizes of regions; the law of small numbers implies fewer extreme values and more inter-regional equality. Moreover, homogenization of preferences, culture and economic structures should result in convergence and lower levels of inequality. However, economic cohesion seems less likely in countries fractured by discontinuities in the quality of human and/or social capital, economies and societies that are under the influence of both endogenous processes (such as transition and EU integration) and exogenous shocks (such as war and embargoes). Indeed, the argument of smallness is dichotomous; growth spillovers (whereby the area around the metropolis benefits from its growth though positive spillovers) contrast metropolitan shadow effects (through which the metropolis stifles growth in the surrounding area through centripetal forces), with the latter prevailing in the case of Croatia.

In the light of the argument, Croatia does not fulfil all the size-determined requirements, as the Eastern (Pannonian) and Adriatic regions are more than twice as big as North-western Croatia. Nonetheless, a roughly even distribution of population among regions was achieved (thus complying with the fundamental NUTS directive). Also, the metropolitan area is not in a separate region but part of North-west Croatia. This makes inequality estimates fairly reliable. In addition, historical data for the pre-1990 period suggest an even more equitable distribution of inhabitants throughout Croatia's regions, with population shares remaining virtually unchanged over the course of 20 years.

Inter-regional inequalities of Croatian NUTS2 regions through time

We recalculated the raw data in the described manner into NUTS2 data for four years. The first three – 1969, 1979 and 1989 – use data from the socialist period and the last – 2008 – from the capitalist one (data for ten-year periods could not be calculated since data for 1999 does not exist). Both the first and last year are determined by data availability: 1969 was the first year data were collected and 2008 is the most recent year for which data are available at the time of writing, which is also the last pre-recession year (the slowdown started in 2009 and was followed by two years of negative growth). As mentioned earlier, there is a serious issue of comparability for data during the period. The problems concern statistical discontinuities. In the chapter we provisionally deal with statistical discontinuities using relative values and assuming a constant linear relationship between GMP and GDP data. This enables us to compare inequalities and use per capita national income (*društveni proizvod*) for the pre-1990 period (for the three data points 1969, 1979 and 1989) and per capita gross value added for the post-1990 period (for the only data point 2008). Since real income on the NUTS2 level cannot be calculated we use this per capita income as a crude measure of real income and approximation of living standards.

First we calculate NUTS2 per capita income in terms of the national average; the results are depicted in Figure 14.2. The figure indicates a period of convergence from 1969 to 1979 and divergence thereafter. The divergence is especially pronounced after 1989 when both the Adriatic and Pannonian NUTS2 regions fall behind, especially the latter. This divergence of Pannonia is not a result of transition but started earlier; transition only seems to have accelerated it. At the end of the 1980s the Adriatic region experienced an acceleration that increased its income per capita above the national average, on what seems like a path towards convergence with the somewhat decelerating North-west region. The transition, war and new borders changed this and increased

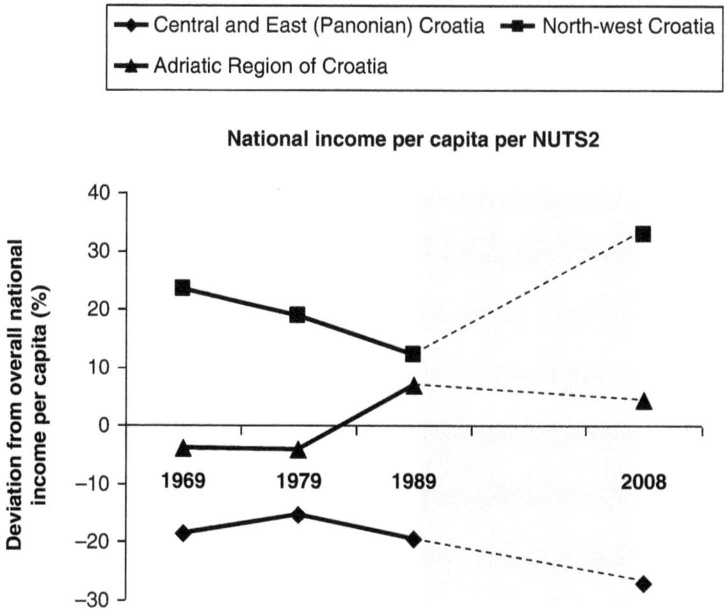

Figure 14.2 Relative income per capita in NUTS2 regions (1969–2008)

the gap between regions, giving the North-west a boost the other two regions could not follow. During the whole period the ranking does not change. The Eastern (Pannonian) region has the lowest values and, even more importantly, continually lags further behind. Thus, even when corrected for size, differences widen over time. Development paths of average counties do not differ noticeably from trajectories of average income per capita for the whole NUTS2 region.

Figure 14.2 takes into account per capita income but not space per se. Another measure of spatial inequality was given by Gallup, Sachs and Mellinger (1999) who introduced the concept of GDP density. Subsequently, recent literature began favouring national income per square kilometre as a good measure of the geographic aspect of economic activity. Results are presented in Table 14.2 where income and employment density are calculated as a percentage of the national average. The income data overestimate the actual dominance because firms register income according to their central office and a sizable portion of the income of Zagreb firms may have been earned elsewhere. Employment densities that are not under this influence still

Table 14.2 Relative economic density in NUTS2 regions

	National income per square kilometre, Croatia = 100				Employment per square kilometre, Croatia = 100			
	1969	**1979**	**1989**	**2008**	**1969**	**1979**	**1989**	**2008**
East (Pannonia)	66.87	67.73	63.21	51.12	69.99	68.41	68.93	53.32
Adriatic	75.31	74.88	85.54	79.70	74.47	76.19	78.31	69.70
North-west	512.42	510.72	473.23	564.42	254.21	253.48	245.94	312.65

show metropolitan dominance. GDP economic density of the Eastern (Pannonian) region slowly deteriorates over the whole period – that is, for almost four decades. The density of the North-western region also exhibits a slight decrease over the socialist period only to rise considerably during the transition period. The data seems to show that the density of economic activity in 2008 is more than ten times greater in the North-western than in the Eastern (Pannonian) region. The data clearly show metropolitan dominance and that the Adriatic region is significantly below average during the whole period. These results are largely affected by population density that varies substantially between counties and regions alike. In order to reduce the effects of geographical size and population density we recalculated the data to compare an 'average county'. The recalculation did not influence the results, giving robustness to the conclusions drawn from Figure 14.2.

Intra-regional inequalities in Croatia from NUTS2 and national perspectives

Clearly, as the previous section showed, inter-regional differences in Croatia are big. But NUTS2 regions themselves are not homogenous. The topic of regional dynamics and differences in Croatia has rarely been tackled and no one has so far concentrated on the NUTS2 level.

The available results on regional inequality deal with inequality on the level of counties. In addition to Bićanić and Pribičević (2009) only two papers, Puljiz and Maleković (2007) and Nestić and Vecchi (2007), compare income inequality. Papers dealing with aspects of regional unemployment are more common: see Botrić (2007), Boršič, Kavklar and Bićanić (2007), Franičević (2007) or Puljiz and Maleković (2007) as examples. The two quoted papers dealing with income inequality compare data for only two years. But in both cases periods are very short – the first paper compares 2000 and 2005 while the second 2002 and 2004; in neither case is this sufficient to determine any long-term changes. In this context it is worth noting the efforts of Puljiz and Maleković (2007) who assess spatial inequalities of income, wages and unemployment rates at the county level. The authors find rising inequalities for the period 2000–5 as well as heterogeneity within counties. They find that the within-county contribution to inequality decreased over time and the influence of between-county inequalities dominated in determining the national Theil index. As expected, the city of Zagreb, Istria and Primorje-Gorski Kotar counties outperform the rest of the country in all parameters, while the eastern part of the country expectedly lags behind. Subsequently, the article describes Croatia as a country of moderate income but pronounced unemployment disparities. The second study by Nestić and Vecchi (2006) uses household income survey data. They explore differences in regional poverty between 2002 and 2004 and find substantial regional variation in poverty rates. Also, when comparing the more recent inequality levels to those of 1998 they find that inequality has risen.

In this chapter we approach intra-regional differences in a more complex way. This was possible because there are enough data points to calculate Gini coefficients and Theil indices (the methodology was discussed previously). Table 14.3 provides the calculated Gini coefficient and Theil index for intra-regional inequality. Population weights are used in calculating both measures. While Gini coefficients can be compared vertically (comparing inequality levels within NUTS2 regions) and horizontally (comparing inequality changes within regions over time) this is not true of the Theil index, which can be compared only horizontally (in contrast to the Gini its value is not calibrated to 1).

Both inequality measures show the same structure. Changes in North-west Croatia and Pannonian Croatia follow the same pattern (first a fall and then a rise) while the Adriatic region changes are in the opposite

Table 14.3 Intra-regional inequality levels

	1969	1979	1989	2008
Gini coefficient				
Central and East	0.083	0.054	0.047	0.083
North-west	0.234	0.172	0.148	0.171
Adriatic	0.145	0.159	0.163	0.091
Theil index				
Central and East	0.011	0.005	0.004	0.005
North-west	0.101	0.055	0.035	0.213
Adriatic	0.036	0.041	0.044	0.018

direction (first a rise and then a fall). Comparing initial and final values gives ambiguous results except for the Adriatic region where both the Gini and Theil indicate a reduction in intra-regional inequality (in this sense a regional homogenization) over the period. Perhaps the changes in the Theil index for the North-west region is a result of its special features. The Theil index is more sensitive to upper-end extreme values – that is, to the influence of the City of Zagreb – so the large increase in the Theil index for the North-western region may be caused by intra-regional migration; but the causes of such developments have yet to be studied, leaving firm conclusions outside of the scope of this chapter.

The final topic concerns the relationship of NUTS2 inequality to national inequality. Again the data allows using both the Gini and Theil indices. Table 14.4 provides the spatial Gini for Croatia based on data for the counties and the decomposition of the Theil index for Croatia 1969–2008.

The Croatian Gini can be derived from the county data in two ways. The first is without population weights while the second uses population weights for the individual Gini. The values for the latter measure are smaller. These two measures together with the decomposable Theil index indicate the same changes in national level inequalities. Overall spatial inequality is slowly decreasing during the socialist period. However, comparing initial and final values, the change is ambiguous. The unweighted Gini indicates a 15% rise while the weighted Gini and Theil indicate a 14% and 12% fall, respectively, over the whole period. Perhaps the fall during the first 20 years speaks in favour of policies aimed to alleviate differences in the development gradient. In the case of the unweighted Gini and Theil indicators, transition implied an increase of national inequality when measured via regional inequality

Table 14.4 Spatial Gini coefficients and the decomposition of the Theil index for Croatia (1969–2008)

	1969	1979	1989	2008
Gini coefficient				
Unweighted	0.468	0.454	0.442	0.475
Population weighted	0.174	0.142	0.142	0.140
Theil index				
Theil Index	0.034	0.022	0.017	0.030
Within group	0.028	0.018	0.013	0.018
Between groups	0.007	0.004	0.004	0.012
Share of within group	81%	80%	75%	60%

while the population weighted Gini shows a slight fall. Inequality of national income per capita exhibits a steady decrease, as less developed regions become less populous due to both aging of the population and migration to new metropolitan areas.

The Theil index is a decomposable inequality measure, so it allows for national inequality to be divided into two components that separately measure the contribution of inter-regional inequality (between groups) and intra-regional inequality (within group) to national inequality. The bottom part of Table 14.4 gives the results of the calculation. The overall Theil index first falls (1969–89) and then rises (1989–2008), so the individual contributions to inequality change. The share of intra-regional inequality decreases over time, while inter-regional disparities emerge as dominant in the post-transition period. Still, total inequality remains driven by within-region inequalities, which illustrates substantial heterogeneity persisting within regions.

Conclusions and policy implications

The results of this chapter show widening inter-regional differences and large intra-regional differences. Thus they confirm widely held preconceptions about regional inequalities on a relatively small area and rising regional inequality that coincide with the process of transition. In this sense the chapter provides hard evidence of these stylized facts.

The chapter offers no rigorous explanation for this apart from indicating that explanations could be found in socialist-related industrialization that created 'enterprise space' that largely collapsed with the transition, regional and development policies which disappeared after 1990 under the transition path chosen and the absence of any regional policies during transition which increased the importance of the region that includes the metropolitan area of Zagreb.

However, with regard to probable future changes in spatial inequality, three things are worth noting. *Firstly*, for two decades Croatia has been without any meaningful regional policy and has shown no interest or awareness about needing one (the so-called areas of special concern is a social policy not a regional policy) and as a result has no social infrastructure geared at developing and implementing a regional policy. *Secondly*, Croatia's EU membership in 2013 means the EU will have a new stable outside border in its South-eastern and Adriatic region. For Croatia, considering the influences borders have on regional inequality (see Blokker and Dallago, 2009), this should give a significant boost further to rising spatial inequality both between regions and within the

Adriatic region. *Thirdly*, there is no awareness about the implications of a NUTS2 division and the discussions taking place about regional divisions still completely ignore this fact of life and still discuss other non-NUTS2-based territorial divisions. Since NUT2 regions will vie for EU funds, a possible discrepancy of NUTS2 regions and Croatia's territorial policies is likely to lead to inefficiencies, coordination costs and, perhaps not surprisingly, to coordination failure.

Finally, there is the influence of the extended recession on regional inequality in Croatia (Bićanić, Spajić and Kukavčić, 2010). With low growth, fiscal contraction and reduced investment incentives, the probability for any meaningful regional policy will disappear and there will be further pressure towards increasing regional inequalities.

Notes

1. A more detailed discussion of the topic is offered by Bićanić and Pribičević (2009), on which this section draws.
2. Galic, G. (2012) 'Ministar Grčić ispravlja Dekana Grčića: koliko regija treba imati Hrvasrtska' [Minister Grčić corrects Dean Grčić: How many regions should Croatia have?], *Novi list*, 29 March.
3. Nacional (2011) 'Hrvatska ukida županije i uvodi pet regija' [Croatia abolished the county and introduces the five regions?]; Petkovic, M. (2011) 'Hrvatske će nakon izbora dobiti 5 regija' [Croatia after the election will get five EU regions], *Vjesnik*, 25 May.
4. For a history of regional divisions till 1990, see Bogunović (1985, 1990), and for the period till 2011, see Bogunović (1985, 1991).

References

Bartlett, W. (2002) *Croatia: Between Europe and the Balkans*, London: Routledge.

Bićanić, I. and Pribičević, V. (2009) 'Multiple shocks and changes in the development gradient of Croatia's regions', in P. Blokker and B. Dallago (eds) *Regional Diversity and Local Development in the New Member States*, London: Palgrave Macmillan, pp. 272–93.

Bićanić, I., Spajić, V. and Kukavčić, I. (2010) 'The impact of the recession on South East European economies', *Journal of Southeast European Studies*, 34(74) pp. 193–221.

Blokker, P. and Dallago, B. (eds) (2009) *Regional Diversity and Local Development in the New Member States*, London: Palgrave Macmillan.

Bogunović, A. (1985) *Regionalni razvoj Socijalističke Jugoslavije i Hrvatske* [Regional development of Socialist Yugoslavia and Croatia], Zagreb: SNL.

Bogunović, A. (1991) *Regionalna ekonomika* [Regional economics], Zagreb: Narodne Novine.

Bogunović, A. (2011) *Regionalna ekonomika* [Regional economics], manuscript.

Boršić, D., Kavklar, A. and Bićanić, I. (2007) 'Estimating determinants of unemployment spells in Croatia', *Papers and Proceedings 9th International Symposium on Operations Research*, Ljubljana, Slovenian Society INFORMATIKA.

Botrić, V. (2007) 'Regional labour market differences in Croatia: Evidence from the 2000–2005 Labour Force Survey data', *Privredna kretanja i ekonomska politika*, 17(113): 26–51.

Cowell, F. A. (1995) *Measuring Inequality*, London: Prentice Hall/Harvester Wheatsheaf.

Dubey, V. (1975) *Yugoslavia: Development With Decentralisation*, Baltimore: The John Hopkins University Press.

Fink, G. and Favlik, P. (1989) 'Alternative measures of growth and development levels: Comparison and assessment', in P. J. Hardt and R. F. Kaufman (eds) *Pressures for Reform in the East European Economies, Vol. 1*, Washington, DC: Joint Economic Committee Congress of the United States, pp. 101–53.

Franičević, V. (2007) 'Being at risk: Institutional and structural uncertainties in Croatian labour markets', in M. Fredotović and Z. Reić (eds) *Seventh International Conference on Enterprise in Transition*, Split: Faculty of Economics, pp. 262–5.

Gallup, J. L., Sachs, J. D. and Mellinger, A. D. (1999) 'Geography and economic development', *International Regional Science Review*, 22(2): 179–232.

Gezici, F. and Hewings, G. J. D (2007) 'Spatial analysis of regional inequalities in Turkey', *European Planning Studies*, 15(3): 383–403.

Lovrinčević, Z., Marić, Z. and Rajh, E. (2005) 'How to regionalize Croatia optimally?' *Ekonomski pregled*, 56(12): 1109–60 [in Croatian].

Nestić, D. and Vecchi, G. (2007) 'Regional poverty in Croatia', in Z. Lovrinčević, A. Mervar, D. Nestić, N. Starc, P. Stubbs, M. Sumpor and S. Švaljek (eds) *Social Policy and Regional Development Proceedings*, Zagreb: EIZ i FES, pp. 65–90.

Novotny, J. (2007) 'On the measurement of regional inequality: Does spatial dimension of income inequality matter?' *Annals of Regional Science*, 41(3): 563–80.

Portnov, B. A. and Erell, E. (2001) *Urban Clustering; The Benefits and Drawbacks of Location*, Aldershot: Ashgate.

Portnov, B. A. and Felsenstein, D. (2005) 'Measures of regional inequality for small countries', in B. A. Portnov and D. Felsenstein (eds) *Regional Disparities in Small Countries*, Berlin: Springer-Verlag, pp. 47–62.

Puljiz, J. and Maleković, S. (2007) 'Regional income and unemployment disparities in Croatia', in M. Fredotović and Z. Reić (eds) *Proceedings of the 7th International Conference on Enterprise in Transition*, Split: Faculty of Economics, pp. 1846–2693.

Terassi, M. (1999) 'Convergence and divergence across Italian regions', *Annals of Regional Science*, 33(4): 491–510.

World Bank (2006) *Croatia: Living Standards Assessment*, Report No. 37992, Washington, DC: The World Bank.

Index

Lightning Source UK Ltd.
Milton Keynes UK
UKHW021117300120
357885UK00006B/368

9 781349 347179